OXFORD BROOKES
A SPORTING MIRACLE?

OXFORD BROOKES
A SPORTING MIRACLE?
From a cowshed on the Thames to the top of the rowing world

PETER SMITH

*With a Foreword by Sir Steve Redgrave
and photographs from AllMarkOne*

First published 2024

Copyright © Peter Smith 2024

The right of Peter Smith to be identified as the author of this work has been asserted in accordance with the Copyright, Designs & Patents Act 1988.

All rights reserved. No part of this book may be reproduced, stored in a retrieval system, or transmitted in any form or by any means, digital, electronic, electrostatic, magnetic tape, mechanical, photocopying, recording or otherwise, without the written permission of the copyright holder.

Published under licence by Brown Dog Books and
The Self-Publishing Partnership Ltd, 10b Greenway Farm, Bath Rd, Wick, nr. Bath BS30 5RL, UK

www.selfpublishingpartnership.co.uk

ISBN printed book: 978-1-83952-862-0
ISBN e-book: 978-1-83952-863-7

Cover design by Kevin Rylands
Internal design by Mac Style

Cover photographs © AllMarkOne
Brookes women's eight winning Remenham Cup at Henley Royal Regatta, 2024
Brookes men's eight winning Championship Eights at Marlow Regatta, 2024

Printed and bound in the UK

This book is printed on FSC® certified paper

Contents

About the Author — vii
Acknowledgements and Thanks — ix
Foreword by Sir Steve Redgrave — xiii
Introduction — xiv

Chapter 1	Jenny and Sam	1
Chapter 2	Rowing hurts	10
Chapter 3	The Poly	15
Chapter 4	Brookes emerges, disaster strikes (1992)	25
Race Report	The 2023 Prince Albert Challenge Cup Final	35
Chapter 5	HRR the First Time (1993)	39
Chapter 6	Brookes, the best boat in Oxford (94–95)	55
Race Report	The 2023 Ladies' Challenge Plate Final	64
Chapter 7	A New Home	68
Chapter 8	Towards the Millennium (1996–99)	80
Race Report	The 2023 Temple Challenge Cup Final	91
Chapter 9	The science of rowing	94
Chapter 10	Haining and Bailhache-Webb (2000–07)	102
Race Report	The 2023 Island Challenge Cup Final	119
Chapter 11	A new focus (2008–12)	122
Chapter 12	Show me the money	131

Chapter 13	The ecstasy and the agony (2013–15)	138
Race Report	The 2024 Grand Challenge Cup Final	146
Chapter 14	The Head of the River	149
Chapter 15	Coxing	155
Chapter 16	Recruitment	163
Race Report	The 2024 Remenham Challenge Cup Final	172
Chapter 17	Onwards and upwards (2016–19)	174
Chapter 18	The Women of Brookes	185
Chapter 19	Selecting the crew	195
Chapter 20	The pandemic years (2020–22)	201
Race Report	The 2024 Temple Challenge Cup Final	211
Chapter 21	The gym and training	213
Chapter 22	The Tokyo Olympics	223
Chapter 23	Brookes' annus mirabilis (2023)	232
Chapter 24	What makes Brookes special?	242
Race Report	The 2024 Stewards' Challenge Cup Final	254
Chapter 25	But is there a dark side?	256
Chapter 26	Onwards to 2024	263
Chapter 27	Henley (and Paris …) 2024	273
Chapter 28	Learning from Brookes	288
Chapter 29	The Future	294
References		299
Index of People		302
General Index		306

About the Author

Peter Smith was born in Sunderland, where rowing is not particularly popular, but learnt to cox at Lady Margaret Boat Club (LMBC), the boat club of St John's College, Cambridge. Luckily for him, LMBC was very strong during his three years there, so he won Head of the Lent and May Bumps medals, the university Coxed Fours, various regatta trophies and medals. LMBC represented Cambridge at the British Universities event and won silver, and Peter coxed the Cambridge Lightweights to victory over Oxford in the 1978 race in a record time (because of the raging tailwind).

After university he joined Mars Confectionery, who showed little enthusiasm for giving him time off to cox an aspiring under-23 GB squad boat. He did some coaching and coxing at a local club, then became simply an enthusiastic follower of rowing. Having become a member of the Stewards' Enclosure at Henley Royal Regatta whilst still a student, he has attended every year since 1977.

His professional life has revolved around procurement and supply chain management, with board-level roles in the public and private sectors, as well as non-executive posts in both sectors. He has advised the National Audit Office, the UK Treasury and Cabinet Office, amongst many others, as a consultant, and ran a successful business website for eight years. He is a top-20 influencer in his field and now lectures at several business schools.

He has also written four business books, including *Bad Buying – How Organisations Waste Billions Through Failures, Frauds and F*ck-ups*, published by Penguin Books in October 2020, lifting the lid on some amazing global stories of disaster in the business (and government) world! His latest passion is how procurement can contribute to wider global issues, and his book *Procurement with Purpose – How organisations can change the way they spend money NOW to protect the planet and its people* was published by Brown Dog Books in November 2021.

Away from procurement and writing, he is active member of Humanists UK, plays the bass guitar, keeps fit (cycling, walking, gym), supports both Sunderland and Brentford football clubs, and attempts to grow fruit and vegetables.

This is his first sports-focused book.

Acknowledgements and Thanks

It was the 2023 Henley Royal Regatta Finals Day that led to this book. I tweeted about the amazing Oxford Brookes University Boat Club (OBUBC) performance and the club's incredible development over the last 30 years. Matt Akers, who followed me on Twitter (we are both procurement professionals) replied, saying, 'Peter, I was the cox in the first Brookes boat to win at Henley, in 1993.'

That felt like fate. I had spotted the absence of any publication covering the Brookes story and, having written several business-related books, I thought maybe I could fill that void. Matt, who turned out to be incredibly helpful and positive, was key. He introduced me to Richard Spratley, the Brookes rowing supremo for over 30 years and now Director of Rowing. Fortunately, Richard felt positive about the idea, as did Henry Bailhache-Webb, Head Coach, so sometime later, here we are.

So thanks to Matt, still rowing competitively in his fifties now, and then to Richard and Henry in particular. Thanks also to other Brookes coaches past and present – including Peter Haining, Dan Janes, Hugo Gulliver, Chris Tebb and Sam Sheppard. Peter Lowe, who recruited Richard into Brookes in 1992, and features heavily in the early chapters, was very helpful, as were Tasmin Bryant and James Symington from the committee of Taurus, the Brookes alumni club. Other interviewees included Haydn Morris, Kevin Morris, Russell Cook, Clive Couldwell, Tim Magee, Alex and Jane Gandon from the Poly days, then David Peill, Andrew Hall, Alex Henshilwood, Jenny Bates, Mike Sweeney

CBE, Rachel Quarrell, Alex Partridge, Matt Hnatiw and Max Bird – all were helpful and provided further insight.

Rory Cruickshank of AllMarkOne provided some brilliant photographs, and in terms of the book production, the team at the SPP and Brown Dog Publishing were excellent again, with particular thanks to Frances Prior-Reeves. Richard Spratley's partner, Jane, also provided invaluable marketing advice. And my wife Jane was as supportive as ever and listened patiently for a year as I held forth on all aspects of Brookes' history.

Rowing does not get the coverage in the mainstream media it once did, but there are excellent websites covering the sport, particularly Row360 and Junior Rowing News, staffed by insightful and committed writers and experts. My thanks to them for valuable source material and general entertainment. The legendary Martin Cross with his podcast/video series *Crossy's Corner* was another source of inspiration and expertise. Thanks also to Henley Royal Regatta which has an archive of results and since 2014 video coverage of every race, a treasure trove of amazing sport.

Very sadly, in April 2024, whilst I was writing this book, the Brookes Director of Sport, Keith Kelly, passed away after suffering from a brain tumour. He was a consistent supporter of Richard Spratley and the boat club and contributed much to the success of recent years. He first worked at Brookes in 1997, was also an international basketball player with Wales, and became Director of Sport in 2008. He was only in his late forties and was highly respected and liked at Brookes. 'One of the nicest guys I've ever had the pleasure of knowing' was a typical comment on Instagram when the news was announced. This book is dedicated to his memory.

There are four chapter 'variants', as it were, within the book. The core is the chronological story of OBUBC, from 1987 or so through to the current day. The early days of Brookes, from 1992–95 and the

Acknowledgements and Thanks

Keith Kelly christens the boat named in his honour in 2022 (© *AllMarkOne*)

more recent years are given the most attention – there had to be some prioritisation to keep the book at a manageable length.

Other chapters discuss key overarching aspects of the Brookes story, such as recruitment, financing and training methods, as well as final discussions around how other organisations of all types might learn from Brookes. Then there are general topics of rowing interest, such as a discussion of the 2021 GB Olympic rowing failure. Finally, interspersed through the book, you will find race reports from the most exciting Henley Royal Regatta finals in which Brookes competed on 2 July 2023 and 7 July 2024.

You may wish to follow the chronology first then dip into other chapters, or miss out elements completely. But I hope the whole book tells the Brookes rowing story, goes some way to explaining how the club has achieved such impressive results and provides a wider context for that success.

Finally, I apologise. A lot of effort went into this book and into trying to get the detail right. But I am sure I have missed some key people involved in the story, got some crews, dates or event details wrong and probably upset someone along the way. I also tried and failed to contact certain people who seemed important to the story. My errors or omissions are regretted and were not deliberate.

Foreword by Sir Steve Redgrave

Since Oxford Brookes became a university in 1992, staff and students have focussed their energy not just on academia, but on sport as well. They have achieved so much in their short history as a university, and within rowing they have been catapulted onto the world map through their focus and achievement.

Guided by Richard Spratley, they have become the go-to university to further an aspiring athlete's rowing career, with their dominance on the domestic circuit, and now rivalling the top American colleges.

More often than not, university recognition goes to Oxford and Cambridge due to their long history and the annual boat race. However, Brookes' results on a year-by-year basis is second to none and it has also proved to be a great pathway to the national team, with some of their graduates going on to achieve honours at World Championships and the Olympics – including in Paris this year.

Their focus, dedication and commitment to excellence while they are studying gives these athletes such foresight and vision for whatever career path they follow once they hang up their oars. Over the last 25 years, the club has won so many titles at Henley Royal Regatta, which is the benchmark for success, and today, any crew racing that comes up against an Oxford Brookes crew know they will have their work cut out to beat them!

Sir Steve Redgrave
June 2024

Introduction

It is Sunday, 2 July 2023, and Henley Royal Regatta (HRR to its friends) is ready for Finals Day. The first race is not until 11 am, a civilised starting time because today the only races are those 26 finals. We will see four hours or so of racing, with a lengthy pause for lunch, and a race every 10 minutes. Two Henley veterans, Richard Spratley and Henry Bailhache-Webb, now the rowing supremos at Oxford Brookes University, just up the river from here, wait slightly nervously to see how their crews are going to get on today.

Members and their guests enter the Stewards' Enclosure, which sits alongside the last 400 metres or so of the course. They admire the manicured lawns, bar and restaurant tents, the military band and the merchandise tent selling its first Henley Teddy Bears, mugs and hoodies of the day. The art gallery features pictures and even sculptures with a rowing theme.

To the uninitiated, Henley looks like an Edwardian garden party, although the Stewards, the purely voluntary, self-electing group that has run the event from its beginnings in 1839, have slowly but steadily modernised the event since I competed there with the St John's College, Cambridge, Lady Margaret Boat Club in the late 1970s.

At that time the regatta was struggling financially and, in 1977, three of us in our bright red rowing blazers were virtually kidnapped and persuaded to sign up as members of the Stewards' Enclosure. As the economy and hospitality industry boomed through the 1980s, membership of the Stewards' became more prized and today there is a substantial waiting list, although a decent-level rower can probably jump the queue.

Introduction

The list of Stewards in the programme still shows the Lord Wigram and the Emeritus Bishop of Menevia (who actually was a headmaster and keen rowing coach), but is in the main a rollcall of great rowers, male and female, including Sir Steve Redgrave, Chair of the Regatta Committee until he hands over to Richard Phelps after the 2024 event, and other Olympians including Matthew Pinsent, Heather Stanning, Dame Katherine Grainger, Mo Sbihi and more.

In 2023, for the second time, the regatta runs over six days, starting on Tuesday. For the first three days races start around 9 am, because of the sheer number that need to be fitted in. This year 732 crews have entered, and although around 300 were unfortunate enough to fail in the qualifying race last Saturday, that still leaves 420 boats in 26 different events to compete.

The first women's race over the full course was back in 1993, but it is only in the last 10 years that the number of women's races and events has grown strongly, and it is now not far short of the men's roster. That is the main reason why the programme was extended to five days in 1986, then to six in 2022.

But the relaxed and convivial atmosphere of the Stewards' Enclosure conceals what is a fiercely competitive sporting event. Athletes have rowed themselves into unconsciousness, and launches at the finish stand by to treat distressed competitors.

Whilst international-level rowing is held on lakes with six boats racing abreast, Henley is gladiatorial. It is a straight knock-out event, one boat against another, on a course that is 1 mile 500 yards, or 2,112 metres, long. That rather odd distance is simply the longest straight course that could be fitted onto this stretch of water. It is also a little longer than the standard international course length of 2,000 metres, something that has been known to catch out crews, who find the last 112 metres just too much.

Oxford Brookes

A fast men's eight can row the course in around 6 minutes, a strong women's crew being 30 seconds slower generally. I was there the day in 1989 when Ruder Club Hansa Dortmund, the German national squad, became the first crew ever to break the 6-minute barrier at Henley. When the announcer said, 'Dortmund win in a time of five minutes …', the cheers from the spectators were almost hysterical. We had seen history made. However, even the best sculler will take well over seven minutes. But the wind and strength of stream can make a huge difference.

The one-on-one nature of the event means that many races, particularly in the opening rounds, are mismatches with easy victories. In the days before an event just for juniors was introduced, we had a memorable quad sculls race, featuring the Army of the Union of the Soviet Socialist Republics versus Windsor Boys School!

But on Finals' Day, with the best crews left to fight over trophies, we expect close, brutal and dramatic races. We won't be disappointed. Rowing history will be made by an unlikely club, one that has totally changed the face of British rowing in recent years. Because Oxford Brookes University Boat Club (OBUBC or simply 'Brookes' to most rowing followers) is aiming to stun Henley today.

As we will see, 2023 turned out to be special for Brookes. I started working on this book in late 2023, and wanted to review Brookes' 2023/24 season as well as focusing on the Henley 2023 events and the club's history. As this book neared completion, Henley 2024 rolled around and, clearly, I hoped Brookes would perform well. But surely they couldn't live up to that amazing 2023 performance. Could they?

Before we look at those recent years, though, we will revisit the origins of the club and the Brookes rowing history. But to begin, two young athletes and their experiences over the last four years illustrates well key aspects of the Brookes story, and how such a successful boat club has emerged.

Chapter 1

Jenny and Sam

'I learnt to row at Reading, learnt to race at Hartpury – and learnt to win at Brookes.' (Jenny Bates, Brookes athlete, GB international and Henley winner)

Off to Hartpury we go …
Jenny Bates grew up near the Thames in Reading, enjoyed sport generally, particularly swimming, and, aged 17, thought she would try rowing. But Reading Rowing Club had no room for novices at that time. However, she saw an article about the GB Rowing World Class Start programme, designed to get young athletes into rowing. She went along to the session in 2016 and quickly got hooked on this new sport.

She was athletic and strong, but although tall by most standards (personally, I dream of being 1.78 m), that height wasn't quite what the programme was looking for, with 1.80 m being considered the minimum for women. But she was highly competitive, and when other girls at the trial session started boasting about how well they were going to do, she vowed to do better. Which she did, and was accepted into the programme.

Her days as a novice were fun, although it wasn't all success – including lots of falling into the river as she learnt how to scull. But she met Olympic gold medal winner Helen Glover, her role model, who was of similar height and build, which spurred her on.

Bates decided that she wanted to apply to a university that would allow her to develop her rowing. She chose to study Physical Education and School Sport at Hartpury University in Gloucestershire, which started life as an agricultural college but developed a strong reputation for sport and business degrees, as well as everything connected with animals and agriculture.

That same autumn of 2017, the slightly younger Sam Sheppard also arrived at Hartpury, but as a boarder in the sixth-form College. He had learnt to row in East Sussex and then chose Hartpury – just like Bates – because of the College's reputation for rowing. Both Bates and Sheppard enjoyed rowing at Hartpury, and Bates enjoyed some success. She raced in the British indoor championships, improved her erg times, and got fit and strong. She rowed in a single scull and also in a quad scull, her crew won some events, rowed at Henley Women's Regatta and the Universities Championships.

But moving into her second year, she contracted mumps, which made her face blow up like a 'real-life fat-face filter', as she put it, but also left her with serious health issues. She suffered from post-viral costochondritis, an inflammation of the chest cartilage, and was out of rowing for around 18 months, half of her time at Hartpury. And when she did return, medics even wondered whether she had cerebral palsy because of her slightly unusual rowing style. She somewhat lost interest in her sport, and then in her third year at Hartpury, in early 2020, Covid struck. Her last few months, supposedly at Hartpury, were spent mainly at home, in lockdown.

Meanwhile, Sheppard improved his rowing during his two years at Hartpury and then chose Oxford Brookes largely for rowing reasons, arriving in September 2019 to study Sports and Exercise Science. But halfway through his first year, Covid meant a pause in serious rowing competition for Brookes.

New beginnings at Brookes

In the early summer of 2020, Bates returned home to Reading to find her father had taken up indoor rowing to keep fit during lockdown.

Jenny and Sam

That provided a challenge for Bates – she didn't want to let her dad beat her on the erg times! She also got back into running and cycling, and started feeling fit and strong again. She got a job as a carer, and set up a pick'n'mix sweets business with her best friend, Elle Nash, who was already at Brookes.

But, after her disappointment at Hartpury, she was ready to say goodbye to her rowing career and had a place at Saint Mary's University in Twickenham lined up to study for a teaching qualification. However, in the summer of 2020, on the weekend that should have been the climax of the (cancelled) Henley Regatta, she and Nash decided to run a marathon to raise money for the MIND charity. By an amazing coincidence, the distance from the Brookes boathouse at Cholsey to the iconic Leander Club in Henley, via the Thames towpath, is exactly the marathon distance.

The day before the run the pair were in Henley and happened to meet Henry Bailhache-Webb, head rowing coach at Brookes. They told him of their plans for the next day. 'I've never run a marathon,' said Henry. 'I'll join you tomorrow!' (Can you imagine being fit enough to just decide on the spur of the moment that you will run a marathon the next day?)

Anyway, the three of them ran together, with Henry complaining most of the way that he was struggling to run at such a slow pace. He did prove useful though because 'he held the gates open for us and he knew the way', as Bates puts it! And by the time the runners arrived at Henley, Bates had decided. Forget St Mary's, she was going to Brookes in the autumn to do a Masters – and get back into rowing.

She was welcomed into the club, loved it, and all initially went well. The crew's time on the water was still limited because of Covid, so there was lots or cycling and working outdoors on the ergs. In early 2021, her crew came third in the intermediate category at the British Universities (BUCS) regatta, which was a decent result, Bates thought.

But the day after the event, back in Oxford, Richard Chambers, then the coach of the women's squad, read out the crew lists for the next event. Bates had been dropped from her boat.

'It wasn't handled particularly sensitively, I had no warning, it was just announced. And at that stage, the women's and men's squads weren't joined up as well as they are now,' she remembers. 'I was disappointed, but I knew Brookes always made the best decisions for the boat, and everything was based on data.' The results from the telemetry in the BUCS event made her one of the weakest members of the crew, and other women in a lower Brookes boat deserved promotion into her seat.

Bates was supported by friends and colleagues in the club, who assured her that she would bounce back. But initially it did not look that way. She found a place in a four, but over the following weeks her crewmates were moved into other boats, and eventually she was left on her own as a sculler – she had done some sculling at Hartpury, but it was not her specialism really. At the Wimbleball training camp in May 2021, she was on her own, feeling lonely as she sculled along behind whilst other eights and quads trained on the lake.

Ups and downs ...
Sheppard had a slightly less stressful year with OBUBC, but it was not trouble free. He struggled with motivation during the Covid period when athletes were training from home or largely on their own, so came back to Brookes with a lot of work to do to get back to racing fitness. By the time the delayed Henley Regatta took place in August 2021, he was rowing in the Prince Albert Cup coxed four 'B' boat. The four beat Aberdeen University but then came up against the Brookes 'A' boat, with the expected result.

At that event, the Brookes top women's eight won the inaugural Island Challenge Cup for student women. Bates was delighted – she bought into the philosophy at Brookes that everybody contributes to

Jenny and Sam

success, and that meant she was delighted for the club and the athletes. She remembers Jordan Simper from that crew telling her, 'Your time will come, Jenny!'

That still didn't seem likely, and at the beginning of the 2021/22 season things got worse for Bates. She caught Covid, followed by lingering post-viral health issues. She felt supported by the club, but it got to the point where she came close to dropping out of university – and rowing – altogether.

By now, Hugo Gulliver had joined as coach for the women's squad. He brought the squad closer to the men's squad, and his emphasis was on making rowing fun. He was also responsible for getting Bates back into the boat, even if he achieved it in a slightly underhand manner! He called her one evening in early December.

'Jenny, I've got a problem. There's been an injury, I'm a rower short for the Bristol Head this Saturday. I need you in the boat.'

'Hugo, I haven't been in a boat for months! I can't do that.'

'Jenny, you don't want to let down the others, do you? They'll be so disappointed if we can't compete.'

So, with some trepidation, Bates was back on the water. The two Brookes women's boats finished first and second at the event, and Bates was hooked again. By the summer of 2022, her crew, the Brookes women's 'B' boat, won the intermediate eights at BUCS and at Henley Women's Regatta. At Henley Royal Regatta the 'B' crew gave their own 'A' crew a good race in the third round of the Island Cup. Bates and her colleagues pushed the first boat all the way, but lost by just over a length.

Sheppard, by now, was in his third year, enjoying rowing, but for much of the year he perhaps did not train as hard as he could. At that same Henley in 2022, he rowed in the Brookes 'B' crew in the Temple Cup, which delivered a great win over old rival Imperial College in the second round, but then lost to Durham University's first boat.

As summer 2022 approached, he decided to stay on and do a master's at Brookes, and he stepped up his effort in the gym. By the end of that academic year he was impressing Bailhache-Webb with his results. As the students disappeared off for the summer, the coach took him aside. If he continued training at this level, 'Sam, you'll be a monster next year.'

Sheppard was motivated by that confidence in him. When the students returned, he told his housemates that he was going to be selected for the Temple 'A' crew this year and they were going to win at Henley. His housemates weren't convinced, as Sheppard had not always applied himself 100 per cent, but something had clicked and he was enjoying himself, even in the gym.

'Training is a means to an end. You wouldn't do it on your own, without something to work for. But the atmosphere and the camaraderie around training at Brookes is so great, it keeps you going. It's competitive, but you're working with your best mates, even if you know you are going for the same seats in the boat.'

Despite the intensity of the programme, the coaches at Brookes try to ensure lives aren't 'consumed by rowing', as Sheppard puts it. Athletes socialise together, have dinner together, and having rowers around who have been there for several years and have already won major events is motivating for everyone.

But in rowing, the coach can only do so much. Ultimately, it's up to the individual. It is the personal drive, determination and commitment that matters. As Sheppard says, 'Only you have the power to decide how hard and well you're going to train.' However, a great coach can help athletes get themselves to that place where they *want* to push themselves to the limit.

Henley 2023 – the light at the end of the tunnel?
As the 2022/23 season started, Gulliver was really bringing the women's squad together, and helping Bates develop her technique.

Jenny and Sam

'I've always had the power, I could see that in my erg times, but my technique wasn't good enough to let me apply it as well as I should,' she says. In November 2022, she decided to enter the GB national trials, in which athletes have to compete in single sculling boats. She borrowed a boat and headed off to Boston in Lincolnshire without any great expectations.

To everyone's surprise, not least her own, and as an unknown in national rowing terms, she came sixth. 'The GB coaches kept checking their watches, they couldn't believe it,' she remembers. She was faster than several current members of the GB squad, and having been close to giving up rowing just a few months earlier, suddenly Bates was being talked about as a future Olympian.

Meanwhile, Sheppard had made another decision at the beginning of the 2022/23 season. As well as pushing himself harder this year, he decided he would give up competitive rowing after Henley 2023. This actually was part of the motivation for him to work to the maximum during the year – he knew this was his last chance of winning a major prize.

One day Richard Spratley took him aside in the gym. 'Are you really not going to row next year? If so, do you fancy doing some coaching?'

Sheppard hadn't really thought about it, but if Spratley had seen some potential in him, it seemed worth giving it a go. That's why, a year later, he is coaching at Brookes, the latest piece in the jigsaw as Spratley looks to maintain the coaching continuity that has served the club well in recent years.

Back to 2023 and, in the run up to Henley 2023, the Temple crew trained with the Ladies' Plate crew, the most senior of the full-time Brookes men's boats. 'We often would beat them in training races,' remembers Sheppard. 'But whenever it came to a crunch event, and a real race, on the day, they would step it up and beat us.' That training would prove useful when it came to Henley itself.

In the women's squad, Bates was in the 'A' crew training for the Island Cup at Henley, alongside Arianna Forde, also promoted from the previous year's 'B' crew. It's interesting to note that three women who were in the 'A' crew in 2022 rowed in the 'B' boat the following year – that shows the Brookes objectivity and ruthlessness coming into play again, but this time to the benefit of Bates. Yet the athletes accept their fate, and seem to genuinely put the best interests of the club ahead of their own feelings. And that top crew was beating everybody in sight in early 2023, winning BUCS by three lengths and beating Harvard, Leander and Thames to win the top event at the Henley Women's Regatta.

So how did Bates and Sheppard and their crews perform at Henley Royal Regatta in 2023? Well, you might have guessed the answer by

Jenny Bates (©*AllMarkOne*)

Sam Sheppard (©*AllMarkOne*)

now, but you can read the race reports for the Temple final on page X, and for the Island final on page Y.

The Brookes secret
How does Bates explain the success of Brookes? 'We keep each other accountable. People post photos of the extra training they're doing on group chats, and everyone is really supportive. We trained with the top rowers and watched them win when we were starting at Brookes; now the new recruits look at us in the same way. It's about role models. We help and push each other up – but we have fun too.'

That squad aspect is emphasised by Sheppard too. 'I've been training from the beginning here with guys who have won gold medals at world under-23 championships. Seeing what they do pulls the standard for everybody up. But equally, the folks towards the bottom of the squad also work hard and the pressure from them pushes us all in that same positive direction too!'

For instance, the Brookes men's sixth boat finished sixteenth out of 300 boats in the 2022 Head of the River race on the London Tideway – faster than all but three other UK university first boats! So being at the 'bottom' of the Brookes squad is still a pretty impressive place to be.

Both Bates and Sheppard have had amazing opportunities and experiences. They've competed against Olympic rowers, raced in Shanghai, at the San Diego Crew Classic, at regattas around Europe as well as Henley, BUCS and domestic events. These are not experiences many student athletes enjoy, in any sport, anywhere.

We will have more on what Bates has been up to in 2024 later. But let's just say the Los Angeles 2028 Olympics is very much on her radar. And Sheppard is finishing his master's, looking forward to at least a few years of coaching, and maybe more. Who knows, he might prove to be the Spratley or Bailhache-Webb of the 2030s and 2040s …

Chapter 2

Rowing Hurts

'Marathon runners talk about hitting "the wall" at the twenty-third mile of the race. What rowers confront isn't a wall; it's a hole – an abyss of pain, which opens up in the second minute of the race. Large needles are being driven into your thigh muscles, while your forearms seem to be splitting. Then the pain becomes confused and disorganized, not like the windedness of the runner or the leg burn of the biker but an all-over, savage unpleasantness.'
(Ashleigh Teitel, writer and rower, quoted on the 10morestrokes website)[1]

Rowing hurts

On hearing I was writing this book, Sheena Smith, a friend who rowed seriously for the University of Washington two decades ago and still coaches today, told me I really should emphasise the pain of rowing up-front to help non-rowing readers understand what it is all about. She said this:

> 'I'd love to read about the physicality of what it's like to pull along the weight of both boat and cox – knives in the lungs, burning quads, calluses ripping on hands, sweat dripping, a million annoyances and adjustments that you can't do anything about and must tune out, because once you're in the race, rowers can't stop ...'

Every sport is unique by definition, but rowing genuinely has unusual attributes. First of all, it really, *really* hurts, more than pretty much any other sport, partly because few other activities use virtually every muscle in the body. Swimming comes close, but even that does not replicate the way rowing engages the legs, the arms (right down to the fingertips, literally), upper and lower body, stomach, back, even the neck and head muscles keeping your head as still as possible. The sport is intense and punishing on your entire body.

Perhaps because of this, it is one of the few sports where athletes can and do reasonably regularly throw up, collapse or even pass out, as we saw in the 2024 Boat Race, where the Cambridge stroke, Matt Edge, was virtually in a zombie state for the last two minutes of the race. Fortunately, Cambridge held on to win and he recovered quickly.

Rowing the classic 2,000-metre course in a race means setting off like a 100-metre sprinter, then settling into maybe an 800-metre runner level of exertion, followed by a last 30 seconds of flat-out sprinting effort again, but with every muscle in your body contributing. Rowing a head race over 15 or 20 minutes means a less dramatic initial effort – but pain for longer!

And it is not just the muscles. There is good chance that your hands will be covered in blisters for much of the season. You will bang your hands and shins on parts of the boat that suddenly leap out to attack you. You might expect back problems to be a major issue, which they are, but tendonitis in the hands is one of the most common ailments.

Yet it is strangely addictive. One athlete at the Brookes boathouse told me she had suffered a succession of injuries. 'I decided to give up rowing last year. I stopped for a whole month. But I was so bored, I missed it so much!' She is now hoping to work her way back up the hierarchy of Brookes boats, subject to maintaining her health and fitness.

Trust is everything

Then, unless you are rowing on your own in a sculling boat, there is the team aspect. You can't stop, as my friend said. This is the second part of the great Ashleigh Teitel quote at the top of this chapter:

'As you pass the five-hundred-meter mark, with three-quarters of the race still to row, you realize with dread that you are not going to make it to the finish, but at the same time the idea of letting your teammates down by not rowing your hardest is unthinkable ... Therefore, you are going to die. Welcome to this life.'

Teitel captures there one of the essential psychological aspects of rowing. Unlike many team sports (football, rugby, cricket, basketball), one amazing individual can't drive victory, but again unlike those sports, one really bad performance *will* cost the team the win. So the pressure on everyone to perform for the sake of their colleagues is intense. That means trust is vital and central to rowing. I *must* trust my crew mates if we are going to succeed. When I feel like I might die imminently, even a momentary thought that someone else is not working as hard can lose the race.

Even if a crew is leading, a couple of athletes thinking 'I can take it easy now, we've got this', can let the opposition back into the race. That is why team spirit, collaboration and the bonds within clubs and crews are vital to successful rowing, and the friendships formed in rowing clubs and crews tend to last a lifetime. (Later, the GB Olympic team performance at the 2021 Tokyo Olympics will be discussed, an example where maybe that team spirit was not in evidence.)

But on the positive side, the sensation when a high-quality boat is really travelling is brilliant, even if you are merely the cox, as I was. Off the start in a race, you feel the G-force acceleration and de-acceleration of every stroke in the cox's seat, as you are bumped forwards and backwards into the back of your seat (wear some padding ...). On a calm, sunny day, the boat seems to glide across the surface of the water, four or eight rowers moving as one.

Rowing Hurts

It is a great experience, as is winning a significant race. The sheer decibels of the Henley Stewards' Enclosure crowd shouting you on in a close finish, or even the Cambridge Bumps spectators gathered around Grassy Corner, cheering as you go for the bump, is incredible. But equally, losing, when you have given your absolute all for six minutes or more, is an awful feeling.

In my first year coxing at Henley for Lady Margaret Boat Club, we came from two lengths down to beat our biggest Cambridge rivals. That felt good. The following year, another College unexpectedly did exactly the same to us. I am not exaggerating to say that was one of the worst moments of my life, and no miserable work experience, for instance, has ever come close to that intense psychological pain.

Here is another excellent description of how it feels, in this case rowing a 2,000-metre 'race' on the erg machine, but it applies just as well to rowing on the water. (It is attributed to Lewis Hynes, although I have not found the original.) Here is one section describing the third quarter of the race:

> 'If you are going to fail it will be here. You don't, but the loss of all hope of control, despair of ever going faster, and the fear of failure; all combine, react and ignite in your tinder-dry throat, the flames leaping into your chest and scorching it raw. The skin on the back of your forearms and shins goosepimples up, some bizarre atavistic reaction to the acid poisoning your blood. You are being drowned by your own exertions, burned alive from within by the byproducts of your muscles, and you must not, will not, ever let it stop. This is the wilderness, the third 500 m, an eternal, blasted wasteland. It is a black place, hope is abandoned, logic is absent, pain is eternal. It is the entrance to the hole that is the last 500 m.'

Oxford Brookes

So, there are intense highs and lows for serious athletes in this sport, but fundamentally, rowing hurts. Bear that in mind as the story of Brookes unfolds and remember that every victory and loss featured here really, really hurt. So how coaches persuade athletes to go through that pain barrier, time after time, working for themselves and for their teammates, is a critical success factor for any serious rowing crew or club.

Chapter 3

The Poly

'Putting up a poster we found three other people with basic rowing knowledge who wanted to row. We were effectively all novices.' (Nick Ryan, quoted by Clive Couldwell in the Taurus newsletter, 2011)

The Poly
In the beginning, there was the Poly.

Oxford Polytechnic always had to fight for recognition alongside its illustrious neighbour, the University of Oxford, an ancient establishment founded in the eleventh century, in the days of William the Conqueror. The forerunner institutions to the Poly date back only as far as the Oxford School of Art in 1865 and, having merged with several other colleges, the institution became a fully-fledged Polytechnic in 1970, with strengths in technology and business as well as health and social sciences.

In the mid-1970s, a number of keen rowers who had competed at school arrived at the Poly. But there was no boat club, so some like Hayden Morris, who joined City of Oxford, gravitated towards local clubs. But in 1978, Morris went along to the Freshers Fair with some leaflets and a positive attitude, and found a number of like-minded oarsmen who were keen to start a club. Nick Ryan, Russell Cook and Alasdair Davies joined Morris, and founded the Oxford Polytechnic Boat Club (OPBC). Quickly, other founding members including Clive Couldwell, Martin Durgan, David Cook and Charles Stimpson came on board.

The club was led by Ryan, as the inaugural Captain of Boats. Sixty enthusiastic novices, men and women, were recruited via an advert in the student's union, and even after some drop outs, the club was quickly one of the bigger sports clubs at the Poly. The only problems were a lack of boats, premises and money.

The City of Oxford club wasn't interested in helping, but others were more generous. The athletes were given their first home by the Oxford Falcon Rowing and Canoeing Club, itself a club with a lengthy and interesting history, as the oldest Oxford 'town' rowing club.[2] The first competitions were entered as a composite Polytechnic/Falcon crew, even though crews were in fact 100 per cent Poly athletes. Cook borrowed a boat from his old school, Reading Blue Coat, and other founders used their connections at schools such as Monmouth. Some Oxford Colleges were also helpful.

It was all somewhat hand to mouth though. Cook remembers being stopped by the police on the Marlow bypass having 'borrowed' a trailer from the Marlow Rowing Club! But the club was established now and, in the 1979–80 season, Oxford Polytechnic/Falcon won the novice men's fours at Monmouth Regatta and novice women's fours at Stratford-upon-Avon. The Poly was on its way in the world of rowing.

By the next season, Tim Magee, who had both rowed and coached, got involved, and a sponsored row enabled the club to buy their first boat, christened *Oxpolycarbonate*. It was an old GB squad training boat, that 'we picked up for next to nothing', says Couldwell.

In that 1980–81 season, the Poly tried to persuade Boris Rankov, captain of Oxford University Boat Club, that the Poly should be allowed to row in the University's bumping races. He wasn't keen, but he agreed that a Poly crew could enter the annual Oriel Regatta – which they promptly won! It is not the most serious rowing event in the world, but when a huge cup was presented to 'the Poly', it was accompanied by almost total silence from the assembled (and shocked) University students. 'Only St Hilda's cheered, because I was coaching them,' remembers Magee.

The Poly

The club entered Henley and by chance came up against Oriel College. Sadly the Poly lost this time. 'We rarely had the same crew one week to the next in those early days,' says Morris today. But the club started entering British Polytechnic Sports Association events, and won championship events at the annual regatta through the 1980s.

Those early days seem like a world away from the experience of Brookes athletes today. But every success story starts with a few faltering steps, and talking to the founders today, they are still rightly proud of the essential role they played in this story.

By the time Alex and Jane Gandon arrived in the mid-eighties, the Poly had a decent men's first eight. Boat bargain-hunting continued with the purchase of an old South African squad eight, a rather impressive carbon fibre model renamed *Poly Folly* that, legend had it, had once broken the Henley Royal Regatta Thames Cup record.

Oxford Poly Boat Club, 1980-81 (*OPBC/Brookes archive*)

Oxford Brookes

Through the eighties, the club continued to put a lot of effort into training novices. Whilst the men's first boat continued to be largely those like Alex Gandon, who had rowed at school, by the late eighties 'we had two men's and two women's novice boats and a women's first eight which was made up in the main of women who had learnt to row at the Poly', remembers Gandon. 'There was a positive feeling as novices, including me, worked our way through the ranks,' says Jane Gandon (Jane Macmillan in those days). 'Looking back, it was all very inclusive.'

During the 1960s, there were probably fewer than 1,000 female rowers in the UK. Whilst that number steadily increased, and women's rowing came into the Olympics in 1976, it was often still a struggle in the 1980s for oarswomen to be taken seriously and find resources in clubs and academic institutions. The Poly was perhaps ahead of its time in its relative equality in this sense.

But it continued to be a struggle to find equipment, for both men and women, and the club often borrowed boats. Everything was very much run by students for students, with a captain of boats and a committee structure, but although students did most of the boat maintenance and much of the coaching, there were already some external coaches, Nick Rogers and Dave Cowell being early examples.

Indeed, the legendary Boris Rankov, who was in the Oxford Boat Race winning crew no less than six times, coached at one point. 'But the coaching was very much focused around a single boat, not the entire club,' explains Alex Gandon. However, the club was competitive, not winning at Henley level regattas but picking up medals elsewhere and developing a reputation as an institution that took rowing pretty seriously.

At Henley Royal Regatta in July 1987, the Oxford Poly boat won a couple of rounds in the student eights event, and Peter Lowe, a keen schoolboy rower on his gap year between school and university, saw this

Oxford Poly 1st boat, 1985 (*Brookes archive*)

Oxford Polytechnic Boat Club, Thames Cup at Henley, 1986 (*Brookes archive*)

and thought 'maybe I'll go there for my degree'. The Poly already had a good reputation for property and architectural studies, Lowe's degree choice.

By the 89/90 season, word had spread that the Poly was a decent place to row, Lowe was stroking the first boat, and Oxford Poly finished thirty-fifth in the Head of the River race on the Thames in London. That was very respectable for a race with over 400 entries, and a higher placing than long-established rowing universities such as Nottingham, Edinburgh and Southampton.

In 1990, the Poly opened the Isis boathouse, giving the club its first home of its own two miles from the centre of Oxford by Iffley Lock.[3] It was a step forward for the club, but the location was not perfect for training, with access to only a limited stretch of uninterrupted water. (In 2004, Brookes sold the Isis boathouse for £400,000 to help fund the developments at Cholsey, but by 2024, it was on the market for £1 million with planning permission to convert the upper floor into a 2-bedroom apartment!)[4]

In that same year of 1990, the club entered the men's first eight into the Ghent regatta in Belgium, where they beat Imperial College, one of the favourites for the student event at Henley (by now named the 'Henley Prize').

But at Marlow regatta Imperial came out on top, and although the Poly performed well at HRR in July there was disappointment, losing to Imperial in the semi-finals by just a canvas. The club seemed to be moving in the right direction though, and there was confidence that the big breakthrough was close.

In 1991, the crew edged up to a thirty-third place finish at the Head in London. But at HRR in July they were drawn against the Japanese students from Nihon University. Lowe's crew was confident, perhaps over-confident, and to their surprise lost badly. Unlike the epic race with Imperial the year before, this really hurt. The University of Bristol

The Isis Boathouse (*2014 Photo © Roger Templeman (cc-by-sa/2.0)*

Oxford Poly at Henley 1990, with Peter Lowe stroking the boat (*Brookes archive*)

went on to beat Imperial in the final, leaving the Poly crew feeling that this should have been their year.

This was the final straw for Lowe, by now a post-graduate student, and his friends. They realised much needed to be done to really challenge for major prizes at Henley and elsewhere. It was time to get serious help.

'Do you fancy doing some coaching?'
After losing at Henley that July, Lowe was in the Bridge Bar in the Stewards' Enclosure drowning his sorrows, when he bumped into a friend of his, Tim Levy, who Lowe had rowed with pre-Brookes. Levy came from a rowing family and had coaching experience already at Thames Rowing Club. Lowe knew Levy had a brilliant rowing brain, with the ability to look at a crew and spot quickly what was needed to increase its speed.

'Tim, we need a coach at the Poly. Do you fancy helping?' asked Lowe. There was no salary, hopefully some expenses, but that was it. Levy thought about it. 'Give me half an hour,' he said, and disappeared. Thirty minutes he was back at the bar, with Richard Spratley at his side.

Spratley grew up in and around Henley and the upper Thames. His father and grandfather were architects and builders covering Reading, Henley and Marlow, and Richard gained a place at the prestigious state grammar school in Marlow, Sir William Borlase's. Whilst the school did some rowing, Spratley really got into the sport as a 14-year-old with Henley Rowing Club. He was keen and dedicated from the beginning. 'There was never a chance he was going to come and see me until he'd been out rowing and done all the gym training afterwards,' recalls Jane, his girlfriend from the age of 15.

Although he was academically bright, he was a practical young man who wanted to pursue rowing and also something useful as his day job. So he left school at 16, studying at Reading College while starting work with a local construction firm. He was selected for national junior trials, but never quite made the GB squad. Joining Leander Club, aged 18, he became a successful rower with Leander, Henley and London Rowing Club crews, rowing at a good club level, winning a national championship and reaching the finals day at Henley one year. His rowing career continued alongside his construction work through his twenties.

But as he approached 30, he had decisions to make. He wasn't going to make it at the very top levels of the sport as a competitor, despite his enthusiasm and technical skill. At 5 feet 11 inches (1.80 m) and weighing around 12 and a half stone (80 kg), he was just too small for the highest level of heavyweight rowing, but probably a little on the large side for lightweight rowing, which was now beginning to be taken seriously as a separate category. And age was against him as well. He also decided to start his own construction business, which was going to be a serious drain on his time and energy. In 1990, he decided to walk away from rowing.

But as it so often does, fate intervened. His two brothers rowed at Kingston, and brother Jeremy joined their father's architectural practice. With his brother and father, Spratley built a small development of three houses near Oxford for the family's use. Jeremy's best friend was the same Peter Lowe, who lodged with Jeremy whilst a student at Brookes.

So when Levy returned to the bar with him, Lowe knew Richard well enough to agree to the arrangement. Levy had the coaching experience, but he didn't have much time to offer, and he wasn't the most organised individual. He knew that Spratley was a good manager and organiser, given his experience in the construction world. They could offer complementary skills.

Spratley was open to a new challenge. He didn't have any formal training as a rowing coach. But he had worked under good, experienced coaches as an oarsman, and he'd observed and learnt from the legendary

Oxford Brookes

Steve Gunn who trained scullers at Molesey and ran training camps at Henley. Spratley was already missing rowing, and this was a way to keep in the game – at least for a couple of years, he thought.

Lowe, Levy and Spratley agreed to get together to talk further about their plans for the boat club. They convened at the Flower Pot Hotel in Aston, a tiny and beautiful hamlet just along the river from Henley. In the bar of the Victorian pub and hotel, the three talked about the training programme that the Poly would adopt, and literally sketched out a plan on a beer mat. 'That programme is still the basis for what happens at OBUBC today,' says Lowe.

Chapter 4

Brookes emerges, disaster strikes (1992)

'If we train twice as hard as everyone else, we stand half a chance.'
(Richard Spratley)

Becoming Brookes!
By chance, Spratley and Levy had joined the Poly at a momentous moment. The UK's Further and Higher Education Act of 1992 allowed 35 polytechnics, including Oxford, to become fully-fledged universities. Oxford decided to name itself after John Henry Brookes, a craftsman, artist and educator who was the first principal of the Oxford Schools of Technology Art and Commerce, predecessors to the Poly, back in 1934.

The brief from Lowe to the new coaches was simple – win the student eights event at Henley Royal Regatta. That event was known as the Henley Prize at the time, but changed its name to the Temple Cup for the 1992 event, which has been its title ever since. That goal motivated Spratley, given his association with the town, and the 'unfinished business', as he called it, after his previous experience at the regatta.

By the winter of 1991, Levy and Spratley were ensconced and making their mark on the boat club. There were about twenty male rowers, as well as a group of female athletes, although at the time they were not Spratley's responsibly. The men still rowed from Falcon, but the Isis boathouse was used for some training and the women boated from that location too.

This was where Spratley's wider capability began to show itself. He was both a strategic thinker, and also a practical, resourceful and pragmatic operational manager. Perhaps that was something to do with his training and experience in project management, essential for his work in the construction industry. He was organised and could think on his feet, but he also had strategic vision, although he claims that he did not initially have a grand plan for the club.

But as a coach, he wasn't going to accept the status quo. He quickly decided that the river in Oxford was not ideal for serious training, being winding, busy and narrow in places. So in the autumn of 1991, Spratley and Lowe negotiated an agreement to use the facilities of Wallingford Rowing Club, 13 miles (21 km) south of Oxford, which gave them access to a beautiful stretch of the Thames, relatively quiet and wide. It is simply a great rowing location.

Now the crews could train more effectively, with longer periods of rowing uninterrupted by locks, tourists or rogue punts. The new coach could quickly see that the crew was promising, and might be able to achieve the goal they had set themselves, to win the student eights at Henley Royal Regatta.

'Sunshine on a rainy day ...'
Spratley told his crews that if they did twice as much training as their rivals over the winter, they stood half a chance at Henley, an early example of both the Brookes mantra of hard work and the underdog spirit that served them so well over the years. Levy was seen as the rowing 'brain', whilst Spratley was the man who made things happen. The training was certainly intensive – 'a run, then sets of squats, hops, squat double jumps, sit-ups, all before we started on the weights'; the programme is embedded in Lowe's memory, thirty years later.

A new agreement with Shiplake College, a private school on the river near Henley, saw Spratley training the squad in eight two-man pair boats hired from Shiplake. Bill Wallace, the boatman at the College was very helpful, Lowe remembers, and racing between pairs, swapping the

Brookes emerges, disaster strikes (1992)

oarsmen around regularly, was a very good way of seeing just who the fastest men on the water really were.

In late 1991, Brookes made the first of what turned out to be a very regular pilgrimage to Wimbleball Lake, near the Somerset/Devon border in south-west England. Richard Spratley had rowed there at the annual Wimbleball regatta in his youth, and remembered how much he enjoyed the experience.

Wimbleball is an oddly shaped reservoir, nestled in the Exmoor hills. When the sun is out, illuminating surrounding woods and slopes, its beauty is heart-stopping; but it can be somewhat bleak in bad weather. It is around 1500 metres long and its width varies from a couple of hundred metres to over 500 metres. If you look at it on the map it looks too irregular to be a good training ground for rowing, but you can get a good straight course of a thousand metres or a little more without too much trouble, and its width means you can have several boats rowing alongside each other for that distance.

As Spratley says, 'there is nothing you can do at other training centres that you can't do at Wimbleball – but there is plenty that you can do or experience at Wimbleball that you don't get anywhere else.' To understand what he means, watch the videos Brookes has made of the training there.[5] The drone shots are stunning, some of the very best rowing film ever made. And going there is an experience for the athletes, building team spirit as well as rowing expertise. There are many unrepeatable Wimbleball stories, I'm told …

So a dozen or so rowers, a couple of coxes, Richard Spratley and Tim Levy travelled down to Wimbleball for the first ever Brookes training camp in late autumn 1991. Most of the party had bed and breakfast accommodation at the Raleghs Cross Inn, a few kilometres from the lake. On the first morning, there was a pre-breakfast trip to the lake to get the boats out on the water for the first training session.

After enjoying the beauty of Wimbleball for an hour or so, and working up an appetite, the crews set off back to the inn for breakfast. Most were in the Brookes minibus, which Peter Lowe had persuaded the university authorities to lend them for the weekend. James Symington was driving, with Lowe in the front passenger seat and Piers Ashley-Carter wedged in between them.

The squad were in high spirits, singing along to 'Sunshine on a Rainy Day', a recent chart hit. But they were hungry, already in calorie deficit for the day. Demands for Symington to 'drive faster because we're starving' were heard, but going down a hill, disaster struck. A large truck pulled out onto the main road, heading in the opposite direction to the minibus, but because of its size, it veered across onto their side of the road. There was no time for Symington to stop, so he desperately steered onto the edge of the road to take avoiding action. But the minibus was out of control, and headed over the grass verge, towards a ditch and trees bordering the road.

Lowe remembers as if in slow motion seeing a large tree approaching his side of the bus as they hurtled towards it. The bus took off into the air, heading for the tree, then landed with a thump in the ditch. Fortunately the vehicle had grounded itself and came to an abrupt stop, but as this was pre compulsory seatbelts days, the rear passengers were thrown into the seats in front of them.

There was silence for a moment. Then, a voice. 'Is everyone OK?'

Incredibly, the answer was 'yes', apart from one athlete with a facial cut caused by his own spectacles. But the rest were shaken, shocked but fine. When Lowe extricated himself from the vehicle, he realised that the wing mirror next to where he had been sitting was now embedded in the tree he'd seen approaching. 'If we'd hit it another two feet to the right, that might have been my head,' he remembers. But the minibus was a write-off, its entire undercarriage ripped to pieces.

Brookes emerges, disaster strikes (1992)

The squad had a couple of cars as well as the bus, so everyone was ferried back to the inn, and the training camp continued with a replacement minibus quickly provided via the insurance policy. But the reaction of the university when Lowe called to explain what had happened to their lovely minibus is not recorded, perhaps fortunately.

That is a genuine sliding doors moment in the Brookes history. That accident might have led to fatalities, the end of Wimbleball training before it had even started, the end of that crew, and perhaps even the end of Spratley's involvement with the club. But after some basic first aid to treat the cuts and bruises, the crews were back out on the water that day.

Wimbleball involved plenty of seat racing, a training and selection tool that became one of Spratley's core processes and has continued through to the present day. You race two crews against each other, and then swap a couple of people around between the boats, and race again. You repeat this until everyone is thoroughly exhausted. Now there must be a clever mathematical algorithm that would show how to find the optimum crew in the minimum number of races. But most coaches will also use some 'feel' as well as hard data (perhaps from telemetry equipment today). Eventually you arrive, in theory at least, with your fastest crew.

The end of 'the Poly'

That weekend at Wimbleball helped to solidify the selection of the first boat. In the Head of the River on the Thames in March 1992, the last time 'Oxford Polytechnic' was seen on that event's results list, the first boat crew moved up to twenty-second place, beating crews from illustrious clubs such as Thames Tradesmen and Vesta, as well as universities including Durham, Edinburgh and Reading. The rowing world really began to take note of 'the Poly'.

Through the next couple of months it all looked good, and preparation was going well for Henley. After the exam season was over, Spratley decided the crew needed some different competition, and different scenery. So off they went, in their minibus, towing a boat behind them, on a grand tour of European regattas. At Ghent regatta in Belgium, the crew won a bronze medal, pushing Lea Boat Club, one of the fastest club crews in England, all the way.

Then Spratley had the bright idea of driving down to Switzerland to enter the Lucerne event, traditionally one of Europe's most prestigious regattas, particularly in an Olympic year. That was rather different from the usual domestic rowing against Imperial or Newcastle University, and just not something that British universities did, even Oxford or Cambridge. The very top-level continental regattas were the preserve of national-squad-type boats, international or aspiring internationals.

'We just wanted to push ourselves as hard as possible, to set our goals as high as possible and measure ourselves against the best crews in the world,' remembers Spratley.

The crew arrived in Lucerne to some strange looks from officials. This was a British student crew they had probably never seen or heard of before, but the boat beat two national crews in the heats, Spain and France, and found themselves in the final up against crews like the German national squad, one of the fastest eights in the world.

Spratley remembers that race. 'We were over the moon to qualify, but we lost in the final, not surprisingly! Some of the crew were desperately disappointed with our performance, but actually I was pleased when I looked at the times.'

Brookes was some 22 seconds slower than the winning German crew. Now that might sound like a lot; it is about seven boat lengths over a 2000-metre course. But Spratley knew that in most years, the fastest student eights at Henley Royal Regatta are some 20 seconds slower

Brookes emerges, disaster strikes (1992)

than the winners of the Grand for the top national boats. So these international performances boded well for the first weekend in July at Henley.

> **The athletes speak**
> 'OBUBC's culture is underpinned by a gritty, underdog mentality. We win races in spite of being Brookes, not because we're Brookes. Every athlete therefore knows that they don't own the seat in which they sit, but are instead borrowing its history, whilst they search to contribute their own.'
> (*Matt Heywood,* 2x HRR winner, GB U-23 and full international)

At the Henley Women's Regatta, held just a week before the Royal Regatta, the Oxford Poly coxed four won the college event, beating Ridley College, Canada in an exciting final. This was the last outing for 'Oxford Polytechnic', before it became Oxford Brookes University, and was also the first major title for the club. It seemed a good omen for the men's crew at the imminent HRR.

'Jump out of the boat!'

After their performances earlier in the year, Brookes went to Henley 1992 as one of the seeded crews in the student eights event, no longer the Henley Prize but now renamed the 'Temple Challenge Cup'. They sailed through the first two rounds without breaking sweat, then came up against Exeter College of Oxford University in the quarter finals. In truth, the early eighties saw the end of the days when individual colleges at Oxford or Cambridge were serious contenders at Henley, as other clubs including Brookes were becoming more professional compared to Oxbridge's generally amateur approach. So Brookes should have won this race comfortably.

Oxford Brookes

The first few strokes of a race are frantic, as the rowers take short strokes to get the boat going and build speed quickly. They slide up and down faster, and if there is some sort of weakness in the equipment, it is often exposed right at the beginning of a race. And this time, after just a few strokes, disaster struck for the Brookes stroke, Ludo Reed, and the entire crew.

The sliding seat carrying him forward and back suddenly broke. He was almost pitched out of the boat, but although he managed to avoid that, he could not row, and realising what had happened, the crew stopped rowing too. Peter Lowe, in the number 2 seat now, raised his hand and shouted to the umpires following in the launch, expecting the race to be halted. In most regattas, there was a rule that if equipment failed in the first minute or 250 metres, the race would be re-started.

But there was no signal from the umpires. So Brookes started rowing again, as best they could. Spratley was on the riverbank. 'I was yelling at Ludo to jump out of the boat, I thought they would go faster without him,' he remembers. In fact, there *was* a rule covering that eventuality and the crew would have been disqualified if it had finished a man short, so that was not really an option.

Indeed, the whole concept of the 'coxless four' was invented at Henley in 1868 when the cox of the Brasenose College four jumped out when the umpire started the race. The boat won easily without the cox's weight, and with a steering device devised by the crew, but was disqualified. However, rowers realised that a four did not really need a cox and that created coxless fours as a category.

Back to 1992, and the Brookes crew laboured up the course, with a non-contributing stroke sitting motionless, losing in the end by around three lengths, remarkably close given their handicap. Most of the crew were in tears, their dream of winning at Henley had gone. But Lowe didn't give up. As club captain, he went to see Peter Coni, the Regatta chairman and a respected figure in British rowing. Surely there should

Brookes emerges, disaster strikes (1992)

be a re-row, he argued. The coach of the Exeter College crew has said since then that he would have been happy to race again. But Coni would not grant Brookes another chance.

At that time, it appears that the rules for Henley were somewhat vague and not well documented. Today, everything is much clearer. Would Coni have been more sympathetic if it had been a better-known boat club affected, a Harvard or Cambridge, perhaps? We will never know. But that was it for Brookes in 1992.

Imperial College went on to win the event, beating Trinity College Dublin in the final. Imperial was a good crew, and we can't know if Brookes would have won. Spratley still remembers the feeling to this day. 'The crew were devastated. I'd sold them the big dream for the whole year, it was in sight, then it was gone in a few seconds.'

A year of tough training with one aim in mind, all gone through a piece of bad luck. Spratley was furious initially, then calmed down. He tried to raise the spirits of the defeated crew, talking about coming back next year to make amends. His own wife assumed that this was the end though. 'You can't do another year of this,' she suggested to Spratley.

He hadn't been thinking really beyond the summer of 1992, and while it is tempting to think that there was some amazing 30-year plan to make Brookes the best club in the world, Spratley confirms there wasn't. 'We've always worked by ticking off small hurdles and achievements, one thing at a time,' is the way he explains it.

However, despite the devastating Henley disappointment, Spratley had thoroughly enjoyed his first year with Brookes. He loved working with young athletes, seeing their enthusiasm and feeling that he could help them thrive and improve. He was a 'people person', who loved the human interaction of coaching, but he was also highly competitive, and saw the potential to win more as a coach with Brookes than he had been able to do as an oarsman himself. 'Let's give it one more year,' he said to his wife and, after some discussion, he agreed to stay on.

Oxford Brookes

And there was one positive outcome that made the 1992 disaster into a turning point. Several of the crew who had intended to leave Brookes decided to stay on and do a master's course so they could row for one more year, vowing to work even harder to make amends the following year. Meanwhile, some of that 1992 crew left, always wondering what might have been.

In September of that year, a handful of strong new schoolboy rowers came up to the university to start their courses. It looked like the 1993 Brookes Temple crew might be even stronger than the 1992.

The 2023 Prince Albert Challenge Cup Final

Dotted through the book, you will find detailed reports of the most exciting Henley Royal Regatta finals of 2023 and 2024 that featured Oxford Brookes. Here is the first.

Henley Royal Regatta, 11 am, 2 July 2023

Race report – The 2023 Prince Albert Challenge Cup Final
Down at the start of the Henley Royal Regatta course, at the beginning of the day, it is quiet, and the crowds in the enclosures and the hospitality tents, the fairground, campsites and bars along the course, all seem distant. With just a few spectators on the riverbank, you can hear the water lapping around the boats, the occasional cry of waterfowl and the umpire in the launch, preparing the crews to depart up the course.

'Both crews, when you are ready, I shall say "attention, go".'

The first race of finals' day at the 2023 Henley Royal Regatta is the Prince Albert Challenge Cup for student coxed fours. The rules mean you cannot select a crew member who has won a non-junior event at Henley previously, or has won medals at international level. The crew must be 'real', current students.

This year, we have a classic UK versus US match-up, with Oxford Brookes University taking on the University of Washington – 'the Huskies', to their supporters. Washington is one of the top US rowing universities, and their four probably starts as slight favourites, but we are expecting a close race. The coxed four is not the fastest type of boat, as four people have to carry the non-contributing cox over the course, so clearly it is slower than four rowers or scullers without that dead weight. But that does not lessen the anticipation of a close race.

With the temperature at about 17°C, and a light breeze, these are good conditions for rowing, and there is little swell on the water from wind or river traffic yet. Both coxes lie flat in the front of the boats, which is aerodynamically effective and gives them a great view ahead

Oxford Brookes

down the course. But that means they cannot see the faces of their own crews, or talk directly to the stroke, which can be an issue tactically as the race develops.

Brookes has the Berkshire station, next to the enclosures, which is generally a slight advantage off the start. The other crew on the Bucks station must row close to Temple Island for the first 30 seconds, which tends to confuse the steering, and tricky cross winds interfere as you hit the end of the island. But crews with coxes who steer should not have too many issues.

There is no messing around from the umpire here. 'Attention, go' is shouted out without hesitation. After three or four slightly tentative strokes, Washington really accelerates powerfully, despite the station disadvantage, taking a small lead. Brookes looks relaxed, but a little sluggish in comparison.

The first timing point on the course is known as 'the Barrier' and Washington leads narrowly at that point in a time of two minutes and one second. Over the next 90 seconds, the crews go stroke for stroke up to the Fawley timing point, which is approximately half way. Washington still leads by a few feet, after 3 minutes and 26 seconds of intense rowing. But the Huskies are failing to increase that lead, and they must start to feel that, despite their own fast start, they have not been able to break the men from Oxford.

Going past the Upper Thames Rowing Club boathouse on the bank, with more engaged spectators now watching events closely, Washington digs deep and extends the lead, but it is still only half a length. That is not a significant lead in a four. But the facial close-ups from the excellent video coverage show two of the Washington crew visibly suffering. The Brookes guys don't exactly look like they're out for a gentle paddle in the park, but their expressions look more composed.

As the boats come level with the Regatta Enclosure, where a lot of rowers and their families hang out, the noise from the crowd hits the

The 2023 Prince Albert Challenge Cup Final

crews for the first time, the Brookes bladework starts to look a little ragged. Some blades are axing into the water from a greater height than is ideal. But the power is really being transferred into boat speed and now the crews draw level for the first time since the very first stroke. The cheers from the crowds build – 'come on Brookes' is the most common cry. The Henley crowd loves a GB versus USA scrap, and this is a classic. The noise grows louder as it becomes clear that the Brookes boat with the distinctive oars is inching ahead.

And now, something remarkable happens. As the crews come level with the Stewards' Enclosure grandstand for the last 200 metres of the race, the Washington crew suddenly cracks. The Brookes four seems to spring forward, moving further ahead every stroke.

Any rower will confirm that when you have been in the lead in a race and the other crew rows through and past you, it is a horrible feeling. (I experienced that as a cox at Henley and it was truly one of the worst experiences of my life.) But usually, the change is gradual. Here, one minute the crews are level, and 30 seconds later, Brookes leads by what seems like a mile. It is a dramatic collapse. The Washington men look like they are still trying as hard as they can, but Brookes has broken them. Six minutes of stroke-by-stroke rowing, pain in every second, and four of the best young oarsmen in the USA have cracked under the pressure from Brookes.

Anyone looking at the final verdict of three and three-quarter lengths (and to be honest, it looked like more) would think this has been an easy win. But watch it,[6] and you can see the war of attrition all the way down the course. And it is a war from which Brookes has come out victorious.

But there is one interesting postscript to this race. It looks like a classic USA versus GB tussle. But how many rowers do you think were actually British in the race? The Brookes boat featured a NZ/GB athlete, Jack Cooper, along with Evan Falstrup-Fisker from the US, the Croatian/New Zealand Arnerich brothers (Marine and Dominiko), and a South

Oxford Brookes

African cox, Bakang Zondi. That is unusually cosmopolitan for a Brookes crew but 'was just how it worked out' rather than deliberate strategy, according to Richard Spratley.

And what about the Washington crew? We will come back to that later when we look at how the top universities recruit their talent. But anyway, Brookes has won the first of its seven races today. How many more will they win, the spectators along the course are wondering?

(All the races covered in the 'race reports' are available on the Henley Royal Regatta YouTube channel.)[7]

Chapter 5

HRR the First Time (1993)

'Just go out and do your job of work. Do what we do in training every day.'
(Richard Spratley)

Matt Akers – Henley Record Holder

Shrewsbury is one of the most beautiful towns in the UK. Circled by the River Severn, its castle and abbey date back to the eleventh century, and its history requires a book of its own (and there are many already). Close to the border between England and Wales, it has been the site of battles, revolts, treaties and royal trysts. It is also the birthplace of Charles Darwin and the home of Shrewsbury School, founded in 1552, one of the nine original 'public schools', so one of the oldest and most prestigious private schools in the country.

The broad Severn flowing through the town has also provided rowing opportunities for centuries, and Shrewsbury School embraced that from 1866, making it one of the oldest school clubs in the country. That tradition has continued, and Shrewsbury remains perhaps the best British rowing school not situated on the Thames. It was dominant amongst schools at Henley Royal Regatta in the early 1980s and remains second only to Eton in terms of number of all-time Henley victories.

However, young Matt Akers did not attend Shrewsbury School. His alma mater was the humbler Meole Brace state comprehensive. But being in the town, he was attracted to rowing and, aged thirteen, his father's friend, Treasurer of Pengwern Boat Club, suggested he should come along and do some coxing. Akers was also keen to learn to row.

His best friend's father was indulgent enough to drive the two boys to training in his ageing Morris Minor, smoking his pipe all the way. But despite the passive smoking, Akers took to the sport and, being young and slight for his age, he had the opportunity both to cox more senior boats and do some rowing himself.

He had ideas of going to Nottingham University, strong academically and with a rowing heritage. But in the sixth form, he realised he might struggle to make the grades necessary for that institution. He saw what Oxford Polytechnic was doing in the rowing world, and rather liked the look of the town planning degree as well as the chance to continue rowing at a decent level. He also knew that, by the time he started, the Poly would be a new university.

But before he moved on from Pengwern, he was about to set a Henley record that has never been beaten (as far as can be determined). Despite his size (or lack of it) Akers was a decent oarsman. Pengwern put together a crew that was good by regional standards, and travelled to some more distant regattas in the south of England. They decided to enter the Thames Cup for club eights at Henley in 1992, and somehow managed to get direct entry, avoiding the deadly qualifying race.

So Akers rowed at Henley Royal Regatta in 1992, aged 18 and weighing just 8 stone 4 pounds (53 kilos). Bear in mind that his weight would be considered low for a cox, never mind a rower, so that makes him, as far as we can tell, the lightest oarsman in the post-war years to row in a men's 'adult' event at Henley. Henley stopped publishing weights in the programmes a few years ago, and as rowers get heavier and stronger year by year, it is quite possible that Akers' record will never be broken. But sadly Pengwern lost to Auriol Kensington in the first round at HRR and, in the autumn of 1992, Akers said goodbye to Shrewsbury and headed off to Brookes.

During freshers' week, he naturally gravitated to the boat club. He went along to the first sessions for new students, and found himself surrounded by huge 14-stone (90-kilo) giants, generally from private schools, some wearing their GB Junior rowing tops. Clearly, he was not going to compete with these monsters, even if his technique had been perfect and they rowed like proverbial threshing machines.

But he was happy to present himself as a cox in any case. He enjoyed that role, and his considerable rowing experience meant he could both sympathise with the pain the rowers were going through and offer coaching from the cox's seat, based on his own experience from five years of rowing on the Severn.

Famous freshers

David Peill took up rowing at Monmouth School, and quickly made an impact. He was selected to row for Great Britain at the 1991 junior world championships, and although his pair did not win a medal, he was clearly a young man with potential. He took a gap year, and went off to Australia, where he coached rowing. But which UK university should he choose? Wanting to study Estate Management, the choice quickly coalesced to either Brookes or Reading University. Reading had some rowing pedigree, but Brookes looked like the better bet.

Peill was recognised immediately as a strong athlete and became part of Spratley's first boat squad for the 1992/3 season. 'In retrospect, Richard Spratley was only in his early thirties – but he was very much in charge. He never tried to be your mate, but he was also motivating and professional,' says Peill. The club thrived on the underdog spirit, and Peill found a strong club culture already in place. The athletes 'enjoyed having a good time as well as working hard,' he remembers.

The ethos of crew selection through tough training, seat racing, testing and data was already in place. 'We also did a lot of running and weights as well as the rowing.' But there was also a high degree of self-motivation amongst the squad, although sometimes the club still struggled with resources.

Peill remembers some mixed feelings about the growing and increasingly visible boat club amongst the wider Brookes sporting hierarchy. 'We were thrown out of the main gym, given some weights and basically told to go and find a new place to use them!' On another occasion, the crew had to borrow a set of oars to row in an event at Nottingham – 'We certainly didn't have anything like the kit you now see.'

After some arguments about use of the university minibus, the boat club bought their own, helped by the generosity of crew member Pete Alvis's father. He also contributed in other ways, both by funding a small regular fee for Spratley, and by introducing the club to his friend, David Telling, the CEO of Mitie, a major facilities management business. Mitie started sponsoring the club, and soon the crew had a new boat with the Mitie name proudly emblazoned on the bow.

This was in the days before laptops and tablets, and Spratley's attention to detail during training sessions was facilitated by copious notes scribbled on paper – 'He was constantly looking at how we could make the boat go faster.' But the technical side of things was still pretty basic. 'If the rigger needed adjusting, you hit it with a hammer,' claims Peill!

But the crew felt that this year, they really were onto something special. Assuming they could avoid 1992-type disasters, of course.

Building the Brookes spirit

The team spirit at Brookes was no doubt already there before Spratley joined, even in the days of 'the Poly', but he took the intensity up a notch. Most weeks, there were two gym training sessions and three on the river. That's not exceptional – at Cambridge, top college boats were often on the river six days a week.

But the quality of the Brookes effort was very different from my experience on the Cam. Part of that is driven by the location. The river

HRR the First Time (1993)

at Cambridge is not suited to long, hard pieces of rowing, unlike the Thames from Wallingford. The gym training at Brookes was similarly tough and focused, as Spratley did not want questions of fitness to hold back his crews. They needed to be as good or better than any rival.

Another key part of the Brookes culture was driven by Spratley from the beginning. In his schooldays, he was invited to GB under-16 trials at Bedford School. He remembers going to get changed and finding a large sign on one door saying, 'First boat changing only. Strictly no admittance to others.'

The young Spratley wasn't impressed by this approach. Whether it was conscious or subconscious thinking, he brought an egalitarian spirit to Brookes. From the beginning, in the gym or on the water, all the crews trained, ate and relaxed together. And today, it still doesn't matter whether you are an Olympic medal winner coming back to the club to train or a first-year fresher, you wear the same kit, train the same way, and yes, change in the same pretty basic changing rooms.

The athletes speak

'For me the reason for Brookes' success is the atmosphere and ethos of the whole club and the coaches. You could be an Olympic gold medallist, or a new 18-year-old fresher, and you will be treated with the same training and respect to reach your goals, no matter how big or small.'

(*Toby Lassen*, 3x HRR winner, 2x GB U23 World Champion)

There is a video of rowing at Yale on the internet which shows their amazing boathouse, with a lounge that looks like it belongs in a five-star hotel. The training facilities are equally impressive, a huge gym building paid for by a late nineteenth century alumnus, with three 'tank rooms' (indoor rowing pools – Brookes does not have any of these).

But the camera lingers on a sign on the door of one of those training rooms. 'Varsity Heavyweight Crew Only', it says.[8] You will see none of that at Brookes.

Follow the data

Even in those early days, Spratley was also an evidence-based coach, even though the data available then was negligible compared to today. He would swap rowers between crews to see what difference that might make, a tactic that also added to the competitive nature of the Brookes set-up. But he also maintained that positive sense of a single squad, avoiding unnecessary negative feelings. 'Athletes always felt Richard was fair,' Matt Akers remembers.

For much of his first year, Akers actually coxed the Brookes second boat. Much of the training was side by side with the first boat, and although generally this was not positioned as formal racing, it was highly competitive. Even if the rating was low for long rows, maybe 25 strokes a minute, as opposed to the racing rate of 36 or so, there was still a desire to show that you could edge ahead of the other crew, demonstrating you had more power in your boat.

Akers found Spratley to be highly organised, drawing no doubt on his experience of running a small business. He knew what he wanted, and discipline was firm, in a 'let's get on with this' sense. He wasn't a bully, but he was respected. 'However foul the weather, the crews would be out on the river as scheduled. If one crew member didn't turn up, we'd get a few seconds of choice expletives from him. Then he was likely to insist that we went out anyway with seven people rowing,' says Akers. Not ideal, but better than wasting a session, was Spratley's philosophy.

Akers was not an overly strident cox who screamed at the opposition during races, but as well as his credibility as in effect a coach in the boat, he was a good and aggressive steersman. Now you might not think that

HRR the First Time (1993)

steering matters too much on a pleasantly wide stretch of the Thames, but the stream is all-important to rowing boats. If you are moving downstream, with the current, you want to be in the middle of the river getting the maximum benefit from pace of the river, which could be as much as 5 kilometres per hour. Going against the stream, you want to hug the bank as closely as possible, where the current is weaker, without running aground or crashing into the odd heron or water vole.

Akers managed that balance between aggression and safety well, and earnt the respect of his crew, but had no real thought of moving up to the first boat, which was coxed by a very capable young woman, Lottie Miller. But then came the fateful Paris regatta in June 1993.

London, Paris, Henley ...
The athletes knew they had a good chance of winning the Temple Cup at Henley in July 1993 to make amends for the 1992 disaster. But Imperial College stood in their way, probably the toughest UK university opposition. At this stage, Brookes had no idea which American or Dutch crews might make the trip to Henley and rain on their parade, but they knew Imperial would stand in the way.

At the London Head of the River event in March 1993, Imperial finished a very credible seventh, whereas Brookes was back in twenty-ninth, 30 seconds behind Imperial and down a few places from 1992. But the Imperial boat contained some rowers who would be ineligible to compete in the Temple, because of their seniority, so the result was better than it first looked. But Bristol University and three University of London crews were ahead of Brookes too, all suggesting there was still much to do if Brookes was going to avenge 1992. Meanwhile, Akers coxed the second boat into a respectable but unexciting eighty-fourth place in the Head.

The Imperial crew was competing at the Paris regatta in June, just a few weeks before Henley. So Spratley wanted to go and take them on, to get a benchmark against their rivals. But Paris was a major international event, and so came under the auspices of the World Rowing Federation. And, traumatic though it may be for us to believe today, the rules said that, in the men's event, all competitors must be men. And that included the cox.

Today, we are used to seeing women coxing men's boats, and indeed men coxing women's boats. We've seen Oxford versus Cambridge boat race days in some years where a men's boat has a female cox and a women's boat is steered by a man. It is all very progressive, and quite right too. To give the sport some credit, I don't remember much nonsense about 'women can't control a bunch of blokes' as the transition to more female coxes happened. The only bit of moaning from male coxes related to weight. Like many male coxes, I struggled to get down to 9 stone or less (57 kg) as a competitive weight, but there were plenty of young women for whom that was no hardship.

Anyway, for Paris, Brookes had a dilemma. Change coxes and compete, or pull out. So Akers was promoted into the first boat so Brookes could enter. Off the crew went to Paris in their minibus, towing the boat behind, with Mike Reynaud hiding under the kitbags at Dover as he didn't actually possess a passport! In the heats of the Open Eights, Brookes rowed well. This international rowing was all quite a new experience for many of the crew, and they were only vaguely aware of the level of crews they were up against. The GB national eight was there, the two French national squad eights, the Germans, Encouragement (the top French club crew, which included two giant Romanian Olympians) and more.

Against this tough competition, Brookes made it through to the final, beating two national crews in the process. Ironically, Imperial did not make it through their heat – so Brookes did not get that chance to measure up directly. In the final, Brookes also acquitted themselves well, and after the race, Spratley approached a couple of his trusted

HRR the First Time (1993)

crew members in the boat. How has it been with Akers coxing, he asked. It was good, they said. Then came the big question. Do you want to keep him?

That was a tough one. The crew had nothing negative to say about their incumbent cox. But Akers had rowed for five years himself. He understood the technical elements of rowing perhaps better than any other cox who was likely to come up against Brookes at Henley. He could genuinely coach the crew, as well as cox. He was a similar weight to his rival; and had a pleasant easy-going approach which concealed a tough competitive spirit. That all went down well with the crew.

Akers would stay, was the decision. That initially did not go down well with everybody in the boat, but the crew comes first. With just a soupcon of tension in the air, the oarsmen got back to work.

Highs – and Lowe

Half the 1992 Henley crew were still around for the 1992/1993 season, but there were several strong new rowers with a junior rowing pedigree who had come up to the university in the autumn, including David Peill and Mike Reynaud. Spratley could see quickly that there was going to be some serious competition for seats, particularly on the stroke side. That is not a bad problem for a coach to have, but it can lead to difficult decisions.

Peter Lowe was now in his final year at Brookes, at the end of his six-year stint. He was never the biggest rower in the crew, and as Brookes athletes began to be noticed at a national level, he saw an opportunity to seek national selection as a lightweight oarsman. The rules for lightweight men require the crew to weigh no more than 11 stone (70 kg) on average and each individual no more than 11 st 5 lbs (72.5 kg).

Lowe started watching his weight in the early months of 1993. The weight loss went reasonably well initially, but his rowing did not. His times on the erg started dropping off, and the problem was that with the new recruits, there was serious competition for places in the first boat. 'It was clear quite early in the season that we had six good candidates for four stroke-side seats,' Spratley remembers.

Lowe entered GB lightweight squad trials with a first session at freezing Ely. He was invited back, but the second trial in Nottingham in May was a disaster. Lowe was struggling to reach the maximum allowable weight, so he resorted to long runs wearing multiple layers of clothing to try and lose a few pounds. Perhaps understandably, he then found he couldn't give his best on the water.

He returned from the selection event disappointed and not feeling 100 per cent in terms of fitness and strength. And matters then came to a head at the Brookes Wimbleball weekend training camp a few days later, just five weeks before Henley Royal Regatta.

The top Brookes athletes raced each other in pairs, up and down the lake, switching over after each race to try and establish a pecking order of the strongest rowers. Sadly, Lowe did not come out well compared to his rivals. Spratley tried different pairs; he genuinely did not want Lowe to miss out in his last year at the club for which he had done so much. But neither he nor Lowe could ignore the evidence.

In their first couple of years working together (and with Levy), Spratley and Lowe as captain were already establishing fairness as one of the pillars of the Brookes ethos and culture. Rowers wouldn't win a seat in a boat because their face fitted or they enjoyed a beer with the captain. This was all about objective strength, stamina and ability to move the boat. After the seat racing, Lowe and Spratley knew what had to happen. Lowe would not be part of the crew for the Temple Cup.

There was shock amongst the other athletes, but they had seen what happened at Wimbleball. Many of us in Lowe's situation would have thrown our toys out of the proverbial pram, and probably thrown the pram in the river for good measure. But Lowe acted in a remarkably

HRR the First Time (1993)

mature, professional and dignified manner. He agreed to move into a good Brookes four that competed at Henley and got to the semi-final. Also in that four was a young man called Alex Henshilwood. He had rowed successfully at Bedford School, but had a gap year and found when he got to Brookes he also did not quite make the first eight. More on him later.

But although the four had some success, it could not compensate Lowe for the loss of his place in the first boat. That experience did change his life, he says today. It drove him on and contributed to his spirit of adventure, of wanting to prove himself and take on the toughest challenges. In 1997, he rowed the Atlantic in 61 days, from the Canary Isles to Barbados, as part of the first ever Transatlantic Rowing Race organised by the legendary Chay Blyth. He has run London marathons, competed in the Devizes to Westminster kayak race and swum the length of Lake Windermere. In 2018 he swam front crawl across the English Channel non-stop solo, non-wetsuit, in 13 hours and 52 minutes. He also chaired Taurus, the Brookes rowing alumni club, for over 20 years.

Lowe is clearly both a hero and somewhat crazy. But would he have done any of this if he had kept his place in the Temple crew of 1993? Or would he have been satisfied sitting quietly in front of the TV for the next 30 years? We will never know.

But the 1993 Henley crew (James Brown, Mark Russell, Jeremy Hepworth, Pete Alvis, Mike Reynaud, David Peill, Alex Hoodless, John Cooper, and cox Akers) was not short of self-confidence or rowing ability, even without the totemic Lowe. Reynaud is probably still the only top-level oarsman who has also competed in the TV show *Gladiators*. He came on as a reserve after another competitor got injured in the first event, and acquitted himself really well until he bombed out in the final handicap race.[9] Reynaud was also runner up in GMTV's 'Hunks in Trunks' competition in 2005 for the best-looking man wearing very short shorts. Oh, for those far-off days when we could objectify beautiful bodies on national breakfast TV.

Reynaud didn't seem too worried about objectification, as he also entered *America's Next Top Male Model* in 2006 when he was studying for an MBA in the US. He came an impressive third. In the interests of decorum, we won't include pictures here, but photographs are available on the internet, if you're interested.

But back to serious – or not so serious business. Whilst Spratley ran a very disciplined operation, we are talking about young men here, even if they were very fit and usually disciplined. But only usually … for instance, Reynaud had the idea of practicing his roller-blading technique by being pulled behind the crew minibus down the steep hill in Headington (near the university), which also happened to be a major road. Fortunately for the future of US male modelling shows, and the 1993 Temple crew, the driver refused.

Preparing for the big day
Back on the river, approaching Henley 1993, one of the favourite Spratley exercises was a timed eight-minute row from above Cleeve Lock back up towards the boathouse. It became a challenge to see how far the boat could go in those eight minutes. As Henley approached, Akers could see the boat getting that little bit further every outing.

After the Paris regatta, the crew made it without too many rollerblading-related scares through to July 1993 and Henley. Brookes had an advantage in that, being based less than an hour away, they did not need to stay in the town. During the regatta, many of the good folk of Henley support the event by offering to accommodate crews from exotic and distant lands: Australia, California, or even Newcastle.

Notwithstanding fantasies about California girls (or boys) using your shower room, the reality is pretty demanding. Having four, eight or nine sweaty, hungry athletes taking over your house and life for two

HRR the First Time (1993)

weeks is an interesting experience, however thoughtful and charming they may be. These days, as the regatta has expanded, more crews use the camping sites that have grown up, but many still stay in private houses. For crews that know they have no chance of winning, there is a tension here. Do they basically come to party, or work hard to put up a good show on the river? It's a tough balance.

When I competed, we were told by the family hosting my crew that Henley had the most pubs per inhabitant of any English town. Certainly, with the iconic, independent Brakspear's brewery still operational in the town, producing a beautiful best bitter, it had dozens of excellent pubs, some little more than the front room of a terraced cottage. The two years I coxed LMBC at Henley, we had a realistic chance of winning as allegedly the best Cambridge college crew, so we took it seriously. However, there are rumours that my college second boat didn't follow that approach, taking the opportunity to sample some of those hostelries, although crew members may have different memories (indeed, one threatened me with libel action if I suggested anything less than total athletic dedication …)

Being local, Brookes did not have to worry about this dilemma, and Spratley again took a professional approach. He didn't want the crew to spend long hanging around the regatta, before or after races. His house was not too far from the town, so the routine was to call in at his place for a cup of coffee on their way from Oxford to the regatta.

He would show them videos of great athletics events, particularly races featuring the rivalry between Seb Coe and Steve Ovett, and tell the crew to watch how those athletes were aware of the competition, but basically ran their own race. He wanted his crews to pace themselves. Don't worry if you are losing in the first minute if you know you are rowing at the right pace to maximise your whole race performance. Akers remembers these sessions fondly – 'they were also good relaxation before we got to the hurly burly of Henley.'

Before the race, Spratley would tell the crew, 'Go out and do your job of work. Just do what we do in training day in, day out. Go and do it today.' He wanted his crews to win, he says, and coached them to believe that they could, even if they had a 'bad row' by their normal standards.

In recent years, we've heard many sportspeople talking about the importance of 'following (or trusting) the process' in moments of stress. The first recorded use of that expression in a sporting context appears to be the American Football coach Nick Saban and psychologist Lionel Rosen who worked together at Michigan State University around 1998. However, whilst Levy and Spratley might not have used that exact expression, what they were trying to do with crews from 1992 onwards was exactly that. Don't worry about the result, do what you've trained to do, focus on that, and the end result will take care of itself. The Brookes coaches were clearly ahead of their time in terms of the methods they were using.

1992 avenged

Brookes came though the heats without too many problems. The quarter final was closer than it should have been. Stroke John Cooper, writing in the Taurus alumni newsletter, remembered the 'only wobble was Thursday against Cardiff where we all seemed to interpret "do enough" as "everyone do your own thing and it should be fine". It nearly wasn't enough, and coming into the enclosures a load of geese got in the way, just as we were trying to make it look like we weren't finding it too hard.'

Then it was Sunday and the final against Trinity College Dublin (TCD). In the boat tent before race, the TCD cox was having a quiet moment away from the excitement on the riverbank, composing himself before the big race. A quiet moment that is until Spratley crept

HRR the First Time (1993)

up unnoticed and coughed very loudly in his ear. Totally inadvertent, of course, but it certainly ruined the moment of contemplation.

Spratley was still only in his early thirties at this point, so whilst he was an authority figure to his crews, he was the same age of many of the competitors and was not averse to behaving in a somewhat juvenile fashion at times. But generally, he approached the role of coaching in a more professional, objective and analytical manner than was the norm in British rowing outside the top national levels at this time.

On the start, the crew members who had experienced the disappointment of the previous year tried to keep that out of their minds. Just remember everything we've done in training, they told themselves. This time, there were no disasters off the start, and again John Cooper tells the story.

'The boat straight, blades set, we were away. High forties off the start and we meant business. Each stroke the cleavers did their work, until by the end of the island we were in control and had really settled into a rhythm you seldom get, when you know every man is at the edge, serving up everything they've got, including Matt (cox) who made sure TCD felt and saw the power being put down by the boys. It was beautiful but savage for TCD, as there was no stopping us.'

And in truth, this was not a dramatic, tense race to complete this part of the Brookes story. Brookes took an early lead and, although Trinity College Dublin fought all the way, Brookes came home with a three length victory.[10] A video taken by the father of crew member Pete Alvis from the umpire's launch following the race shows a very dynamic and powerful crew, even if the bow side timing is a touch off at times! But OBUBC had done it, and their name was on the Henley Royal Regatta roll of honour at last, with what would be the first of many such successes.

Brookes first win at Henley – the Temple Cup, 1993 (*Brookes archive*)

The 1993 Temple final commemorated (*Brookes archive*)

Chapter 6

Brookes, the best boat in Oxford (94–95)

'We've always worked to maintain a good relationship with Oxford University Boat Club, their coaches and athletes. But of course it's good to beat them!' (Richard Spratley)

Oxford beats Oxford – hurrah!

After the glory of Henley 1993, the club re-assembled in Oxford in the autumn of that year. But there was a dilemma now in terms of the 1993/1994 season generally and Henley 1994 specifically. Several of the winning crew from July were still around, too many to allow the Brookes first boat to enter the Temple again in 1994. There were also some newcomers who made their way straight into that first boat, notably Fred Scarlett, as well as internal promotions, including Alex Henshilwood.

The name 'Fred Scarlett' has a certain resonance, perhaps a reminder of the pioneer Thames scullers from the 1800s, men who worked on the river, with sturdy names and sturdy bodies. But no, Scarlett was born in 1975, his father was an Oxford University rowing blue and Fred attended Kings School Canterbury, a very good rowing school. Scarlett's ability was recognised, and by the time he arrived at Brookes, he was already a GB junior international.

With the Temple out of bounds, the decision was taken to step up to the Thames, which at the time was the event for club crews and also the first boats of 'top universities' – basically meaning the US giants,

Oxbridge, University of London and Nereus in Holland. This was the first time that Brookes was considered amongst that elite.

But before Henley there was another important historical moment for Brookes in 1994. The Oxford versus Cambridge race, held on the Tideway in London every March, is the most watched rowing event in the world with the exception perhaps of the Olympics. The two crews train on the tideway course for the last two weeks or so before the event, with occasional trips to London before that.

For the earlier part of the year, the Oxford University boats train on the same stretch of river as Brookes. So the crews were aware of each other, and Spratley knew the Oxford coaches quite well personally. In 1993, he convinced Oxford that Brookes could help them in their final training by racing them informally on the Boat Race course in London. Oxford agreed to try that, but only with Isis, their second boat. Cambridge decided that if Oxford were doing that, they probably should too, so Brookes took on both Isis and Goldie, the Cambridge second boat.

The Boat Race is unusual in that it is a two-boat, side by side race, but with no marked course or lanes for the boats, unlike Henley for example. It is also held on a not very straight bit of river in London that has interesting tides and currents, and the water can be very rough. A good friend of mine, Robert Ross, who I rowed with at LMBC, holds the record as the youngest ever Boat Race competitor, in 1977, but also a less enviable record as part of the crew that sank dramatically in 1978!

That is why you see the two boats, with coxes playing key roles, jockeying for position to avoid turbulence and maximise their speed, given the bends in the river and the need to stay in the part of the river where the current is fastest (The Boat Race is timed to allow the crews to have the benefit of that tidal effect).

Brookes leading Oxford, 2019 Boat Race practice (© *AllMarkOne*)

Brookes leading Cambridge, 2020 Boat Race practice (©*AllMarkOne*)

So the idea of practice races with other top crews on the Boat Race course developed. Competing with Brookes (and others) was a good chance for the Oxbridge boats to practice their starts and that side by side, stressful and challenging racing that they would experience in the main races against each other.

The sessions with Isis and Goldie went well, and in 1994 Oxford asked if Brookes would race against their 'blue boat', the top crew that would face Cambridge. Matt Akers coxed that day, in quite blustery conditions, and there is a brilliant photograph of that tussle, which was used on the front cover of Regatta magazine (number 66, March 1994).

To the surprise of many, Brookes won comfortably, in a landmark event that the magazine covered enthusiastically. Alex Henshilwood also remembers racing Cambridge, although that did not get as much coverage – 'but we beat them too'!

Following the Henley win in 1993, this added to the wider realisation amongst the rowing community that something impressive was going on at Brookes. Oxford University had been rowing for over a century, and many casual observers of The Boat Race assumed that Oxford and Cambridge were the fastest university boats in the UK. Brookes was showing that this was no longer always the case.

Unsurprisingly, that outcome in 1994 was not well received by the dark blues themselves, and that fixture was not resumed again until 2016. Brookes won that contest too, as the Oxford Mail newspaper reported,[11] and the club has triumphed in most of these practice races against Oxford and Cambridge since then, which now also include the Oxbridge women's and lightweight boats going up against various Brookes crews.

Back to 1994, and at the Head of the River race in March 1994, Brookes leapt up to fourteenth, the club's best ever performance, winning the Ortner Shield for the fastest university crew. The Brookes second eight made an even bigger leap up the table, going from eighty-second in 1993 to forty-eighth, winning the university second boat prize easily and finishing within one second of both Bristol and Durham University first boats. Brookes was starting to build real strength in depth, not just a hot first eight, and their rowers were also getting noticed by the GB under-23 national selectors, the start of another long relationship.

Back to Henley

The competition in the Thames Cup Henley in 1994 was tough. In those days, with the regatta held over just 4 days, the events with 32 entrants had 5 races which meant 2 races had to be held on one day. The same was true back in the days when I coxed, and the Ladies' Plate (for student crews in those days) included five rounds over four days.

That means I coxed a crew on Henley finals day. But my personal experience was actually competing in the semi-final, one of the first races on finals day, with the final later in the afternoon. My crew, Lady Margaret Boat Club, including one crew member who wasn't feeling well, tragically lost by a third of length to Yale in a classic race, which we could have won. But we exhausted Yale nicely for Imperial College, who had a much easier semi-final and then beat Yale that afternoon.

Anyway, in 1994 at Henley, Brookes got through the first two rounds on Thursday and Friday in the Thames Cup without much trouble. But the format meant Brookes potentially had to row both their quarter- and semi-final on the Saturday. In the quarter-final on Saturday morning, they came up against the London Rowing Club Lightweights, effectively the GB national lightweight squad. It was a desperately tough race, but Brookes held on to win by a quarter of a length, a fine victory.

However, that exertion took it out of the crew, super-fit though they were. Later that day, in the semi-final, they came up against the Brown University crew. Brown was having an unprecedented year of success in the US. As their website[12] still says today:

'In the long and storied history of Brown men's crew, which dates back to 1859, there have been countless numbers of impressive oarsmen, coaches and crews. However, what transpired at Marston Boathouse in the spring of 1994 can be considered miraculous. The entire program achieved perfection, as all five Brown crews (varsity, second varsity, third varsity, freshman and second freshman) ended the season unbeaten in every dual race and championship event, a total of 48 victories.'

It was the freshman eight that pipped Brookes, a sign of the strength in depth the top US universities had in those days. Whilst their top boat was very fast, Brookes in the nineties still had some way to go to get to the point where – like Brown – they could field five highly successful boats.

On that Saturday morning, Brown had also experienced a much easier race than Brookes. So it was no surprise that although Brookes put up a good fight, the Americans were too strong. They went on to win the final comfortably too. For the Brookes athletes who had tasted glory at Henley in 1993, including cox Matt Akers, this was something of an anti-climax. But for those 1993 winners leaving in the summer of 1994, their place in Brookes history was already secure.

AAAAGGGGHHH!

When the rowers re-assembled in Oxford in September 1994, there were some new faces, fresh from school and, in some cases, already junior international rowers. Most notably, Steve Williams arrived from Monkton Combe School in Bath, a good rowing school, although not quite in the top league. Williams impressed immediately, and quickly established himself in the first boat. Based on having fewer Temple winners in the crew this year, Brookes could enter that Henley student event again the following July. David Peill, Mike Reynaud and cox Matt

Brookes, the best boat in Oxford (94–95)

Akers were still there from the victorious 1993 crew, along with Scarlett and Williams, with Oliver Jenkins, Henshilwood, John Watchhorn and stroke Phil Baker completing the crew.

Spratley's coaching was developing too. 'He always gave very clear messages and set clear standards. There was a clarity of purpose – he always made sure we knew what we needed to do in terms of training and racing,' says Alex Henshilwood.

At the 1995 Head of the River, Brookes finished fifteenth, one place lower than the previous year, but the second boat dropped back to ninety-first. As Henley approached, the regatta was having one of its occasional struggles with eligibility for the different events. That year the final of the Thames was fought by Imperial College, who pipped the University of Washington. Meanwhile, in the 'intermediate' Ladies' Plate, Princeton University lost out to a very fast GB national squad lightweight boat that maybe should have been in the Grand. With major university crews spread out across multiple eights events, Brookes went into the regatta as one of the favourites for the Temple.

The crew sailed through the four days without too many worries. In the final it was the old rivals, Trinity College Dublin (TCD). It wasn't an easy race, but Brookes triumphed, winning the Temple for the second time in three years. The 1995 crew was very strong, still remembered as one of the best Brookes has produced. 'In some sense, that crew set the benchmark for everything that followed in Brookes,' says Henshilwood.

A note of sympathy for TCD, who were runners-up in the Temple four years running from 1992 to 1995, twice behind Brookes and twice losing out to Imperial College London. Indeed, 1977 remains the last time that fine Irish university won the student eights event at Henley.

Mike Sweeney, who served as chairman of Henley Royal Regatta from 1993 to 2014, was also the Umpire for that 1995 final. After Brookes won, he took Richard Spratley aside. 'Next year, I want to see you in the Ladies', not the Temple!' he said.

This was indicative of the Henley Stewards' struggle to get the right crews in the right event to maximise competition and fairness, an ongoing battle to this day, and one that will feature later in the story too. As Sweeney says, 'We've had a continuing battle to maintain a level playing field and drive good competition. But as fast as we change the rules, coaches – who understandably just want to win – will try and find a way round them!'

But not everything went to plan for Brookes in 1995. At that time, certainly for the first couple of days of the regatta, coaches could follow crews for most of the race by riding bicycles along the towpath. That is impossible today because of the commercialisation of the event with campsites, bars, retail outlets and fun fairs along the river almost as far as the starting line. At the weekend, you can barely walk along the towpath, let alone consider cycling.

Spratley was a man who liked detail, and he was not content to sit in the enclosure near the finish and listen to the announcer telling spectators what was happening in the race. These were the days before YouTube live video, of course, so we got something like this.

'At the end of the Island, the crews are level, both striking 38 strokes per minute. (Silence for a minute or so.) At the Barrier, Harvard lead Reading University by half a length. Time to the barrier, two minutes two seconds. (More silence) At Fawley, the crews are level.'

There would be a few more updates, then a final formal announcement of the winner, the time and the winning distance. You might occasionally get some indication of the rating (strokes per minute) from the commentary, particularly off the start, but as Spratley explains, this wasn't enough for him.

'Was the leading crew really trying, did they go flat out? Or were they just treating it as a practice row? Did they have a very fast first 20 strokes, then settle into a relaxed rhythm once they were ahead? What was the wind like? Were there any steering issues?'

Brookes, the best boat in Oxford (94–95)

With his love of data, he wanted to understand all aspects of the race and the strength of each crew Brookes might face, and tactics the opposition might use. So to get intelligence on crews, Spratley would follow every race in relevant events on his bicycle. That's quite a feat when there are 16 Temple races on the first day, for instance. But by the end day two, he felt he could assess pretty accurately who the threats might be.

In 1995, on semi-final day (Saturday), the crowds were building on the bank, but Spratley was still navigating the course on his bicycle. He was dodging spectators, following the Brookes race, when his front tyre hit a pothole and he went flying over the handlebars – luckily, not into the river, but into the vegetation alongside the narrow towpath.

Felling dazed, he got back on his bike, although his shoulder hurt like mad. But he needed to get back to the boat tent to lead the debrief with his crew. Clutching his shoulder and pretending there was nothing wrong, he made it through the session, but then decided he really needed to get to hospital. Sitting in A&E later, he got a message that the Henley Stewards wanted to speak to him – some issue with the race perhaps? He decided he wasn't in an ideal state to speak to them, and fortunately the issue, whatever it was, went away. The following day, with his broken collarbone diagnosed, painkillers and strapping in place, Spratley and his crew were presented with the Temple Cup again.

Oxford Brookes

Henley Royal Regatta, 12.10 pm, 2 July 2023

Race report – The 2023 Ladies' Challenge Plate Final

After several other finals without Brookes, we move onto the final of the Ladies' Challenge Plate. Confusingly, this event is not rowed by women. Even though there are now 10 events for girls or women, the Ladies' (as it is known to afficionados) is believed be so named because the cup was first presented by the wives of the Stewards who organised the regatta. Or maybe it was 'the ladies of Henley'. It dates back to 1845, so a little vagueness as to its origins is excusable.

For a century or so, this was the eights event for students, but from 1985 it became defined by HRR as the 'intermediate' eights event for men. Now 'intermediate' in some contexts indicates a level of competence but not particularly special skills. (I describe myself as an intermediate skier and bass guitar player, for instance.) But that is misleading here.

The crews in the Ladies' are for the most part just below full national squad level. Some may be international under-23 crews, or crews made up of rowers who are on the fringes of national selection but not quite Olympic level. Or we see the first boats of top clubs or international universities – Washington from the US, Nereus from Holland, Cambridge from the UK – and of course Brookes. The standard is certainly not comparable to my skiing aptitude.

The Brookes boat contains previous winners of the Temple, the Prince Albert and even the Grand. Jamie Copus, Jake Wincomb, Matt Heywood, Sam Bannister, James Doran, Sam Nunn, Evan Olson, Matt Rowe and cox Will Denegri are not lacking in experience down this course. (Interestingly, Doran rowed for Oxford University in The Boat Race, but asked if he could join up with Brookes for the summer season.) The match-up here is a regular Henley event, with Brookes taking on Leander.

The 2023 Ladies' Challenge Plate Final

The Leander club is based at Henley, just 100 metres from the regatta winning post, and has traditionally been one of the best two or three clubs in the UK, providing numerous crews and rowers for the GB national squad. Indeed, GB crews are often badged as 'Leander' when rowing at Henley. Leander is also famous for its pink tie and socks, so spotting a Leander member in the Stewards' Enclosure is usually easy.

It was for many years the bastion of the formal British rowing establishment, whilst producing many excellent athletes. It still has a somewhat upper-class image, but is very much an active rowing club. On the river, Leander are always tough competitors, and this is their home course and home crowd. Their Ladies' crew is mainly British, full of junior international and full GB squad members. At the Head of the River in London in March, Leander was less than two seconds behind Brookes, who won, and these two boats appear very evenly matched. So no-one is risking their shirt, or their pink socks, on this race.

At 1210 precisely, the two fastest eights in the UK, outside the GB Olympic eight, head off. Brookes has the Bucks station, furthest from the bank and the enclosures, which is a small disadvantage as they will have a little more stream running against them. But we can instantly see both the sheer power and the smoothness of both crews. They are rating around 48 strokes a minute – extremely high, and there is nothing in it for the first minute, perhaps Leander just leading. But Brookes have settled into their mid-race rhythm early and look good too, despite a tricky crosswind and the Canada geese sailing calmly across the course ahead of the boats.

The time to the Barrier, the first checkpoint, is 1 minute 47 seconds, which turns out to be the fastest of the day. There is still nothing in it as the crews approach the Fawley timing point, around halfway. But now Brookes puts in a 'push', increasing the stroke rate a touch. Over the next 30 seconds or so, they open up a half-length lead, with a time to Fawley of 2 minutes 59 seconds, also the fastest of the day. Brookes

Oxford Brookes

clings on to that lead despite attempts from Leander to get back on terms. The next two minutes are intense, and this is turning into the head-to-head battle we hoped for.

As the boats come level with the Regatta Enclosure, with about one minute to go, that lead is maintained, and for crews of this quality, that is usually a safe enough margin for the leading crew. Time is running out for Leander. We have seen the 'decisive move', according to commentator and multiple GB gold-medal winner Mo Sbihi.

But you've put eight international level men in a boat, to race against their biggest rivals, on home territory, in what is probably their biggest event ever. You don't think they will just give up, do you? There is huge determination, strength and sheer will power in the Leander boat. With 200 metres to go, the crew basically go berserk.

Even though every individual must feel like he is already at absolute maximum effort, somehow they find more and lift their stroke rate well above the Brookes crew. In the stands the crowd can see Leander gaining with every stroke and also go crazy. The commentators have woken up to this, and their tone switches suddenly to incredulity. Could Leander do it?

But there are only a few strokes left. Are the Brookes crew feeling comfortable, do they think they have it tied up? It isn't easy to go from an exhausting but fundamentally comfortable rhythm into something more urgent. Is there last-minute panic as they see Leander crew gaining fast? The noise from the crowd is deafening, and there is no way the rowers can hear any final demands from their coxes. It is all in their own heads and bodies now. All down to the years of coaching and training. Four strokes to go, three, two, one … and it is the first photo finish of the day.

It looks to those watching like Brookes crossed the line first. Just. And after a few seconds, that is confirmed. But by how much? This will turn out to be the closest finish of the entire regatta. Three feet is

The 2023 Ladies' Challenge Plate Final

the verdict. These boats have covered 6,930 feet over the last 6 minutes and, at the end, one boat was 0.04 per cent faster than the other. If the finishing line had been one stroke further on, Leander would probably have won.

But no problem, Richard Spratley says Brookes had it totally under control, never in doubt. Brookes had plenty in reserve. I'm not quite so sure, but it's two out of two for Brookes.

Chapter 7

A New Home

'It was clear we'd outstayed our welcome at Wallingford – they'd been good hosts, but we needed to find our own place before we got kicked out!' (David Peill, OBUBC 1992–95)

6 December 2023
The weak December sun, already sinking westwards at 2.30 pm, is breaking through the light mist floating over the Thames. I'm driving north following the river towards the Oxford Brookes boathouse, near the town of Wallingford. Across the river, I see a gleaming white egret standing in the shallows by the far bank. After weeks of rain, the river is high and flowing fast – probably around 3 miles per hour (5 kph). I'm wondering whether it might be too dangerous for rowing today.

I've done my reconnaissance, thanks to Google Streetview, so worked out how to spot the unmarked turning off the main road. The warning signs about CCTV and private property indicate that something interesting is here and, turning into a parking area, I see two dark barn-like buildings with Oxford Brookes Boat Club lettering on the side of one.

This is the relatively unostentatious HQ for one of the best rowing clubs in the world. Now many boathouses today include gyms and training facilities, but not in the case of Brookes. This site is all about the rowing on the river, and its history is another example of how Richard Spratley's personal attributes of vision, opportunism, management ability and persistence helped drive the growth of the club. But let's go back to the 1990s and start the boathouse story properly.

A New Home

The Wallingford Years

The early days of the Brookes club, and the association with Falcon in Oxford, were outlined earlier. By the time Richard Spratley came on board in 1991, Brookes men still rowed from the Falcon club and the Isis boathouse was used principally for the women's squad, and storing boats. The first two erg machines were then housed in a portacabin 'out the back of a general-purpose Brookes university gym,' remembers Spratley.

But rowing from a base in the city has its drawbacks. In the centre of Oxford, the river is relatively narrow with twist and turns, hence the adoption of bumps racing for the college championships every year. (More on bumps racing in Chapter 15.)

However, for serious training, you want a wide stretch of clear water, where boats can row hard side by side and with a good, uninterrupted distance between locks, waterfalls or weirs. It is also ideal if you don't have to worry about punting tourists, or drunken revellers testing the depth of the water.

So in late 1991, Brookes came to an agreement with the long-established and successful Wallingford Rowing Club to hire a few boat racks in the boathouse along with the use of the changing facilities. The Isis boathouse was maintained for novices, the women's crew and some land training. Boating from Wallingford, a lovely Thames riverside market town some 14 miles (23 km) downstream from Oxford, means there is some 7 miles (12 km) of uninterrupted rowing to be done between locks. The river is wide too, so two or even three boats can comfortably row side by side.

The only problem is the occasional flood, which makes the Thames unsafe for rowing boats, even those powered by experts. Once Spratley had secured the use of Wallingford's facilities, much more effective training on the water could be undertaken from the new site.

That Wallingford base saw the seminal Brookes successes at Henley in 1993 and 1995. But as the club grew, the facilities came under pressure. Brookes wanted to recruit more rowers into the programme, but that meant more changing space and boat racks at Wallingford, and more erg machines and weights somewhere appropriate.

It became clear that the arrangement with Wallingford was becoming untenable. Whilst that club was a good host and deserves credit for its role in the Brookes story, there began to be some muttering amongst members. At weekends in particular, the facilities were getting very crowded. Wallingford is a long-established and successful club in its own right, so maybe there was a feeling that the tenants were now squeezing out their hosts.

There was another issue. Matt Akers, the cox of those winning Henley crews, remembers training and the competitiveness between the two Brookes men's eights. The rules of the river tell boats to stay on the right-hand side but, to maximise speed, the Brookes coxes would try and hog the middle of the river when going downstream, and keep in towards the banks when going against the stream. If there was an unofficial 'race' going on, the rules of the river might have been bent just a little. You can imagine the Wallingford captain not being very happy about their misbehaving tenants when complaints were made from other inconvenienced river users!

Bowbridge and the cowshed

By 1995, Brookes really needed to find their own place. This was a mature, expanding club, not a fledgling teenager any longer. On his coaching launch following the boats, Spratley started looking out for another potential home. Near the village of Cholsey, with wooded riverbanks on the west side, just a mile or so south of Wallingford, he could catch a glimpse of what looked like an old shed of some sort. It was only 30 yards or so back from the bank, but partially hidden

A New Home

by trees. There never seemed to be any activity around it, as far as he could see.

David Peill, part of those winning crews, was studying Estates Management at Brookes, so he took on the task of researching potential boathouses. One night, looking through a local newspaper, he spotted a classified advert – 'building for sale by the river near Wallingford'. Peill responded and discovered that this was the building Spratley had spotted and was owned by Errol Facy, a well-known local businessman and owner of the only department store in Henley itself. The shop in The Marketplace opened in 1896 and has somehow survived, unlike many other department stores in the UK.

The riverside building had once been a punt repair workshop, but Facy had ideas about development of the site. He had worked with a developer to try and gain planning permission for light industrial development, but had been turned down flatly by the planning authorities. We might hypothesise that the application was rejected on the basis that it was:

- in a designated green belt area
- situated on a flood plain within 50 metres of the biggest river in England
- on a site of special natural and scientific interest, no doubt chock full of frogs, bats, wildfowl, badgers, bearded newts, and more; and
- right in the middle of one of the most aesthetically beautiful stretches of the Thames.

To paraphrase what we can assume the report said: 'You must be mad if you think we are going to allow you to stick up some corrugated industrial sheds here!' Whatever the exact wording, there was no doubt that this was *not* going to become the Bowbridge Industrial Park. So Facey decided to sell.

The "cowshed" at Cholsey (*Brookes archive*)

But for a Brookes boathouse, Peill suspected the planning issue would be different. The council might be much happier with leisure use, by an organisation that by now had a growing and positive national reputation. Much better than a bunch of car repair shops and printing centres. So Spratley and Peill negotiated with the owner and initially took out a one-year lease on the site, paying £3,000. The deal was done in Peill's name, the first property deal of his long career in that sector, as it happens.

The 'cowshed' turned out to be an empty but sturdy brick-built construction, with electric lighting, and once Spratley had personally installed some racking for the boats, using scaffolding from his building firm, it was a serviceable if basic site from which Brookes could boat. Peill applied for planning permission for a pontoon from which boats could be launched, measuring the existing structure at Wallingford Rowing Club to design one for Cholsey. Spratley used his construction skills to knock together a workable pontoon, and Brookes athletes were now boating from their own premises.

A New Home

Most importantly, it allowed the crews direct access, whenever they wanted, to a lovely stretch of water. The boathouse is almost equidistant between Benson Lock and Cleeve Lock, a six-and-a-half-mile stretch of water that is the longest on the navigable Thames between locks. So boats can row for 30 minutes or so at a good pace without needing to stop or turn.

Brookes moved in during early 1996 and, within a couple of years, the university was negotiating to buy the site. Again, the deal was

The boathouse just after Brookes moved in (*Brookes archive*)

fronted by Peill – 'We thought if the seller knew the university was putting in the money, he might want more!'

In 1999, the deal was finally done, with a purchase agreement for a price of £100,000. Spratley remembers some university colleagues thinking it was a lot of money for a 'cowshed', as some still disparagingly called it. Whilst planning restrictions make it hard to value the site, it looks like an absolute bargain in retrospect. With several acres of land and over 100 metres of river frontage, it is an amazing location. The only disadvantage is the distance from Oxford, requiring a fleet of minibuses to transport athletes the 16 miles or so from the Brookes university centre in Oxford to and from the boathouse.

We need a better cowshed ...

It is hard to over-estimate how important this development was to Brookes. Without their own boathouse, it could not have grown from the two or three boats that made up the squad in the mid-nineties. If the location had not been so beautifully situated, the training and ethos of the club may well have been different too. The ability to have several boats out rowing together, with regular side-by-side competition, could only happen on the right stretch of water, and that helped to define and support the Brookes style of training.

Sharing with Wallingford, then having basic facilities for years more in the cowshed, also built the underdog spirit and the all-in-it-together motivation that still pervades the club today, despite it being a long time since Brookes was genuinely an underdog in rowing terms.

But it wasn't too long before the boathouse became a constraint on the growth of the club again. The 'cowshed' was not a long-term solution and did not provide space for changing facilities, offices and more. So with Spratley and his brother, an architect, leading the process, eventually planning permission was granted for a new building to replace the cowshed.

A New Home

However, the planners said that the basic 'footprint' of the building had to remain. But after more floods when the Thames overflowed onto fields around, the planners agreed the building could move back some 50 feet from the river and change its configuration slightly. That gave a little more flexibility in the building design.

The Head of Estates at Brookes was generally an ally, but insisted that the university needed to get competitive quotes rather than just giving Spratley's firm the work (quite right too, I say as a procurement professional myself). But Spratley's quote was a five-figure sum cheaper than the alternatives, so he was awarded the contract. And of course he had a huge, vested interest in doing a good job, as he was, in a sense, his own client. As the Head Coach he wanted as good a boathouse as the builder could possibly provide. Any internal conflict was all resolved positively and by 2002, the club could move into the new boathouse.

For several years, the Brookes athletes had endured basic facilities, so the new boathouse was much appreciated. Carla Devlin (née Ashford), one of the first Brookes female stars, winner of the Remenham Cup in 2002, remembers the change like this.

'The Brookes facilities were also VERY different to what they are now! We used to call the old boathouse 'The Cowshed' – there was no heating, no showers, green mould caked on the walls, it was pretty dire, we'd all escape to the Benson cafe in-between sessions, scare the heck out of the local clientele, eat copious amount of bacons butties and try and recharge our batteries. The new boat house was a godsend, I even remember a bunch of us helping paint it."

But of course, as the club grew through the noughties, the pressure on space re-emerged. There was nothing for it. Brookes would have to go through the tedious planning process again and attempt to build a larger boathouse.

The original plan, developed by Spratley himself, was to knock down the 2002 building and build a new construction, more than twice the size of the current boathouse. But councils were becoming much more concerned about the flood risk, and any new building had to stand up to the 'once in a hundred years' scenario test. That meant the new boathouse would have to be built on stilts, to raise it clear of potential flood waters.

That wasn't a problem from a design point of view, but it did matter in terms of the cost. Again, Brookes went out to tender. £1.6 million was the lowest cost proposed. The University wasn't prepared to pay that, so an appeal went out to the alumni of Brookes, particularly those who had rowed. But there wasn't the centuries of history that an Oxford or Cambridge college might call on, and not enough filthy rich Brookes alumni, sadly. Some £200,000 was offered, but this wasn't enough.

Spratley applied his pragmatic and creative thinking again. He asked the finance and estates heads at the university the big question. How

Artists impression – the planned new boathouse, 2010 (*Brookes archive*)

much could you afford? £800,000, they replied. Half the quoted cost. Right, said Spratley, let's build half of it!

I'm not quite sure how Brookes pulled this off in terms of planning permission, but they went back to the council planners, explained the situation, and gained agreement to build the half of the new building that did not require the current structure to be demolished. Then, Brookes said, when we have the dosh, we'll do the demolition, put up the other half and link the two into the single building that had been originally given planning permission.

The new construction was finally opened in 2013, and that's why, when you arrive at Bowbridge today, you see two buildings, separated by about a 5-metre gap. At some point, that may disappear, and a single, amazing building will finally provide the ultimate home for OBUBC. But the new building provided more vital space for boat storage, changing, a crew area and even some limited office facilities for the coaches.

You could eat your lunch off the floor …

Back to my visit in December 2023. When you enter the ground floor of either of the two buildings today, your first thought will almost certainly be 'what a lot of beautiful boats'. And the second will be 'and they're all bright yellow'. All the boats are Empachers, a top-quality carbon-fibre boat constructed by the long-established firm Bootswerft Empacher in Eberbach, near Heidelberg in Germany.

Not every rowing club has followed such a strong policy of standardising equipment, which runs deeper than simply the boats. All the oars are the same, as is every other item connected with the boat. That brings several benefits. Obviously being able to swap equipment easily helps from a point of view of cost. Boats are not cheap; a new eight can cost £60,000 plus, but depreciation is quite low, so ten years later you might be able to sell a well-maintained boat on for £20k or more.

Standardisation also means rowers can switch between boats without having to worry about a different set up or 'feel'. It makes repairs and maintenance easier too, and reduces the cost of holding spares. Going back some years, Spratley explains that there were many different types of oar in use. Spratley and Bailhache-Webb, by then coaching alongside him, decided that this was not sustainable, so made a decision to go for 'fat twos'. They have stuck to that, despite various oar salespeople no doubt trying their best to change that decision.

The second observation you might make is the cleanliness of the boathouse. The main boat storage areas are immaculate. The level of cleanliness reminds me more of the Mars food factory where I once worked, rather than the boathouses I remember from student days. The boats too are sparkling clean, not a spot of dirt or damage to be seen.

Yet there is no boatman (or woman) here, although most traditional clubs of any reasonable size employ someone in that role. It is the man (until recently) or woman (possible today) who cleans the boats, carries out minor repairs, does the technical tasks around getting the rigging right and more. Some boatmen also do some coaching. Indeed, the legendary boatman for many years at Lady Margaret Boat Club where I rowed, Roger Silk, coached the Cambridge University women's crews, as well as various of our own college crews.

But that role does not exist at Brookes. The crews are expected to fulfil most of those duties themselves, including cleaning the boat as well as more technical work. If serious repairs are needed, they are outsourced to a couple of friendly local boat-repair firms. One young British junior international told me that during his year at one of the very top US universities, 'I didn't touch a spanner.' Not only that, but also, 'I had to fill in a form if I wanted to get my footplate moved a centimetre or two.' At Brookes, an athlete would just make that adjustment without even thinking about it.

A New Home

The boathouse at Cholsey today (©*AllMarkOne*)

That seemingly minor point is quite profound really, as it demonstrates the ethos of personal responsibility which certainly pervades Brookes and forms part of the 'Brookes magic', I suggest. That doesn't mean everything is serious and devoid of fun; but it does mean treating rowers as adults, and expecting them to behave in that way, including taking care of the equipment. Perhaps the traditional boatman role runs the risk of almost 'infantilising' rowers?

The changing facilities are still somewhat spartan today, as is the limited office space. But the other impressive aspect is the pictures of winning Brookes crews up on the walls wherever it is possible to fit them. 'We're running out of space,' Spratley says, which applies both to the pictures and room for the growing squad too. To which the reply might be, 'You're gonna need a bigger boat … house!'

Chapter 8

Towards the Millennium (1996–99)

'Building the club has been like constructing a tower of cards. If just one card gives way, the whole thing collapses.' (Richard Spratley)

Focusing on fours

After two Henley wins, Brookes, under Spratley, was developing its own ethos. The club had been seen as a feisty underdog, a mere polytechnic going up against the might of Oxbridge and London, as well as the huge, well-funded US universities. Now, with those Henley wins, and becoming a university, in truth Brookes wasn't really deserving of outsider status. Spratley continued to encourage that thinking however, allied to a tough training programme, going back to 'train twice as hard and we'll have half a chance'.

Looking back today, he feels that building the club fitted the old analogy about the tower of cards. 'Take one piece of the puzzle away, and the whole thing would have collapsed,' he says. There were so many different interlocking elements contributing to success, and if just one had not been in place, the whole edifice might have collapsed before it established success.

The need for pragmatism was one of those elements. By the mid-nineties, the programme was attracting strong junior rowers, but there were limitations. Athletes did (and still do) have to work, and Brookes academic leadership really wanted the institution to live up to its new university status. Whilst the burgeoning reputation of rowing was positive from a public recognition point of view, building the academic reputation was key. Rowers were certainly not allowed to think that their studies didn't matter.

Towards the Millennium (1996–99)

'There is no point having a great crew member for their first year and then finding they have flunked their exams and been chucked out,' Spratley says. That would be a waste for the club, the university and the unfortunate individual. There were practical constraints too. Only certain times were available for training, with the issue exacerbated by the 30 minute each way travelling time from university to boathouse. The boathouse itself was a constraint, as discussed, but the numbers of athletes in the club was limited by a number of other factors too.

Spratley tried training at different times of day. But early morning outings on the river, given the time needed to get to and from Oxford, just left the athletes exhausted or missing lectures. So gradually a training programme developed that allowed a reasonable combination of rowing and work.

His pragmatism extended to recruitment too. Dr Rachel Quarrell (now a renowned rowing writer and commentator as well as an Oxford University academic and teacher) was one of the top coxes in the country, having coxed Oxford women to victory in the 1991 Boat Race. She and her crew had got to know Brookes rowers, and indeed she remembers that the Oxford women generally preferred spending time with Brookes athletes, rather than with their own men's crew, after somewhat ill-considered remarks from a senior member of the Oxford men's boat, who had the temerity to suggest that the women only rowed in order to meet oarsmen!

'Even back then, rowing at the Poly had a sense of purpose – and a sense of humour,' says Quarrell today. They enjoyed designing rowing kit that mimicked other, more famous, crews, but with a twist. Their take on a top with a 'Beefeater' gin logo, for instance, is sadly not suitable for a family audience today (use your imagination …).

Quarrell had coxed for Molesey, Leander, London and other top crews post-Oxford when she received a call from Richard Spratley in the autumn of 1995. Would she like to come and help out at Brookes?

Matt Akers had left that summer and Brookes was short of coxing experience, although young Rowley Douglas from Monkton Combe was a developing star. Quarrell was now doing postgraduate study and could bring experience in the boat and in terms of coaching. She would not be able to cox for Brookes in restricted student events, but that left other options open.

Quarrell liked the Brookes approach. 'There was a notable lack of mucking about. Richard's favourite expression was, "Come on, we're not making a watch!" He hated people spending too much time fiddling about with the rigging or seats, he wanted us to get on with it.'

She also enjoyed the way coxes held considerable responsibility, designing the warm-ups, for instance. 'Richard was inspirational rather than being a highly technical coach,' Quarrell remembers. 'There was a lot of steady state rowing, and 8-minute pieces during which the rating would be varied. With two boats side by side, the aim was to show you could move ahead of the other crew at the same rating, demonstrating greater power. Then the leading crew would drop the rating so the crews came level again. As coxes, we played our part too – trying to position our boat in the best place on the river to maximise or minimise the effect of the current.'

Over the winter, the rating for those pieces would gradually increase, preparing the crews to row at higher rates (36 strokes per minute or more) for substantial periods. 'I think Brookes practiced higher rates earlier in the season than most,' Quarrell says, which set the crews up well for the race season.

At the London Fours head race in 1995, there was a dispute about the eligibility of Brookes' crews in different categories, so Spratley's response was decisive. Brookes would simply enter 'open' categories from now. Quarrell sees that as a key moment for Brookes, as 'it reset their ambition, and made the club focus on how to win at the highest levels'.

Towards the Millennium (1996–99)

In 1996, Brookes edged up to thirteenth at the Head of the River, the club's best result ever. The second boat finished forty-seventh, but the third boat was thirty-fifth! That must have caused some interesting dynamics in the pub afterwards, but the exact reasons for that reversal have been lost in the mists of time. The chaotic nature of the Head (see Chapter 14) means there is every chance the second boat was impeded by another boat, ran into a rogue grey seal or had a minor equipment failure.

Rachel Quarrell and her crew win the Britannia at Henley, 1996 (*Brookes archive*)

At the Evesham Regatta, two Brookes eights dominated, with Quarrell coxing one. 'Richard managed to persuade the judges that the final was a dead heat. I'm sure he just wanted the two Brookes boats to have another battle, he was always looking for ways to test us competitively!'

Then, at Marlow Regatta in 1996, Brookes took 10 oarsmen and won the eights, the coxed and coxless fours (with rowers doubling up and competing in two events) and the pair. That was quite a statement of intent. For Henley, Spratley decided to put his four best athletes into a coxed four.

'Once you start winning, of course the pressure is on to keep that going,' he says. With what was still a relatively small squad, the goal was to juggle the crew formations both to suit the rowers and to provide the best chance of winning something. The Britannia Challenge Cup was not restricted to students, so Quarrell was allowed to cox a four with David Allen, Alistair Ross, David Bushnell and Dan Marett, which competed and duly won at Henley. That was the first men's Brookes win at Henley outside the Temple, signalling the start of a period when Brookes achieved several victories spread across various fours events.

A national dilemma

In the 1996/7 season, Brookes had a men's eight that was a level above anything Spratley had coached previously. At the Head of the River in March 1997, there was a significant breakthrough, with the club's first top ten placing, finishing sixth, only 20 seconds behind the winners, Leander. Brookes beat international-level crews from several countries.

The crew could not enter the Temple again because of the qualification rules, but Spratley felt they were capable of winning the Ladies' Plate, the eights event at Henley that ranked higher than the Temple or the Thames for eights. But four members of that Brookes crew (Brown, Baker, Henshilwood and Ben Webb) were on the fringe of selection for the GB national lightweight eight.

Towards the Millennium (1996–99)

As Henley approached, Spratley was contacted by the coach of that boat. He wanted the four Brookes rowers to compete in a GB national lightweights eight at Henley and Lucerne regatta as a prelude to the World Championships later in the summer. But there was an ultimatum – if the Brookes guys wanted to be selected for the 'worlds', rowing with the squad at Henley was non-negotiable. If they rowed at Henley for the Brookes eight they had trained with through the year, they would not be considered for GB selection.

This was probably the first, but definitely not the last, time that there would be some divergence of interests between Brookes and the GB national set-up (the same applies to other clubs too, of course). Spratley tried to persuade Brian Armstrong, who ran GB rowing, that this wasn't the right approach. But Armstrong was unmoved, and clearly there are two sides to this argument. Ultimately, Spratley felt he could not stand in the way of his athletes gaining national recognition, so they would row as part of the GB boat. But that left him with the four heavyweight members of his crew.

One solution was to put those guys into a four. But meanwhile, a similar discussion had taken place between Armstrong and Nottinghamshire County Rowing Association (NCRA), the established home club for top lightweights, who also had a promising crew that was targeting the Ladies' Plate at Henley. They also had four rowers wanted by GB for that lightweight eight. And of course, that left them in the same position, with four surplus oarsmen. So after some discussion, Brookes and NCRA teamed up with their non-GB squad rowers to form a new crew that would also race in the Ladies' Plate.

That led to the slightly crazy situation where, in the 1997 semi-final of the Ladies Challenge Plate at Henley, the records show NCRA and Oxford Brookes University (in effect, the nascent GB national lightweight boat) narrowly beat Oxford Brookes University and NCRA (the guys who were left behind)! That was one of the strangest racing results ever seen at Henley.

In the final, the GB lightweights came up against the top crew from the University of Washington, probably the best US university eight that year. The lightweights took a small lead, the Huskies came back in the middle of the course and went ahead, and the crews were level all the way past the enclosure, with the crowd going crazy. No-one was sure who had won, but the verdict in one of Henley's best-ever finals was a win for the NCRA/Brookes crew – by one foot (0.3 m)!

More success came in the Visitors' Challenge Cup for coxless fours, where Scarlett and Williams teamed up with Gareth Curry and Toby Carson to win that Henley event for Brookes for the first time. Indeed, that was the beginning of a great run for Brookes in the Visitors'. They were to win that title (including with composite crews, teaming up with other clubs) in no less than seven of the next ten years.

The case of the 1997 lightweights highlights the potential tension between club and international rowing. It exists globally, and has increased recently, perhaps most evidently in the US where top university crews are highly international and indeed can beat most national boats. Yet the USA does not dominate rowing at Olympic and world championship events. In terms of the UK, that relationship between clubs and the GB national set-up has waxed and waned over the years – more on that later, particularly when we get onto the GB rowing performance in the 2021 Olympics.

Who the hell are Bowbridge?

Having mentioned Brookes' strength in the Visitors', in 1998 the club did not carry off that title at Henley. However, Brookes fielded two strong fours, a coxed four in the Britannia and a coxless four in the Wyfold. This is where more of the Henley peculiarities come into play, because if you look at the results from that year, you will see that Bowbridge Rowing Club won the Wyfold, beating Worcester Rowing Club by a length. So what's that got to do with Brookes?

Towards the Millennium (1996–99)

Read this book carefully, and you will be well positioned to make 'the rules of Henley Royal Regatta' your *Mastermind* specialist subject. And if you get to that point, you will know that the Wyfold Challenge Cup for coxless fours is restricted to club crews. No universities, colleges or schools are allowed to enter.

But for years, top rowing universities have run linked but supposedly independent clubs. That fulfils several objectives. It provides a means for athletes to continue training and competing with the university club even if they have technically left the institution. It can also facilitate composite crews, maybe with a couple of current students and a couple of 'old boys' (or girls). And it means those crews can row in events such as the Wyfold which are restricted to 'club crews'.

So Cambridge University has Crabtree Boat Club, which has become a force in British masters rowing in recent years. Oxford has the 1829 Club, Imperial College has Queen's Tower and so on. And Brookes created Bowbridge – named after the address of the boathouse. There is also Taurus, the current Brookes alumni club, which has appeared in regatta winners lists every now and again, including at Henley.

Bowbridge was a crew of recent Brookes graduates, still rowing from the Brookes boathouse and benefitting from the same coaching capability. Gareth Curry, David Allen and Danny Marett were all previous HRR winners with Brookes, and they teamed up with Sutherland who stroked the four to victory.

More recently, the Henley Stewards tried to get to grips with this and exclude university-linked crews from events designed for 'true' clubs. Sir Steve Redgrave (in his role as chair of the Stewards) took Richard Spratley aside at one point and told him that Bowbridge would not be welcome in the club events. Whether that would have stood up in a court of law is doubtful, but you don't argue with the greatest oarsman the world has even seen, do you?

The coxed four victory in the Britannia, after a tough final against Neptune Rowing Club from Ireland, was satisfying as none of that crew were previous Henley winners. But they went on to achieve a huge amount between them – indeed, two of them, Jonno Devlin and Jo von Maltzahn (who was born in Oxford, despite the surname), became the first Brookes undergraduates to win Henley medals three years running. Gareth Corry and Mark Clarke were the other successful oarsman, whilst cox of that crew, Rowley Douglas, also went on to greater things, coxing the GB eight at the 2000 Olympics.

Meanwhile, Fred Scarlett and Steve Williams formed a pair, and were selected to represent GB at the world championships, where they finished a very credible sixth. Not bad for their first international experience, and the start of two glittering careers in GB vests.

A lightweight digression

Going back to that slightly crazy 1997 Ladies' Plate event, it is interesting to note the history of lightweight rowing, its rise and unfortunate fall.

I coxed the Cambridge University Lightweights to a narrow victory over Oxford back in 1978, just the fourth of those races, when lightweight rowing was getting established. The logic was that in rowing, a strength-related sport, a good big 'un would always beat a good little 'un, as they say. This was particularly thought to discriminate against nations whose people tended to be smaller than global averages.

So how could an Indian or Japanese crew compete against hulking great Americans, Brits or Germans? Or indeed how could any skilled 5 ft 9 in (1.8 m), 11 stone (70 kg) oarsman compete with his 95 kg (15 stone), 2.0 m tall (6 ft 6 in) friend, who had the weight advantage and also those long 'levers', arms and legs that could drive the boat effectively and faster than his slighter friend? So the lightweight category was introduced, with men's crews needing to average no more than 70 kg, with no individual over 72.5 kg. The women's equivalents are 57 kg and 59 kg.

For a few years, it looked like lightweight rowing might establish a parallel path to the open or heavyweight class. But then several factors

Towards the Millennium (1996–99)

combined to derail that trajectory. Firstly, lightweights got too good. Peter Haining (see Chapter 10), for instance, started beating all but a handful of heavyweight scullers. The top lightweight coxless fours or quad sculls were posting times that, over a 2,000 m course, were only seconds different from their heavyweight equivalents.

And quite a lot of 'lightweight' rowers were actually capable of competing successfully as heavyweights if they ate more pasta and built muscle. I rowed with some 'lightweight' individuals who would have been under 70 kg whether or not they rowed, being naturally that build. But there were others who were 190 cm tall and whose healthy weight was probably nearer 80 kg, but could starve themselves down to lightweight eligibility to make the team. That probably wasn't healthy for them or the sport. At junior or university levels, the issues were even more worrying in terms of encouraging unhealthy behaviour in young people, which might even lead to anorexia or body dysmorphia.

Secondly, the argument about certain countries not being able to compete started cracking. Japan produces decent rugby front row forwards these days. The Indian cricket team, which used to have small, wristy batsmen and crafty, skinny spinners, now has batsmen who count amongst the most powerful hitters in the world and muscular fast bowlers.

Finally, the Olympics has increased its dominance over many sports, including rowing. Understandably, the Olympic movement does not want to see unshackled expansion of the overall rowing programme, so it regulates events. Rightly, Paralympic rowing has grown in recent years, along with an increasing number of women's categories. But that has been in part balanced by a reduction in the number of lightweight events.

Generally, the Olympic movement does not like categorisation by weight unless it is a pure 'strength' event like weightlifting or boxing. Lightweight events were only introduced in the 1996 Olympics, but in Tokyo 2021 the men's lightweight programme was cut from two events to one, the double sculls. We lost the coxless fours, so that meant there were only two lightweight men's medals and two women's (the two double sculls events). The same applied at Paris in 2024.

There is also a view that including lightweights did not actually increase national participation at Olympic level, which the IOC wanted to see. We did not see India or Japan dominating the lightweight rowing events, as some had hoped. Instead, the UK, New Zealand, Netherlands and so on won those medals, just as they did the heavyweights.

Now the 2028 Los Angeles Olympics has dropped lightweight events altogether. World championships still include lightweight events, but funding at national level is highly related to the Olympics, so lightweights are in retreat, which seems a shame. I don't see this coming back either, so we will probably look back on Peter Haining and his ilk (including the Cambridge crew of 1978 of course) as part of a brief but golden age of lightweight rowing.

The end of the millennium

So the Brookes story heads towards the end of the century and the millennium. In 1999, that Britannia winning crew of 1998 were back at Henley, this time having jettisoned their cox, swapping Clarke for Marett, and rowing as a coxless four in the Visitors'. This was an exceptional crew, demonstrated by their thrashing of old rivals, Imperial College, in the final by over four lengths.

By now, Steve Williams, star of the 1995 eight and the 1997 four, was looking for national recognition and selection. He teamed up with Simon Dennis, an Imperial College graduate, for the 1999 season and they entered the Silver Goblets and Nickalls' Challenge Cup for coxless pairs at Henley. The pair comfortably beat two Australians in the final, making this the first time the Brookes name featured on that Henley cup, and the first Brookes win in what are known as the 'open' events at Henley, those aimed at the very best athletes.

The 2023 Temple Challenge Cup Final

Henley Royal Regatta, 12.40 pm, 2 July 2023

Race report – The 2023 Temple Challenge Cup Final
Brookes has won the last three races now, three finals, two of them after very exciting races. Can the club make it four in a row?

This is the Temple Challenge Cup, the men's eights events for students. On paper it is not as prestigious as the Ladies' Plate or the Grand, but it has a special place in the hearts of many college and university coaches, crews and supporters. Because it has quite strict qualification rules, it is a very 'genuine' student race that excludes the most experienced rowers, even if they are still studying. So you can't be in a crew if you have won the Temple previously, or if you are an under-23 international, for instance.

It therefore is a good indicator of the talent that is coming through each club. Win the Temple, and that may lead on to even greater things. And Brookes has won the Temple at five of the last eight regattas at Henley, a record that no other club can touch.

This year, to get to the final, by a fluke of the draw, Brookes has already defeated three US universities in tough races, Princeton, Washington and Harvard. The race against Harvard was a real battle, and the semi-final against Washington was seen by many as the 'real' final. But Brookes rowed brilliantly and won by almost two lengths, far more comfortably than anyone expected.

Meanwhile, in the other half of the draw, Syracuse has been the dark horse of the event. The crew was unseeded, perhaps surprisingly, but left a trail of seeded crews behind, starting in the very first round, when University of London was surprisingly taken out by a third of a length. Syracuse got ahead and then hung on grimly as they approached the finish, so they are obviously a tough and fit bunch of athletes. That was a race that should have been a quarter or even semi-final in retrospect.

Oxford Brookes

In the actual quarter-final, Syracuse hammered the seeded Dutch rowers from Nereus after being down at halfway. And in the semi-final, Syracuse despatched the Brookes 'B' crew (also seeded!) quite easily. The Brookes 'B' crew is slower than the club's 'A' boat, for sure, but not by very much. So no-one at Brookes is expecting an easy win here.

The Brookes eight sets off like a train. A rather damp train, to be sure, but the pace is impressive. However, Syracuse has sped away 'like an orange rocket' according to the commentator. After 30 seconds Syracuse just lead, but that isn't going to last for long. Around the minute mark, we can see Brookes edging ahead. It's hard to tell if Syracuse has slowed a touch or Brookes are pushing harder, but we can see the gap growing. After that, it is inexorable. We know Syracuse will never give up, and they don't – Brookes never really pulls away. But at Fawley, virtually the halfway point, Brookes has a lead of about a length.

Around this point on the course, as you pass the Fawley timing point, on finals day certainly, you start getting close to the party boats that are cruising up and down the river (outside the boundaries of the course, it goes without saying). It can be a strange experience. You are absolutely shattered by this point, muscles, heart and lungs all flat out. On one side, you have the Upper Thames boathouse and Remenham Club, where genuine rowers and ex-rowers plus their smartly dressed guests clap politely with the occasional encouraging shout.

On the other side, you have pleasure boats full of extremely drunk revellers who frankly would not know the difference between a quad scull and a Viking longboat. There may well be an Elvis impersonator belting out Hound Dog from a boat just as your cox is calling for a 'hard twenty'. So this is a time to really keep your concentration, focus on your rowing, your colleagues, your boat. For goodness' sake don't start looking around (or singing along).

Back to our race, and the legendary Syracuse toughness comes into play one more time. In a last-ditch attempt to get back on terms, coming

The 2023 Temple Challenge Cup Final

up to the mile signal, Syracuse manages to narrow that gap somewhat. But the Brookes athletes are fully focused, and as they come alongside the enclosures, we see them push on again and increase the pressure, as we've seen the club's crews do time and time again this week.

Syracuse are giving everything, and continue to do so to the line. There is no collapse in the final strokes here. But there is no way Brookes is giving this one up. The rowers look relatively comfortable (given what they've just done for six minutes) and they come over the finishing line a length-and-a-third ahead.

So at the end of six days of tough competition in the Temple, the score is Oxford Brookes four, the US university system (Princeton, Washington, Harvard, Syracuse) nil. And that is also the fourth triumph in a row this morning for Brookes. Quite incredible.

Chapter 9

The science of rowing

'Never sacrifice work to appearance; but of course style is effect, and honest hard work will give true style eventually.' (Steve Fairbairn, Steve Fairbairn on Rowing)

The basics

I said earlier that rowing is fundamentally a simple activity and sport. But we should consider the science and technical aspects to help analyse Brookes' success over recent years. Has the club and its coaches discovered some magical secret of rowing that makes their boats go faster?

The scientific principles behind rowing are reasonably simple. Newton's Third Law of Motion states that 'whenever one object exerts a force on another object, the second object exerts an equal and opposite on the first'. Rowing works on the basis that the rower exerts a force on the water in one direction through the blade of the oar, using the shaft of the oar as a lever, and that creates an opposite force on the boat, propelling it through the water. So looking at it simplistically, the more force the rower creates by pulling their blade through the water, pushing the water away, the greater the force that is making the boat go faster.

The rower starts the stroke sitting upright, leaning forward slightly, with knees tucked up towards the chest and arms extended. They lift their hands so the vertical blade of the oar drops into the water, 'behind' the rower, so it is just covered. This is known as the "catch", and going too deep with your blade is just wasting energy. Then they slide back on

The science of rowing

their seat, flattening the legs (the 'leg drive') and pulling the oar handle into their chest as they do so. Arm, back, stomach and leg muscles all come into play.

Once the oar handle is pulled into the body, the rower pushes down with the hands, which moves the blade up out of the water. Again, you don't want the blade to go too far upwards, which would simply waste energy. On the other hand, not far enough and it might clip the water when you slide forward, slowing the boat. You also want to minimise the amount of water you flick up into the air as you remove the blade – more wasted energy again.

Once the blade is just clear of the water, it is "feathered". The wrists rotate so the blade turns through 90 degrees, from vertical to horizontal. It stays in this position to minimise air resistance as the rower slides forward on their seat and the blade moves towards the back of the boat through the *recovery phase* of the stroke. But just before the next stroke starts, the rotation is reversed so the blade is square as it enters the water again. If you forget to do this, as I did a few times when I was learning to row, your horizontal blade really doesn't want to go under water, and the consequences can be rather unpleasant.

Anyway, assuming the blade is vertical as it enters the water, the next stroke has started. Rinse and repeat some 200–250 times for a normal 2,000 metre race.

As well as the basic force applied through the oar and blade, other forces come into play, principally friction. The boat loses energy to overcome the friction between its surfaces and the water – fluid dynamics is a whole branch of mathematics, within which the behaviour of boats is a key topic. (My late father-in-law was a globally renowned expert in this field, particularly in terms of submarine design.[13] He was fascinated by rowing mechanics too.)

There is also the aerodynamics – the friction caused by the boat, the oars and, of course, the rowers (and the cox if there is one) in the boat simply moving through the air. These aspects are influenced by the design of the boat in terms of its weight, shape and composition.

Friction is the main reason why a boat that is not well balanced, where crew members are not working together smoothly, is slower. If the boat tips slightly whilst the rowers are moving up the slide and the oars are out of the water, then more of the boat, or indeed the oars themselves, will come in contact with the water and create more friction. A lack of balance might also mean the rowers are not getting their blades into or out of the water at the optimal moment, so are not able to apply force as well as they might.

Making the boat go faster ...
So competitive rowing is all about getting the maximum possible force applied through the water during a race, whilst maintaining that smoothness and balance. Then the big questions start to emerge. Do I simply select the biggest, strongest people I can find? They can apply more force, but the boat weighs more so needs more energy to move it, and if they are uncoordinated we will lose through the friction effect and their lack of ability to apply the force usefully. Actually, there are very few top-class oarsmen over about 100 kilos in weight.

Should we look to do as many strokes per minute (the 'rating' in rowing jargon) as we can, sliding up and down on our seats as fast as possible without falling off? But then each stroke will be shorter, the blade is going to be in the water for less time as we rush to get onto the next one, so that might not be sensible. Rushing also makes errors more likely, and the energy expended in moving up and down the slide is not contributing to the speed of the boat.

Perhaps the trickiest issues are around how to exert that maximum possible force during the second or so that the blade is in the water, although there aren't too many variables really. If we examine the rowing stroke, from a position of relative ignorance, we might ask:

The science of rowing

- How far forward should I lean before I put my blade in the water?
- Which muscle groups do I engage and when during the pulling part of the stroke – how do I sequence applying force from the upper body (shoulders and back), arms and legs in particular?
- How long should my stroke be? How far back should I lean before I push my hands down to release the blade from the water?
- How fast should I proceed back up the slide to the beginning of the next stroke (the rating question)?

In truth, today the difference between the best crews and their preferred style of rowing, usually driven by their coaches, is not that great. Watching videos from 20 years ago, commentators talk of the 'relaxed' Dutch style, the rough and ready (yet powerful) Canadian style and so on. But some of this even then seemed like rationalisation of beliefs rather than anything very analytical.

Go back much further, and there certainly were different approaches. The battle between the adherents of the English Orthodox style and the followers of the legendary Steve Fairbairn over the 'ideal' rowing stroke went on for decades around the turn of the twentieth century. Reading the story now, it seems incredible, for instance, that many of the 'Orthodox' proponents thought it was better for rowers to learn in a boat with fixed rather than sliding seats until they were quite expert. And other technical points that today no-one would argue about (such as the need for smooth hand movements around 'the turn', as the blade is extracted from the water) were debated with as much favour as religious sects would once argue over angels and head of pins.[14]

Today at the higher levels of rowing, there is not much difference between the top clubs and crews in terms of technique. Some key success factors seem to be generally accepted.

- To deliver the force, the rower needs to, in effect, 'lock onto' a chunk of water as quickly as possible when the blade enters the water. It is the pushing away of that weight that generates the opposite force and the speed. That means you don't want to chop vertically down into the water from a great height and then have to change the direction of your blade. You want to enter the water quickly and be able to 'lock on' to your volume of water and get the movement going in the right direction almost instantly.
- Then, to drive the blade through the water, you need to get the various muscles groups moving harmoniously. Most coaches now would be looking for the legs to engage immediately, with the rower driving them downwards, the upper body also contributing as early as possible and through the stroke, with perhaps a little final arm action right at the end of the stroke.
- You want a long stoke, accelerating through the water, then a quick exit, and transition to moving back up the slide for the next stroke. But an exaggerated lean back at the end of the stroke probably puts the back under unnecessary pressure and slows down the transition. So you rarely see that 'lean back' now other than in practice sessions or when crews are showing off – it does look very good!
- Coaches often talk about 'relaxation', which is probably a red herring. You can't really be 'relaxed' at the business end of a race and you feel you will die imminently. But 'smoothness' is certainly a factor. Keeping all movements controlled and smooth, even when the muscles are anything but relaxed, will help to balance the boat and makes it less likely that it will tip and see that additional friction mentioned earlier. It also helps to achieve the co-ordination between the crew members, that beautiful sight of eight oars entering and leaving the water as one, and eight bodies moving in harmony.

The science of rowing

Spotting a good crew

So what has this diversion into the technical side of rowing taught us? Well, the key message is that, in its most basic terms, it genuinely is a very simple sport. One basic action repeated, ad infinitum (or ad nauseum in the case of some athletes).

And yet, there have been doctorate level papers written about the relationships between human physiology and rowing ability, about the implications of boat shape on fluid dynamics, or describing the power outputs generated by the blade at various phases within the stroke. At a detailed level, rowing can seem surprisingly complex.

However, if you are watching rowing as a non-expert, you can quickly see a good crew by the length of the strokes even when the rating is high. If the crew is rating at 36 strokes a minute or higher, and you can see that the strokes are still long, then that's a good sign. The co-ordination and timing is the next thing to look for – are the blades entering and leaving the water in synch throughout the crew? Perfect harmony, in that sense, is immediately noticeable.

Then look for balance. Does the boat lean from side to side as the athletes slide; can you see one or both sides crashing down towards the water every few seconds? Not a good sign. And finally, is the moment the blades enter the water almost impossible to see precisely? With the best crews, it seems to happen as a fluid continuous movement rather than as a clear 'chop' downwards into the water. But ultimately, you can tell a really good crew. They're the ones going faster than everyone else, and that ultimately is what sets Brookes apart.

So does the club have some great technical secret concerning the rowing stroke? I don't think so, although to be perfectly honest, if there is a secret, I don't think the Brookes coaches would have told me. But if there is a secret, one assumes that their athletes who have gone on to row and coach elsewhere in the UK and the wider world are spreading the 'Brookes technique'. The secret would be out if there really was some special sauce.

Expert commentators observing Brookes races tend to mention a very smooth but quick catch (the blade entering the water) and immediate power going into each stroke, as well as superb co-ordination between the rowers. But that isn't exactly unique to Brookes, and indeed would be what every coach would like to see in their crews.

Telemetry

In recent years we have seen the introduction of amazing technology, generally known as telemetry. By attaching a tiny device to the oar, huge amounts of information relating to every stroke taken can be captured and transmitted to be analysed on a data platform.

That information can relate to:

- the speed and acceleration of the boat at every point during a race or training session
- the speed of each individual oar through the water at every point in the stroke – and related to that, the power being generated by the athlete
- the 'flight path' of each blade including its depth in the water
- the speed of the rower on the slide during the stroke both whilst the blade is in the water and during the recovery phase.

This enables coaches and rowers to obtain detailed data about every aspect of their stroke and technique, enabling examination and improvement in a way that was unimaginable twenty years ago. My feeling is that, although they have no magical technique, the Brookes coaching team has probably been better than anyone at understanding this data and using it to optimise every detail that contributes to making the boat go faster.

The science of rowing

Alex Henshilwood, who rowed at Brookes in 1992–5 has gone on to become a very successful junior coach at Pangbourne College and Eton College, winning the junior eights at Henley with both crews, and was the first to buy the telemetry system in the UK for Eton back in 2013. He supports this theory. He does not see anything unique in the technicalities of the 'Brookes stroke' but he does feel that Henry Bailhache-Webb has developed real expertise in using that telemetry data.

Bailhache-Webb, Brookes' head coach since the late 1990s, has a coaching philosophy which is very focused on personal improvement for every rower. The detailed data that he can access, analyse and use to identify small improvements each person can make is a key element in that approach. For instance, one rower might have a tendency to work too hard early in a race, then see power drop off towards the end. Another might 'save' too much energy early on, and show greater power later, but without optimising overall performance.

Telemetry enables a coach to advise the athlete on issues like this. Indeed, I'm writing this the day after a dramatic Oxford versus Cambridge Boat Race when the Cambridge stroke basically stopped rowing for the last minute or so, absolutely spent. Perhaps this was the first time it happened to him, but watching out for a tendency to put too much effort in too soon is the sort of insight that telemetry can provide. (We will see a parallel Brookes case later in the book too.)

Chapter 10

Haining and Bailhache-Webb (2000–07)

'Henry, travelling is for wankers. You know it is.' (Richard Spratley)

A Millennium baby – and a surprise benefactor
In 2000, Richard Spratley and his wife were delighted to welcome their first child into the world, their son Joseph. Two years later, a daughter, Emily, was born. Spratley was also working hard with his construction firm, feeling more responsibility now there were two more in the family. The UK had been growing reasonably well in the late 1990s, but the end of the dot-com boom in 2000 sent the economy into something of a reverse.

At times, Spratley wondered whether he could keep all the proverbial balls (or maybe oars) in the air at once. Brookes was an established force in British rowing now, but there was more he wanted to do. However, his business and home life were important too. He was being paid by Brookes now, but nowhere near enough to support the family.

At this point, an unlikely benefactor stepped in. Jurgen Grobler was by this time recognised as a very successful rowing coach on the international circuit. In 1992, he joined a GB rowing set-up that had under-performed on the global stage, and quickly took it to unprecedented success at subsequent Olympics.

Spratley and Grobler knew each other through the rowing circuit and there was obvious mutual respect. Indeed, Grobler had asked Spratley to get involved in GB coaching when Scarlett and Williams

Haining and Bailhache-Webb (2000–07)

from Brookes made the national team in 1998. But Spratley had to turn down the chance – 'I couldn't take weeks out from Brookes and my own business to go to international regattas,' he says.

So Spratley was pleasantly surprised when Grobler called him in 2000 to suggest that Brookes should become a high-performance centre for the GB development programme. The concept was to nominate a small number of clubs who would receive funding from the centre and, in return, would work with the national set-up to develop the next generation of international-level rowers. The clubs, including Brookes, signed up to a loose set of goals and ways of working and, in return, received a small annual payment, around £20,000 in the case of Brookes.

That wasn't a lot, but critically the money from Grobler would enable Brookes to recruit a paid assistant rowing coach for the first time. That would take some of the pressure off and enable Spratley to put a little more effort into his construction work. Shortly after Brookes gained its new status, Spratley recruited Kevin McWilliams, who had coached the Oxford University women's crew, as the first Brookes assistant coach.

It was also a historic year in other ways for the club. In the Temple Cup at Henley, a hard-fought semi-final victory over Brown University was followed with an agonisingly close defeat by Yale in the final. But the success in the fours continued, with Tom Burton, Devlin, Marett and von Maltzahn winning the Visitors'. By this stage, Brookes alumni were also making a mark at international level. At Henley, Fred Scarlett and Steve Williams were in the GB squad four that won the Price Philip cup for top coxed fours.

By the time the Sydney Olympics came around, Fred Scarlett, Ben-Hunt Davis and cox Rowley Douglas from Brookes were all in the eight, which to most observers' surprise won the gold medal in impressive fashion, the first time since 1912 that GB had won the top men's event at the Olympics. The eight powered away from the start and was never headed, building a lead of almost a length then holding on to win by a quarter of a length at the end.

So Brookes had its first Olympic medals, although Hunt-Davis did not row for Brookes whilst he was a student, being based at Leander. Williams just missed out on Olympic selection, but his consolation was a gold medal in the world championships, rowing in the coxed four, a boat that was not included in the Olympic schedule. His day would come before too long, though. And 2000 saw what turned out to be another key event in Brookes Boat Club history, as Henry Bailhache-Webb enters the story.

Partridge and Bailhache-Webb come onboard

Richard Spratley is clearly core to the story of Brookes since 1991, but Henry Bailhache-Webb has played an equally important role in the development of the club over the last 20 years.

My first experience with Bailhache-Webb at the Brookes boathouse was memorable. I was meeting Spratley and had not expected to be introduced to other key people at the club. Bailhache-Webb was in the boathouse when we walked in and, on being introduced, my two first thoughts were that he was somewhat intimidating and that he could absolutely play himself in the Hollywood film of the Brookes story, being unfeasibly tall, dark and handsome, with chiselled features and a lean, athlete's physique. Aged 41, he still looked like he could jump in the boat and row pretty damned quickly. But let's backtrack and see how he got to this point.

As a young man at Monkton Combe school in Bath in the late 1990s, Bailhache-Webb was more interested in rowing than academic study. Although he attended a fee-paying secondary school, his early years were certainly not privileged. His parents divorced when he was two years old, and his mother raised three children on her own, initially in a council house and with little money. She was brilliant however at

Haining and Bailhache-Webb (2000–07)

bartering, scrimping, and saving and being efficient with everything they had.

She had an agreement to take out-of-date stock off the hands of local shops, 'To feed my goats,' she told them. But the 'goats' were principally her three children! Bailhache-Webb remembers his amazement at going to a friend's house in his teens and finding them throwing away slightly damaged strawberries that would have been the very best fruit in his house. She also found a state-funded academic scholarship which young Bailhache-Webb won, taking him to the private Monckton Combe school.

Bailhache-Webb showed some obsessive tendencies as a boy. He loved collecting – bees, hundreds of moths, whatever interested him at the time. But he was also full of energy. Playing at flanker in rugby matches 'my aim was to be at every tackle, every breakdown', he remembers. Not actually the best strategy in rugby, but that was Henry's style.

He also loved rowing and, as he grew to 1.91m, lean and fit, he seemed to have the raw material to be a successful rower at senior levels. Monkton Combe was a decent rowing school, but not one that regularly won the top schools' events. His housemaster told him "we know you're not the brightest", which only made him laugh and become more determined, ending up with the best grades in his house that year.

When a friend of his family suggested he should look at Oxford Brookes, where the rowing programme was delivering real success and might suit his talents, he was interested. He had planned to go to university somewhere on the coast, as surfing was his other real passion. Oxford is about as far from the sea as you can get in the UK, but after discussions with Richard Spratley, somehow in 2000 he was enrolled in what he thought was a Fine Art degree course at Brookes. He was enjoying his Art A-level studies, so that seemed like a reasonable choice.

When he arrived in the autumn of 2000, he discovered his course wasn't Fine Art at all but History of Art, which was not in all truth something that inspired him. 'I've never seen the point in studying anything you don't want to do later on' he explains. He eventually managed to switch to Sports Science, which was much more appropriate and enjoyable. But his main focus at Brookes was rowing.

He quickly made it into the top crew that was aiming to win the Temple Cup at Henley in 2001, and by this time Spratley had come up with another cunning plan. Rachel Quarrell, the ex-Oxford University cox, had stepped back from Brookes after winning the Britannia in 1996 with the club, but Spratley suggested that she might like to consider doing a master's at Brookes. That would enable her, as a student, to cox the Temple crew. She had been considering a change of career direction, so she signed up for a master's in Education and Publishing.

However, the Temple proved a disappointment for Spratley, Quarrell and Bailhache-Webb, with the crew losing both finals in 2001 and 2002 to Harvard University. In 2001, the weather was dreadful, and Brookes raced on the Bucks station at Henley, contending with a strong stream and a very good Harvard crew. That race has stayed with the Brookes athletes involved to this day, and the frustration for Bailhache-Webb hit hard. He felt Brookes could, and maybe should, have won, but the margin between success and failure was tiny. He felt that the training was not quite optimised for the unusual 2,112-metre Henley course and the demands of a high-pressure race.

But there were other Brookes successes in 2001 at Henley. Devlin and von Maltzahn had moved up to GB level and won the Prince Philip with the legendary Matthew Pinsent and almost as legendary James Cracknell. Meanwhile, Brown, Corry, future Olympian Alex Partridge and Burton maintained the Brookes winning streak in the Visitors'.

Partridge went up to Brookes in 1999 from Monkton Combe school, where he was a year above Bailhache-Webb. They became lifelong friends, and Partridge remembers young Henry as 'something of an out-there guy, all or nothing, a big personality. He was always an independent thinker, not restricted by the usual parameters'.

Partridge also recalls the intensity of the Brookes training programme. 'Three hours doing weights. Six sets of 60 power cleans, bench press, squats. A six-mile run. But Richard taught us how to have fun in competing against each other and training hard,' explains Partridge. 'But I didn't realise that Henry was really thinking about the training programme. What made sense, what didn't. Most of us just got on with it, but he was analysing what worked for him – and eventually he got the chance to implement that more widely, of course.' In fact, Bailhache-Webb's Sports Science degree project was about the Brookes training programme, so he had another motive for thinking deeply about it.

The Visitors' win in 2001 was notable for Richard Spratley's tactical and organisational nous. The crew was strong, but one of the four rowers was clearly the weakest. It looked like they were not quite fast enough to win the Henley event, but Spratley wasn't content to settle for that. Three weeks before the regatta, Richard announced that James Brown would be joining the crew. He was in the 1993 Temple crew and the 1998 Ladies' Plate winning crew and was a world silver medal-winning lightweight who had left Brookes years ago, but was persuaded to come back by Spratley.

Alex Partridge calls his Visitors' semi-final that year at Henley his 'best ever race'. The crew were a length-and-a-half down to an international-level Imperial college crew, but took the stroke rate up to 46 as they rowed past the enclosures, winning by half a length in a dramatic finish. They were down again in the final against Molesey but triumphed by a more comfortable length and a half. And in the same year, Richard Spratley was made an honorary Fellow of Brookes, at the same ceremony where Sir Steve Redgrave received his honorary degree.

Sir Steve Redgrave (on the right) receives an honorary degree & Richard Spratley becomes an honorary Fellow of Brookes in 2001 (*Brookes archive*)

At this point, Brookes still had their underdog culture, which was justified in some ways – 'We were still welding pieces of metal onto bars to make heavier weights,' says Partridge. 'It was us against the world.' But the club had not yet worked out how to turn enthusiasm and tough training into regular, expected wins at the highest level.

In 2002, Devlin retained his hold on the Prince Philip in a GB squad four, whilst Baker, Marett, Burton along with Gillard won the Visitors' yet again. That year was also noteworthy for another reason, as Brookes won the Remenham Challenge Cup for women's eights. There is more on that in Chapter 18, but this was the first win for the Brookes women at the Royal Regatta, as opposed to Henley Women's Regatta, which had seen several previous successes for the club.

The sequence of Henley wins for Brookes in the fours events was broken in 2003, a lean year for Brookes generally. The club was rebuilding the squad, with many of the best rowers having left, and this

Haining and Bailhache-Webb (2000–07)

was the first year without a Henley trophy since 1994. Having a paid assistant coach was relieving the pressure on Richard Spratley, but it was not proving to be a guarantee of success.

But in 2004 Bailhache-Webb finally got his Henley winner's medal, in a Visitors' crew with Marett and Burton (again) and Andrew Stubbs from the Oxford blue boat. Bailhache-Webb had already represented GB at junior level and at Brookes he made the GB under-23 squad. After he left Brookes, he made the full GB national squad in 2005, rowing in the eight at the world championships. At Henley in 2005, he actually stroked the GB eight that lost by less than a length to the German national crew in a classic Henley final shoot-out. But he started to have back problems, not unusual for rowers, and he took the decision to retire from competitive rowing in 2006.

During this period, other Brookes athletes were also making their mark at international level. In 2004, Steve Williams teamed up with Matthew Pinsent, James Cracknell and Ed Coode in the coxless four at the Athens Olympics. Brookes star Alex Partridge rowed in the four up to the World Cup event in Lucerne, but he suffered a collapsed lung and sadly missed the Olympics, being replaced by Ed Coode.

In the fours final, it was a classic race against the reigning world champions, Canada, and there was nothing in it for the first half of the race, with GB holding a tiny lead for the first 100 metres. But Canada took a small lead after halfway, and were half a second up at 1,500 metres, with the Italians pushing in third place too.

But with just a minute of the race left, GB lifted the stroke rate again. Commentator and Olympic medal-winning cox himself, Gary Herbert, said, 'This is the pain part of the race, the legs hurt, the arms hurt, the whole thing is just going to be going black for them, at this stage though, Olympic gold medallists are made …'

GB took the lead with 200 metres to go but, showing incredible tenacity, Canada mounted a fierce last-ditch push, and with a few strokes left looked like they might have gone back ahead. As they crossed the line, the naked eye could not tell who had won. Photo finish.

When the result came through, GB had won by 0.08 seconds, about a foot (or a third of a metre). It was perhaps the best Olympic rowing final ever – do watch it if you haven't already.[15] I'm not sure any head-to-head sport gets better than this. (Mind you, the Searle brothers in Barcelona is pretty special too ...)

Unfortunately, the other Brookes representative at Athens, Jonno Devlin, had a less happy time. He was in the eight which could not replicate the success of the 2000 GB Olympic crew, and disappointingly failed to make the final. Williams was the only member of that winning four to continue rowing after Athens, and he joined Alex Partridge (once fit again), Pete Reed and Andrew Triggs Hodge in a four which continued the GB run of success with that boat, winning the world championships in 2005 and 2006.

Peter Haining – the world's greatest lightweight sculler

By 2005, assistant coach Kevin McWilliams had moved on, and Brookes hired Peter Haining as Spratley's deputy. Haining was an incredible oarsman, one of the UK's greatest ever. He came from a relatively humble and tough background, learning to row at the Loch Lomond Rowing Club in Scotland, where his father competed.

He left the Value of Leven Academy and became an apprentice painter and decorator, but his rowing prowess soon got him noticed. Haining was a lightweight, but when designated lightweight races weren't available often had to race in the open category against heavyweight oarsmen. He moved to Nottingham as a young man because the Notts Country Rowing Association was the centre of GB national lightweight rowing, and by 1986 was in the England four that won gold at the Commonwealth Games.

In 1988, he and Christopher Bates won gold in the UK championships in the pair, beating much heavier crews. He was then part of the Henley-

Haining and Bailhache-Webb (2000–07)

winning GB lightweight crew in 1989 that beat Harvard heavyweights after a controversial re-row. He always came out on top in the strength and power tests amongst the crew but, as Haining himself told me, 'because I was the strongest in the boat, perhaps I didn't always put 110 per cent into it.'

So his coach, Raymond Simms, felt Haining would be more motivated in a scull where it would all be down to his own efforts. Simms was also a boat builder, and actually built a new sculling boat for Haining. According to other rumours, Haining was always late for training, so the coach felt he might be better off in an event where he wasn't causing problems for others with his timekeeping!

Whilst writing this book, I discovered that a friend of mine, who I didn't know had ever rowed, was in Haining's under-16 prize-winning crew at school in Scotland. He confirmed that Haining's lack of organisation was not a myth. But his rowing prowess was not at all in doubt. He was a three-time world lightweight sculling champion and I recall seeing him – all 11 stone of him – thrashing much larger oarsmen at Henley, particularly if there was a tailwind.

His most famous race was probably the final of the world championship single sculls in 1993. (The film of the race is not of top quality but is well worth watching.)[16] He took the lead and looked reasonably comfortable, a length up after 1,500 metres. But one of his blades hit the lane marker buoy and he virtually stopped rowing for two or three strokes. Several other competitors stormed past him and suddenly he was a length down, lost all his boat speed and 'His chance has gone,' said the commentator.

But Haining says that he and his coach actually rehearsed for exactly this eventuality. Training on the leg press machine, his coach would shout 'you've hit the buoy', Haining would stop dead, then restart the exercise with maximum power.

So he remembers that he wasn't fazed by what happened in the race. He got back into his rhythm, and the practice, adrenaline, anger and determination kicked in. Over the last 300 metres, Haining stormed back, overtaking two of the very best scullers in the world, and won by half a length at the finish. It really is one of the most impressive recoveries you will ever see. Haining retained his world title in 1994 and 1995, making him GB's greatest ever lightweight, and maybe pound for pound the greatest GB oarsman ever, although Redgrave and Pinsent might have something to say about that!

Spratley had persuaded Haining to row in a couple of Brookes Head of the River crews in 1999 and 2001, when he stroked the boat. Haining hit the headlines again at Henley that year, rowing in the pair sculls event. This is from Daniel Topolski's report in the Observer (I should say that I'm not sure it was a 'seven stone per man' weight difference! Seven stone in total seems more likely)[17]:

> 'But the shock of the day was the way veteran lightweights Peter Haining and Nick Strange rowed away from 1998 heavyweight world Pair champions Dietlef Kirchhoff and Robert Sens. Conceding a massive seven stone a man to the combined 30-stone power of the giant Germans, the diminutive Brits sprinted again and again, sapping the confidence and power of their rivals to win by a length and a half. "We may look small but we're six-foot-nine inside," yelled Haining, shaking his fist as he crossed the line.'

Haining and Strange could not quite overcome Redgrave and Pinsent in the final, but they had a good try. After that epic, Haining retired from serious competition in 2002, and had come to admire Spratley's ability to manage 'men, material and money' as he puts it. 'Richard is brilliant at seeing the critical path.'

Haining and Bailhache-Webb (2000–07)

But when Spratley asked him if he was interested in coaching in 2004, Haining wasn't sure. He was going through the process to join the police force, but decided that he could always come back to that if coaching didn't work out. The two met at Henley Regatta, Spratley confirmed that yes, he was serious about the offer, and Haining signed

Peter Haining (right) in 2024 with Alan McDougall from his U16 Loch Lomond crew (*©Peter Smith*)

up in 2005, to the excitement of the athletes at Brookes. A multiple world champion as a coach was a big deal.

However, 2005 was actually a little disappointing for Brookes in terms of Henley Regatta. The Brookes Temple crew made it through several rounds to the semi-final, but were trounced by Trinity College Hartford, a very strong US crew who went on to thrash Yale in the final. In the Visitors', the Brookes four lost in a close final to the University of Galway boat.

Haining coached Bailhache-Webb for a short period, and both remember the mutual 'winding up' that went on. Haining was running late for the gym session one day, so Bailhache-Webb climbed up into the rafters of the old boathouse with his dumbbells and started doing his arm curls there. When Haining arrived, he could sense something was up. 'OK, where the f**k is he?' At that point, Henry dropped a dumbbell a couple of feet away from Haining. 'Right, you can f**** well stay up there for the whole session!'

After one of Haining's legendary 'mega-hard' training weeks, Bailhache-Webb would wind him up the next Monday by saying, 'Oh, I thought this week was mega-week, I thought last week was just the medium week!'

But despite the banter, there was mutual respect too, and with Haining on board, matters improved. For the 2005/6 season, he selected a crew that he felt were strong and coachable individuals with potential rather than the best technical rowers. 'Tough guys who liked a drink,' as Haining puts it. Spratley wasn't convinced about this approach, but Haining told the crew, 'I'm willing to put the work in if you are. That means extra training, but you can go and win the Temple.' Haining developed a tough programme. 'I loved the concept of taking a university crew and getting them disgustingly, international-level fit,' he says.

Haining and Bailhache-Webb (2000–07)

But although the crew was strong, they lacked rhythm. Haining tried different crew members in the vital stoke position, but something wasn't quite right. He wasn't getting consistent times over a 2,000-metre course, the eight 250 metre splits that he was looking for.

At the Metropolitan Regatta, he was watching the Brookes third boat, when inspiration struck. Although the boat wasn't anywhere near as fast as his top crew, they had rhythm. At stroke was Ruben Reggiani, a young Anglo-Italian athlete. At the next training session, Reggiani was plucked out of the third boat and put in at stroke of the Temple crew. Spratley was dubious – Reggiani's erg times were nothing special. But to Haining's delight, his crew went faster than ever.

So Reggiani, who was not even expecting to row at Henley, found himself stroking the top crew, including Messrs McKinnon, Moffatt, Holden-Smith, Merchant, Cordey, Drea, Bryant and cox Ford. The Dutch from Proteus-Eretes were seen off in the quarter final, but then an epic semi-final against another Dutch crew, the legendary Nereus, saw Brookes come through by just a third of a length.

In the final, the Cornell eight, which had looked ominously good all week, fought hard, but Brookes held on to win by just half a length. It was only in the last ten strokes that the race looked settled. After Brookes, Reggiani went on to act as a translator in the football world, including working with Fabio Capello, then England manager. Sadly a back industry halted his dreams of international rowing recognition, but a Henley medal wasn't a bad reward for his rowing career.

That selection decision demonstrates the combination of art and science that top coaches need. The technical and analytical side of the job is vital, but so is that ability to look at a rower, who maybe is not the strongest physically, and see something that will make a boat go faster. Haining also made other lasting contributions. Richard Chambers was rowing in the Brookes Temple 'B' crew in 2004, a lightweight oarsman like Haining. Chambers had talent, but also enjoyed socialising and a few drinks, Haining remembers.

One day after a particularly frustrating training session, Haining grabbed hold of Chambers. 'You remind me of me,' he said. 'You've got so much talent but you're lazy, you're not making use of it.'

With Haining's encouragement, Chambers got his act together and by the following year he was in the GB under-23 squad. By 2007 he was a world gold medallist, and he won silver at the London 2012 Olympics in the lightweight coxless four, alongside his brother Peter, in one of the most exciting Olympic rowing finals ever, with four boats finishing within a few feet of each other, and South Africa winning their only gold rowing medal ever with a final sprint to the line.

Back to Henley 2006, and more senior Brookes oarsmen popped up in other crews too, in a composite with Oxford University which reached the semi-final of the Ladies' Plate, and in the GB squad eight which narrowly lost the Grand to the Dutch national eight.

But perhaps the most significant aspect was Brookes winning a men's eights event and a fours event at Henley for the first time. A Visitors' Cup crew with three Brookes men (Ryan Davies, Robinson and Tucker) and an Oxford University escapee won that event yet again, beating Cambridge University fairly comfortably in the final. Now OBUBC had proved it could win multiple events at Henley, not just one per year.

Bailhache-Webb doesn't go travelling

In 2006, Henry Bailhache-Webb retired from rowing with back issues that ended his Olympic hopes. He felt this was surely the time to go surfing, his other passion (although that doesn't sound particularly good for your back either). He had planned to take a gap year before university and pursue that interest, but Brookes got in the way.

After his graduation and then retirement from rowing, he was living in Henley, ready to go travelling and get back into the waves. He remembers walking across the car park in Henley after a visit to the doctor's surgery to discuss jabs needed for travelling, and getting a call from Richard Spratley, his old coach at Brookes.

'Henry, what are you doing?'

'I'm off to get some jabs to go travelling, do some surfing.'

'Henry, travelling is for wankers. You know that. Come and coach our novices at Brookes.'

We can argue about whether Spratley was correct in his assessment of travelling. Maybe his view was a little extreme, but the prospect of staying involved with rowing was too much for Bailhache-Webb to resist. He had loved his time at Brookes and had great respect for Spratley. He had never applied formally for a job in his life (that still applies today), and whilst the call of the sea was strong, this sounded like an opportunity that was too good to miss. And the surf would still be there if this didn't work out. So he said yes, and weeks later was heading back to the boathouse.

British Rowing had introduced a set of formal qualifications to bring some accreditation to coaching. Spratley himself had been through that in 2000, when Brookes obtained high performance centre status from British Rowing. Bailhache-Webb obtained his certification too, and (as he puts it) realised over the next couple of years that however bad he was at many things, he was actually quite good at this coaching thing.

However, after the Henley successes of 2006, maybe a touch of complacency crept into the club. Some of the best athletes were lost to the GB squad, and Temple winners could not compete in that event again, so Brookes entered the Ladies' Plate as well as the Temple in 2007. But with a much weaker crew, Brookes made their earliest exit from the Temple for many years. Unluckily drawn against the Americans from Colgate University, eventual semi-finalists, the crew were defeated in the first round.

Oxford Brookes

Meanwhile, Bailhache-Webb was greatly enjoying his experience coaching the novices. Indeed, he still calls this couple of years the most enjoyable period of his coaching life. With his degree in sports science, he had coached a little whilst a student, and he loved working with the novice rowers. He got a particular thrill out of athletes like Tom Jefferies, who started as an absolute novice, but within the academic year was rowing in the Brookes first boat in the Temple at Henley in 2007. Bailhache-Webb coached both men and women, and a women's novice coxed four won the intermediate event at Henley Women's Regatta in 2007, to his and their delight.

Peter Haining helped the young coach, lending him books on biomechanics and rowing technique. Haining had rowed at the highest level, so helped to get Spratley and Bailhache-Webb to understand the requirements to compete at that intensity. Bailhache-Webb started thinking about how Brookes could develop towards top-level performance themselves, but after the relative failure of 2007 at Henley, some tension was building in the club.

Was it the athletes' fault that other UK universities seemed to be catching up with Brookes again? Was it simply they weren't working hard enough? Bailhache-Webb, becoming more confident about his own coaching, started being more outspoken in discussions with Haining and Spratley. This couldn't just be blamed on the athletes, he said. The club as a whole was underperforming its potential, despite its successes over the previous years. Bailhache-Webb wanted to structure the coaching differently, pushing harder in terms of the smaller details and building a more rowing-specific training programme. He also felt strongly about tailoring coaching to each individual, rather than the traditional, more crew-based approach.

It was time for some tough decisions.

The 2023 Island Challenge Cup Final

Henley Royal Regatta, 1.00 pm, 2 July 2023

Race report – The 2023 Island Challenge Cup Final
It's been a long morning at Henley Royal Regatta. Well, not that long. For the first three days of the event, rowing starts at 9 am and runs through till 1 pm in a continuous flow of races. But on the last day, we have just two hours of rowing, all finals, before the chance to head for the lunch tents, the fast food stands outside the enclosure (a fairly recent innovation) or, for the majority of spectators, a picnic in the car park. Picnics can range from a sandwich and a beer to the full works – gazebo, tables, silver service, salmon, champagne and strawberries.

I remember years ago, some Stewards' Enclosure members turning up in an old Rolls Royce, with their own butler to serve the drinks. Two parking spaces would be reserved, one for the car and one for the gazebo protecting the 10-seater table and chairs, with tablecloths and silver cutlery. But ostentation is perhaps a little more muted today. The fancy car is now more likely to be a Tesla or McLaren owned by Oxbridge blues or Harvard luminaries who are now 35-year-old hedge fund maestros.

Anyway, back to the racing. The sixth Brookes crew of the morning are taking to the water. This time it is the women, competing in the Island Challenge Cup. This is the equivalent of the Temple, with entry restricted to college and university crews. The Brookes crew has had a tough route through to the final, as this has proved to be an incredibly competitive event, with many crews of a similar standard. On Thursday, Brookes beat an Edinburgh crew that pushed them all the way, which contributed to Brookes breaking the course record to the Barrier and Fawley.

Another tough race saw the crew beating the University of Texas by one and a third lengths on Friday; then the semi-final on Saturday

Oxford Brookes

was a UK race-off, with Brookes coming out on top against Durham University – but again by only one and a half lengths.

This event really matters. The Brookes women's programme is less mature than the men's, and although there have been successes, Brookes women are not as generally dominant as the men. The coaching team, with Hugo Gulliver now in charge of the women's squad, are keen to establish Brookes as regular favourites and winners of this event, just as they have achieved that status in the Temple for men's student eights. Jasmine Bowers, Orren Smeding, Arianna Forde, Jenny Bates, Rhianna Sumpter, Grace Richards, Martha Birtles, Brenna Randall and cox Cameron Moffatt hold that responsibility in their hands today.

In the final, the University of Pennsylvania 'A' crew (Penn) faced Brookes. The Brookes 'B' boat had beaten the Penn 'B' crew on Thursday in an incredibly close race, so there was a bit of extra needle here. That indicates how Brookes is building strength in depth in its women's programme, just as it has for the men.

But as in the case of the men's recruitment situation, the top US universities are getting more and more aggressive in how they look for the top European junior women, and make them offers they struggle to refuse in terms of scholarships. That includes girls at the top British rowing schools. However, this Penn crew is largely all-American by background, and is determined to take the battle to Brookes.

So off we go, with Brookes getting a slightly dodgy start on the tricky Bucks station, nearest Temple Island. Whether it is the alignment of the boat or stroke side pulling harder than bow, the boat slews across towards the island. The cox has to apply the rudder earlier than he would like (yes, it is a male cox), slowing the boat down, and Penn takes an early lead.

But the Brookes rowers are quickly into their stride, demonstrating a long, powerful stroke. However, Penn row at a slightly higher stroke rate per minute – but can they keep that going? Soon the crews are absolutely level, and that remains the situation at Fawley, the halfway mark. But as the crews go past Remenham and Upper Thames clubs, Brookes takes the power up. Now they are moving ahead by a foot or so every stroke, and quite quickly the boat has a third of a length advantage.

Coming level with the enclosure, it looks good for Brookes, but Penn aren't done yet. Just as we saw in the Ladies' earlier, the losing crew puts in a huge final effort as they shoot past the Stewards' Enclosure grandstand. And again, we're not quite sure if the Brookes athletes felt comfortable – or were they clinging on for dear life? But cling on they do, to win a brilliant race by just a canvas, the distance between the bow of the boat and the bow rower. Not much at all, after seven minutes of flat-out rowing.

So, that's it. Time for lunch. Break out the very civilised picnic of smoked salmon, champagne and strawberries, which always seems slightly incongruous when we've just seen super-fit athletes working to the limits of their bodies all morning, gasping for breath, looking and feeling as if their legs are made of lead. But Oxford Brookes University has participated in six finals this morning, and the club has won every one. This, as far as we can tell, has never been done before in a single session on finals day at Henley. It is truly remarkable.

But there is one race more to go – can Brookes make it the magnificent seven?

Chapter 11

A new focus (2008–12)

'At Brookes we will help you become the best you can possibly be.'
(Henry Bailhache-Webb)

A big decision for Brookes

Matters came to a head in 2008. Trinity College Hartford was the latest US conqueror of Brookes in just the second round of the Temple at Henley. For the second year running, there were no wins to celebrate at the most important regatta of the year. And to Bailhache-Webb's regret, the novice programme was halted too, largely for financial reasons (although as we will see, it did return more recently). But he was taking on more and more responsibility, and putting forward his own ideas about how the club could progress.

So in 2008 Spratley made what turned out to be a highly significant decision in the historical context of Brookes rowing, making Bailhache-Webb his deputy. Haining was inspirational, a great rower, a brilliant motivator of a crew. But he was perhaps less interested in the day-to-day management of the club, the boathouse and the whole squad. As Spratley at times had to delegate whilst he was trying to keep his construction business afloat, he needed someone who could be a manager as well as a coach, and he decided that Bailhache-Webb was that man.

It was time for Bailhache-Webb to put up or shut up, as he got the chance to implement his ideas. He took up the role with his usual somewhat obsessive diligence and focus. He started itemising every second in the gym, to the point where there was not enough time for

A new focus (2008–12)

the athletes even to socialize. Even he accepts this was a step too far, but came through his laser-like focus on time efficiency.

But his structured way of thinking transferred into his development of the Brookes training programme, which is where individual and team dynamics got interesting. Spratley gave his new head coach considerable freedom but, with his years of experience, was there to point out gently every so often that maybe Bailhache-Webb should back off a bit or look at a different approach.

'I love working on the quality of the training,' Bailhache-Webb says. 'Frankly, I would do that all day every day.' But that single-minded focus has its drawbacks if you are a crew member. Training is not just hard work – it can be boring. Long periods on the erg are intrinsically dull, even if you are enjoying the background music. At one point, Bailhache-Webb tried to squeeze two gym sessions a day into the student programme, which was just too much.

Bailhache-Webb, impatient to take the reins fully, also told Spratley, 'You might as well piss off now.' In a friendly way, we assume! But both realised quickly that there was a strong synergy if they worked together and played to their respective strengths, and really, that is the basis of all the Brookes success since those early days. But, 'It wasn't always easy letting go, after 15 years or so,' Spratley remembers. 'Stepping back and then finding out how Henry and I could work together took some time.'

Spratley could be less involved day to day with training, but his contribution was vital both in management planning and activities, and also to balance Bailhache-Webb's sometimes intense approach. Spratley would suggest that maybe the crews needed a change. He would pick out events, perhaps go off to a minor regatta and do some proper racing, just to break up the monotony of training on the ergs, weights and paddling up and down the river at Wallingford.

Some even called it a good cop, bad cop scenario with the two coaches. But it is more complex than that. Spratley has a naturally open and easy manner, but is quite capable of being tough when that is needed. Bailhache-Webb is the focused, performance-driven, technical and analytical genius, yet he also has sensitivity and empathy in the way he handles athletes. However, both are leaders who are capable of inspiring both love and that little bit of fear, the ideal combination (according to author and philosopher Machiavelli).

It was, and still is, quite a team, as the results over the last 15 years show. And great credit should go to both men for working out how two such strong personalities could work together in harmony. If Spratley had found it impossible to relinquish control, or Bailhache-Webb had not accepted the assistance that was offered, the Brookes story might have gone down a very different pathway.

It's Olympic time again …
After his Athens disappointment because of injury, Alex Partridge moved to the GB eight for the 2008 Beijing Olympics. He was replaced in the four by Tom James and, despite a succession of injuries in the crew, Triggs-Hodge, Reed, Steve Williams and James won again. They were down for much of the race but made a perfectly timed run to the line, winning more comfortably in the end than in 2004. So (at time of writing), Steve Williams is the only Brookes athlete to have won two Olympic gold medals, an all-time rowing great.

Partridge won a silver medal in the eights, with GB losing out to a superb Canadian crew who never looked in danger. GB and the USA had a great race for the silver, with Partridge and co pipping the Americans by two feet on the line, and two other Brookes rowers also featured in that eight. Tom Lucy was a rowing prodigy. He did not win a Henley medal with Brookes, in part because he was already a GB international aged 19. Indeed, he won a senior world championship

A new focus (2008–12)

medal at that age and a gold world championship, as well as his Olympic silver aged 20. He then retired from the sport to fulfil his childhood dream of joining the Royal Marines, making him a great loss to rowing.

Alastair Heathcote was the other Brookes medal winner in the eights; again, he was at Brookes briefly but did not feature in the club's boats at Henley. Meanwhile, Richard Chambers came fifth in the lightweight coxless fours, and the same position was achieved by Carla Ashford and cox Caroline O'Connor in the women's eights, a notable first Olympic representation for Brookes' women.

Despite the reflected glory from GB athletes, the next couple of years after the Bailhache-Webb appointment were not easy for Brookes. Spratley had to keep his business afloat through the 'great recession' of 2008/9, not an easy task in the construction sector. He had a young family too, so simply did not have as much time available for Brookes as in the past.

Meanwhile, the new responsibilities for Bailhache-Webb weighed heavily on him at times. The job was all-consuming, and for several months at one point he barely spoke to anyone outside the club. Moving on to the next level of performance wasn't going to be an easy or short-term matter.

Brookes was struggling by its own high standards after the disappointing Henley Regattas of 2007 and 2008. In 2009, it was the Dutch of Nereus that stopped the Temple crew, this time in the third round. Brookes just wasn't the underdog anymore, but a worthwhile scalp to be taken by other, ambitious UK crews like Newcastle University, as well as the top US, Dutch and German universities. The progress made over the last 15 years seemed to be slowing, or perhaps even going into reverse. Had OBUBC gone as far as it could?

But Brookes did at least get back on the trophy board in 2009, with a strong crew in the Prince Albert student coxed fours comprising Scott Durant, Matthew Tarrant, Chris Abraham and Karl Hudspith, with

Hannah Clewes coxing. Peter Chambers was also the latest old boy to win at Henley in a GB crew in the Prince of Wales Challenge Cup.

But the biggest shock came in 2010 Temple Cup at Henley. Brookes drew Nihon University of Japan in the first round. Now you never know at Henley – have the crews that have travelled a long way done so because they think they might really win? Or is it a holiday really, perhaps to celebrate 100 years of their boat club, or some similar reason. Well, it didn't look like Nihon were only in Henley for the beer and English scenery, as they beat Brookes comfortably by over four lengths. However, some of the best Brookes rowers were in a composite eight with Oxford University competing in the Ladies', so there was some excuse.

'F*** this for a game of soldiers'
In 2010/11, Brookes had what they felt was a strong first eight crew, combining some of the 2010 Temple crew with rowers from the composite Ladies' crew. The athletes in the Brookes boat also had the chance to gain selection as the GB under-23 crew for summer international events. As part of the trial process for selection, the squad coach asked the Brookes boat to race against the Newcastle University crew that had also performed well over the season.

Spratley and Bailhache-Webb were confident as the crews met for the race off. But to their surprise and embarrassment, Newcastle won comfortably. As the Geordie crew rowed back to the boathouse after their win, they saw the Brookes coaches on the bank, and various obscene gestures and rude remarks were angled towards them.

Spratley still recalls that experience, more than a decade later. 'Henry and I looked at each other. "Fuck this for a game of soldiers," I said to him. We went away vowing that this wasn't going to happen again.'

This was the point where Bailhache-Webb really took on lead responsibility. A couple of years into the head coach role, he was gaining confidence and, with Spratley, he went through every aspect of the programme. How could they improve the recruitment process, identify the best school rowers and attract them to Brookes? How could the gym work become more focused and drive higher levels of strength and stamina? How could they get more out of the hours on the water each week? To move on, more strength in depth was needed, so the squad needed to be larger – how could that be achieved?

Bailhache-Webb realised there was much to be done to move Brookes to the next level. For instance, he had barely looked at the boat club website. But kids were internet-savvy now and young rowers at school would be looking at websites, thinking about choosing their university. Bailhache-Webb realised that the Brookes website was really not helping. 'In fact, it was so bad, it was worse than having nothing,' he remembers. It certainly wasn't selling the success of the club.

He also changed the emphasis of the recruitment effort when Brookes addressed the potential young recruits. Rather than thinking in terms of 'how could you help Brookes win more?' it needed to pivot to "how can we help you become the best rower you can possibly be?" Indeed, that ethos has permeated the club ever since, in recruitment, but also followed through in behaviour and process, and is undoubtedly a critical success factor for Brookes. There were other lightbulb moments. Another coach mentioned that using a spreadsheet for recruitment was useful, maybe essential. Well of course it was, that seems obvious to us today. But that wasn't how Brookes had been doing it.

The timing was right, in that Bailhache-Webb had not wanted to over-promise to prospective rowers whilst he wasn't certain he could actually meet their aspirations. But by now he knew how to make a boat go faster and the technical detail of effective coaching. 'I felt I understood enough to say, this is what we do, and this is how we do it,' he explains.

The style he adopted with athletes was honest, but sympathetic. 'I ask athletes to write down their goals for the year, and I talk to every one of them about that. Sometimes they will say they want to be in the first boat by the end of the season, and I have to tell some that, given where they are now, and how they are training, that looks unachievable.' But that is always done in an empathetic manner, and handled well, those conversations can spur on athletes who perhaps have not realised just what is necessary to get to the very top.

So Bailhache-Webb now embraced this leadership role. But it isn't easy when there is no 'transfer market' to just go and sign up some ace rowers.

Henry Bailhache-Webb (*Brookes archive*)

It takes time to recruit, train and mature a squad and move to the next level of performance. But he and Spratley put plans in place that they were convinced would pay off.

Indeed, Bailhache-Webb actually started thinking more ambitiously then Spratley. 'I think we should be looking at winning the Ladies' Plate at Henley, not just the Temple.' Spratley wasn't sure. Whilst he does not lack confidence, Spratley has a natural humility. 'Don't get too up when you win, then you won't get too down when you lose,' is one of his aphorisms.

Winning the Temple was proving difficult enough, never mind stepping up to the Ladies and competing against the top varsity crews from US universities, the GB under-23s and the best clubs globally. But this goal was informing Bailhache-Webb's thinking and planning now. It would need a broader base of athletes, which also meant better gym facilities, more resources, more boats, more minibuses, more funding from the university. Spratley wasn't sure this was all achievable.

A new focus (2008–12)

That was where the partnership came into its own. Bailhache-Webb was proving himself with his coaching and crew development. Spratley was a strong coach too, but he was also an excellent manager. He could organise that infrastructure needed to expand the club, and he was also effective in terms of managing the club's relationship with the university hierarchy. Without appearing to be an overtly 'political' operator, he was persuasive in managing diverse stakeholders in a positive manner. The two were beginning to form a real team, playing to their complementary skills.

However, the US dominance of the Temple Cup for student eights at Henley had continued through the noughties. Between 2000 and 2012, North American crews won eleven of the thirteen events, (including one victory for the Canadians from Western Ontario) and, in seven of those years, a US crew held the runner-up spot too. At one stage, a number of UK university coaches approached Mike Sweeney, Chairman of Henley Royal Regatta, with a plea to change the rules to make the Temple a UK-only event.

Sweeney listened carefully and then spoke. 'My suggestion is that you all go and try a bit harder to beat these Americans,' was his judgement. Well, Brookes at least did take the advice to heart, as we will see.

But progress was slow and the next couple of years were actually disappointing for Brookes. In 2011, the University of Virginia knocked out the Temple crew in the second round, and there were no other Henley trophies, for the second year running. And, in 2012, after a couple of easy races against domestic opposition, it was the unusual experience of losing to St Petersburg University. The Russians then lost to Brown University, who themselves lost to Washington in the final. There was still quite a gap between Brookes and the top US crews, that was clear.

However, Brookes had something to celebrate that year at Henley, providing three of the four members of a GB squad four that won the Visitors' fours, with the Durant bothers and Matt Tarrant adding to their collection of HRR medals. And at the London Olympics, the Chambers brothers won silver medals in the lightweight coxless fours, whilst Alex Partridge added to his Beijing medal with a bronze in the men's eight, joining the elite club of Brookes multiple Olympic medallists. Caroline O'Connor also coxed the women's eight (again) to fifth place.

Tamsin Bryant (then Adams), who studied architecture at Brookes from 2004 to 2010, recalls on the Brookes website the positive effect of having Olympic athletes around the club. 'It was quite something as a young student coming to Brookes to realise the rower literally sitting next to you on the erg in the gym was an Olympic competitor.' That undoubtedly had a positive effect on the junior members. 'Until you have seen people like that at close quarters, you can't really understand just how hard it is possible to train. It was inspiring.'

Matt Tarrant himself makes says the same point, quoted on the website. '… after winning my first international medal as a junior, I made the decision that one day, I wanted to compete at an Olympic Games – Oxford Brookes had already created champions of the sport, and I wanted to become one of them.'

It is impossible to over-estimate the way success has bred success at Brookes. The inspiration that the previous generation provides to the younger athletes is tangible and contributes hugely to the club's success. But whilst the Brookes alumni were thriving, it was still proving difficult to produce student crews that could consistently match the Americans.

Chapter 12

Show me the money

'We think the boat club makes a very positive financial return to the university, as well as providing reputational benefits.' (Richard Spratley)

OBUBC – a bargain?
What does OBUBC cost? The club employs four managers and coaches (including Richard Spratley) plus some further occasional coaching support. Then of course there are accommodation and facilities costs in terms of the boathouse, gym and so on. Transportation between Oxford and the boathouse, entry fees and other event costs. Training at Wimbleball, Henley, the capital cost of boats and other equipment …

If I had guessed the budget a year ago, I might have gone for something around a million a year. In fact, the club receives about £400,000 from the university. Clearly, being a coach at the best rowing club in the world does not make you rich, a point the coaches reinforced during our discussions.

As a comparison, the Cambridge University Boat Club reputedly has an annual budget of £750,000. That supports a squad of around 60 rowers, about half the size of the Brookes squad. CUBC is also historically only active for around half the academic year, from halfway through the first term to the Boat Races at the end of the second (Easter) term, although this appears to be changing somewhat.

Now you could argue that even £400,000 a year is a lot for a university to stump up for a boat club. However, it seems likely that the club is actually a net positive financially for Brookes. The 120 squad members all pay fees to the university. British undergraduates pay £9,000 a year, overseas students and post-graduates considerably more. That is in basic tuition fees and doesn't take account of any profit the university makes from student accommodation, meals or 'peripherals'.

If we take an average of £12k for those 120 people, probably conservative, that is £1.44 million income annually, more than three times the cost of the club. That also does not take account of other students who might be attracted to Brookes for the chance to learn to row, particularly as the novice programme is now getting stronger, or just for the reflected glory of being there alongside some of the top athletes in the country.

In any case, we cannot point to wealth as a driver of the Brookes success, although it may be that *lack* of money has held back other university boat clubs. Indeed, perhaps because of Spratley's background as the owner of a relatively small business in the tough construction sector, and Bailhache-Webb's own childhood circumstances, it is clear that the attitude to spending is cautious. 'I've always been keen that we prove ourselves before we ask for more money,' says Bailhache-Webb. He wanted to show clear progress at each stage of the women's squad development, for instance.

The first day I met Spratley in person, he was checking on accommodation for a training trip to Wimbleball. That involved a youth hostel and various other hotels and rentals – but he was very concerned about getting a good deal. The squad self-cater too for the weekend away, which must be fun with around 100 hungry young rowers to feed!

'We've had consistent support from the university, even though we've seen a number of different senior people being in key decision making roles over the years,' says Spratley. 'That's been invaluable – essential really – to helping us achieve what we have.' Knowing that the club is not constantly fighting for funds has allowed the coaching staff to get on with their core business of winning races.

Show me the money

Who's got $2 million going spare …?
The situation is very different with American universities. The luxurious Yale boathouse was mentioned earlier. It's not just Yale though. The Harvard website explains that 'a gift of $2 million will establish a named head coach endowment …" and Harvard has 30 of these positions, including 4 in the rowing club. The model is that endowment is invested, and the income funds the coach's salary, in whole or in part, forever.

That provides certainty and stability. Unfortunately, the culture of giving a few million to support your old university athletic club has not really caught on in the UK. So unless there is a friendly ex-Brookes billionaire reading this, the financial situation is unlikely to change. We might expect more to come from the alumni network as it becomes larger year by year. But so far, it has proved positive and supportive without providing any major funding for the club.

But what about sponsorship? Might that provide a route for additional income? In Spratley's early days, the club received some helpful sponsorship from facilities management firm Mitie. Why has that form of funding not continued? The Mitie connection was through a good friend of the father of Pete Alvis, one of the ground-breaking 1993 Temple crew. The agreement was fairly informal, and not too demanding for either party.

There were some other modest successes along the way. In 2001, the Wyfold Galleries, situated by the river in Henley, generously contributed to a new eight for Brookes, christened not unreasonably the Wyfold Galleries. In June 2001, the Oxford Mail reported[18] that 'Judith De Paul, chairman of Wyfold Galleries, which is at Thames Side, Henley, near the regatta's finish line, has paid for a £12,000 top-of-the-range racing boat and has also bought the men's eight crew £2,500 worth of kit'.

The boat was christened *Wyfold Galleries* not unreasonably, and De Paul managed to get top model Jordan (Katie Price) to come along to the

Wyfold Galleries sponsors a boat in 2001, Katie Price included? (*Brookes archive*)

boat naming and sponsorship announcement, leading to an (in)famous photograph with the crew. But despite some positive partnerships, Spratley also had some bad experiences with potential sponsors.

'We had a pizza business that said they wanted to sponsor us. I put quite a lot of effort into writing them a proposal, which was based on something like a £30K a year sponsorship. When I presented it to their guy, he almost fell off his chair. He said he'd been thinking about offering our crews a "buy one get one free" deal if they ordered pizzas!'

There's also the issue of how any sponsorship would work today in the club. Is it just to support one boat? How would that make others in the club feel? The coaches rightly value the egalitarian ethos and the excellent team spirit at the club, and would not want to put that in any jeopardy.

Show me the money

Money (and love) can tear us apart

Indeed, sponsorship has had its positives and negatives in the UK rowing world. Back in the days of Redgrave and Pinsent gold medal-winning fame, a few athletes at the very top of the sport were making good money from personal sponsorship deals, and some of that flowed into the squad level too. But this was a source of potential tension in the wider team.

In *Four Men in a Boat*, the very good book about the gold medal winning GB coxless four at the 2000 Sydney Olympics, written by Tim Foster with Rory Ross, there is considerable discussion about money and sponsorship.[19] Sir Steve Redgrave won his fifth gold medal in that event, and along with Pinsent, they were very much the stars of the GB squad. In general, the book presents the financial issues as negative factors in terms of motivation in the squad.

At one stage, Pinsent and Redgrave had a £1 million sponsorship deal from Lombard Finance. Rowing in the same boat, with the same effort and the same impact on the chances of winning, Foster and Cracknell initially got no sponsor's money. That eventually changed and they made £16,500 a year, paid by Lombard and the lottery, then in the Olympic year received £3,000 from Lombard. This all created some ill feeling and some athletes felt that Redgrave and Pinsent had become 'bigger than the team', as it were. That is perhaps not surprising given their success and public profile, and we can hardly have expected them to donate their income to others, but it may have caused some issues too.

Any chance of tension between colleagues in the squad was resolved in recent years by insisting that athletes could not have any personal sponsorship if they wanted to receive the lottery-funded 'salary'. However, that stands (in 2023) at around £32k a year, tax free, equivalent to nearer £40k pre-tax. So that's not exactly minimum wage levels, but neither is it enough to support the sort of mortgage you need in the south-east of England to live comfortably, or indeed to buy any sort of house.

No more Redgraves or Pinsents

That is one reason why we are seeing very few rowers competing through multiple Olympic cycles today. Consider Constantine Louloudis. He has a remarkable record, one of those rare rowers who made every boat he stroked go faster. Eton won everything when he rowed there. He won four boat races with Oxford, never losing. He stroked the GB eight to world championship gold then stroked the GB four that won gold at the Rio Olympics.

In Redgrave terms, he had at least two more Olympics in him, maybe even three; he would have been 33 at the Paris Olympics in 2024. But after Rio, in 2016 and aged 25, he retired from international rowing. He is now working as a director of a start-up that is 'building cheaper grid-scale energy storage to enable a 100 per cent renewable energy grid'. I do hope his considerable talents are being well used.

Fred Scarlett, the Brookes man, also retired aged 25 after winning gold, this time in the Sydney Olympic eight. It's a very tough life at the top of rowing, and if you are also intelligent (Louloudis has a first from Oxford University) there are many other potential routes. Scarlett worked for Moet Hennessy and Krug champagne for some years, which sounds like more fun than doing hours on the erg in Caversham every day for £32k a year.

So, in Richard Spratley's opinion, we may never see another Redgrave, soldiering on for five Olympics. In fact, there is a bit of a Catch-22 at international level. If a crew wins a gold, there is every chance many will retire. If they don't win, they may stay on for one more cycle. Scarlett's compatriot at Brookes, Steve Williams, did not retire after Sydney because he didn't win a medal. He did win gold at Athens though in 2004 and, being a glutton for punishment, did the same at Beijing four years later. That makes him the most feted Brookes athlete ever. But we may not see many gold medal winners like him who want to postpone their entry into 'normal life', with the chance to pursue other interests and make money, once they have achieved that Olympic goal.

That suggests the GB squad needs to plan for a regular turn-over at the top levels. We will talk about the problems with GB rowing in Tokyo 2020/21 later. Not all were caused by a lack of crew experience, but certainly British Rowing cannot rely on Redgrave- and Pinsent-type athletes coming back time after time. So having a constant 'feed' of top-level younger rowers coming through into the GB system is essential, and Brookes is now contributing to that significantly.

Returning to the funding situation, Brookes as a university appears to obtain a good return from the boat club. But losing the funding at some point is obviously on the club's risk register. That's why Richard Spratley's political skills are another vital element of his overall capability and personality profile. He has adapted positively to changing priorities from the university, such as the desire to see more women rowing, and recently the push to grow the novice rowing programme.

The university is happy to be seen as a centre for a range of high-performance sport, including others such as men's and women's hockey, women's lacrosse, and men's cricket. But rowing obviously stands out, and to an outsider, the relationship between OBUBC and the university itself appears to be positively synergistic. But it cannot be taken for granted that it will continue forever. Let's leave the final word though to Professor Alistair Fitt, Vice-Chancellor at Brookes since 2015.

'The university's senior team has been delighted to see rowing at Oxford Brookes gaining such strength over the years. Our performance at Henley in 2023 was a standout moment for the university and a personal highlight for me. While maintaining success is as challenging as achieving it, I have full confidence that Brookes rowing will continue to stay at the top of the medals table.'

Chapter 13

The ecstasy and the agony (2013–15)

'Stick the knife in!' (Rory Copus, Brookes cox, 2014 Temple final)

Brookes beats the Browns
Even though Bailhache-Webb was driving positive changes at the club, Henley success was proving elusive. In the Temple Cup quarter-final at Henley in 2013, Brookes lost to Delftsche Studenten Roeivereeniging Laga of Holland, who then comfortably beat Harvard in the final. Brookes against Laga was the closest race of the entire event, and really should have been the final, but that's just how the draw can go. Although the loss was disappointing, Bailhache-Webb could see the progress. His crew had been the second fastest in the Temple that year, he was certain. This wasn't like some previous losses.

Henley 2013 was a slightly odd year for the club in general. The Brookes Hall of Fame website lists four winning crews at Henley with Brookes representation, which looks like an amazingly successful year, which it was in some sense. But all is not what it seems. The Britannia club coxed fours was captured by a 'Taurus' crew of Brookes current and ex-students – Sybren Hoogland, Tim Broughton, Brian Wettach, Henry Hoffstot and cox Jack Carlson.

Other alumni continued to excel at Henley. Matt Tarrant and Scott Durant, by now serious GB internationals, won in the Stewards' as part of a GB squad boat. Mason Durant and Lance Tredell featured in another GB squad boat, an eight, which won the Ladies Challenge Cup, beating Northeastern University of the US in a great race by a

The ecstasy and the agony (2013–15)

canvas, coming from behind to triumph in what was then a record time for the event.

It is also worth noting a couple of other names. A young cox, Harry Brightmore, only just 19, steered the Brookes 'C' eight in the Temple, losing to Harvard in the second round. More on him later. And at bow in the 'B' crew, which lost to Brookes 'A' also in the second round, was a certain Rory Gibbs.

Now Martin Cross, Olympic gold medal winner, has an excellent series of videos on YouTube known as Crossy's Corner, and in October 2021 he featured a fascinating interview with Richard Spratley.[20] Spratley explained that he was introduced to Gibbs, aged 16, at the Wimbleball training session by the Millfield School coach who was ex-Brookes himself. He explained that Gibbs had just taken up rowing, having sustained injuries that halted a promising rugby career. He was a skinny kid, but enthusiastic. Spratley and Bailhache-Webb talked, and decided, 'If he's up for it, we're up for it.'

Gibbs' 2,000-metres time on the erg was then a mere 6:40, but Bailhache and Spratley showed excellent judgement. They could see the raw materials and potential were there in the gangly youngster. But as a virtual novice in 2012/13, Gibbs had to work his way up the Brookes crew hierarchy, hence the Temple 'B' crew.

The Brookes women got in on the act, too, at national level in 2013, with Olivia Carnegie-Brown (subsequently a silver medallist at the Rio Olympics) stroking a GB squad crew also containing Katherine Douglas to victory in the Remenham Challenge Cup at Henley. Carnegie-Brown, quoted on the Brookes website, says that 'the atmosphere and winning mentality at Oxford Brookes Boat Club brings us together and raises the level of performance. Brookes taught me how to race hard, and made me the dogged athlete I am today.' Douglas had started rowing as a novice at Brookes in 2009, was a U-23 international within two years, and ended up an Olympian at Tokyo 2021 – quite a remarkable rise to fame.

And so 2014 came around. The Temple crew that was selected to row at Henley featured six of the strong 2013 crew – Tim Grant, Ed Grisedale, Richard Hawkins, James Martyn Smith and stroke Joel Cassells, plus cox Rory Copus. His brother Jamie Copus, a brilliant junior international lightweight, joined the crew, as did Sybren Hoogland, who had won the Britannia the previous year, and Callum Jones completed the eight.

The crew dealt with Newcastle comfortably in the first round, then came up against the Brookes 'C' crew in the second round. The strength in depth Bailhache-Webb had been building was now coming through, with the 'C' crew having already beaten Magdalen College, Oxford comfortably in the first round. Not surprisingly, Brookes 'A' triumphed, then won a good race against old university rivals Durham in the quarter final.

The semi-final turned out to be the toughest and best race of the event. The Cornell University boat was the varsity lightweight crew, although they weren't weight-watching for this open event. But it was a startlingly good crew, unbeaten in the US the entire season, winning the Eastern Sprints and the National Universities Championship. Cornell put up a great fight, but the mature and calm approach that Bailhache-Webb was now instilling in his crews showed as Brookes held on to win by half a length.

Brown University, another old rival and always one of the top US universities, awaited in the final, having beaten crews from England, Scotland, Canada and Holland on their imperious route to the final. But their semi-final time was 15 seconds slower than Brookes', and whilst that isn't always a good guide at Henley, in this case, it proved a good indicator. Brookes led from the start and came home to win with an almost three-length advantage.

The ecstasy and the agony (2013–15)

There is a brilliant video of this race on YouTube with the Brookes cox Rory Copus miked up for the race. This is as good as anything I've seen in terms of showing exactly what a good cox can add, as long as you don't object to the odd rude word.[21] As they approach the last couple of minutes of the race, with a decent lead, I loved Copus screaming this at his crew, in time with their strokes of course, as they started their final drive.

'10 months … Every erg … Every session … Together … For this one f*****g moment!'

If you have ever rowed, and probably if you haven't, that will get the hairs on the back of your neck going. Then, as the noise of the crowd hits them as they row past the enclosures, he shouts, 'Take it all in and feed off it!'

It's interesting, though, that he doesn't say anything about the other crew until halfway through the race, when he gives the call to the crew, 'Stick the knife in!' But the vast majority of his words relate firmly to his own crew's technique and plans, rather than the other boat. That approach reflects Bailhache-Webb's philosophy of relaxation and focusing on your own rowing. It would be good to know if Copus approached matters differently during that much tighter semi-final race though.

Jamie Copus is another athlete quoted on the Brookes website, and he emphasises that club spirit that keeps coming up as a critical success factor. 'The programme is the best in the country – it has given me the physical jump and mental resilience to be a senior international. But above all, the camaraderie is unlike any other. At Brookes, you're a family. A family with a winning tradition.'

However, there was disappointment at Henley that year. In the Prince Albert coxed fours, Brookes lost in the semi-final to one of the best crews Newcastle University ever fielded, who went on to beat Harvard in the final. And Brown got some revenge as their top boat narrowly beat a Brookes and Taurus composite in the Ladies'. On the positive side, Matt Tarrant, now rowing with the GB squad, added a Grand Challenge Cup medal to his ever-expanding collection.

But that first win in the Temple since 2006 meant a lot to the club, to Spratley, and perhaps most of all to Bailhache-Webb. It was a vindication of his approach, and his first Temple triumph. But it would be far from his last.

2015 – the highs and lows

The Henley rules now meant that Temple winners could not row in the event again, so Brookes needed a totally new crew for the following year. Brightmore, the cox, and Rory Gibbs moved up the Brookes pecking order, and there were other strong oarsmen coming into the Temple crew, notably future internationals Matt Aldridge, James Stanhope, Henry Swarbrick, Michael Glover and Morgan Bolding, along with Ben Reeves and Will Hall.

With the benefit of hindsight, this was an incredible crew. But at Henley in July 2015, the draw was unkind. Brookes faced old archenemies Nereus of Holland in the quarter finals. Nereus went off strongly, and broke the course record to the Barrier. Another course record was set at Fawley, and the lead was still half a length or so. Nereus stretched that lead and Brookes did not seem to be making much progress. But as the crews rowed alongside the enclosures, Brookes upped the rate and an incredible comeback looked possible. But Nereus hung on to win by a canvas, a great race and a new course record. (We've got to the point where brilliant Henley videos for every race are available on YouTube, if you want to watch.)[22]

Nereus beat Cornell University in the semis then hammered Lyon of France in the final. So again, Bailhache-Webb knew that Brookes had clearly been the second fastest crew in the event. But that doesn't win you the trophy. The Brookes Prince Albert crew lost to another

The ecstasy and the agony (2013–15)

Dutch university in a tight race (Delftsche Studenten Roeivereeniging Proteus-Eretes, Netherlands, if you must know), and after the delight of 2014 this was not proving to be a successful follow-up. And worse was to come.

In the autumn of 2015, with Brookes starting a new academic year and looking to put together crews for the 2016 regatta season, scandal hit the boat club. On 9 May 2015, when Brookes had competed at Ghent regatta as usual, two of their team, Tim Grant and Sybren Hoogland, were suspended after random drug tests. Both were members of that 2014 winning Temple crew and were GB under-23 internationals now as well.

In November 2015, it was announced that both would be suspended for two years from all sports. The UK anti-doping organisation said Hoogland tested positive for benzoylecgonine, a metabolite of cocaine, whilst Grant tested positive for the stimulant modafinil, which was approved as a wakefulness-promoting drug. Neither were taking the drugs with performance enhancing aims, but as UKAD chief executive Nicole Sapstead said, 'Hoogland and Grant are young athletes who clearly made the wrong choices in their personal lives.'

It was sad for both. Hoogland was banned for two years after admitting taking cocaine at a party on 7 May. He had been drinking, which impaired his judgment, and did not think he would be required for the regatta on the 9th. But he was called on to row after all, and should have owned up to his coaches and explained. But he didn't and was then chosen for the drugs test.

Grant was perhaps even more unfortunate. He explained he was under a lot of pressure with academic work, and when struggling with a deadline on 7 May, a friend had suggested a couple of pills would help concentration. Modalert was the brand name under which modafinil was marketed and sold in India. It was a prescription only drug, but had recently become popular with students as a 'smart drug' as it increased concentration and focus. Grant did not realise he was taking modafinil, and said he had completely forgotten taking the pills, which he saw as completely unconnected with his rowing. So he did not declare that he had done so prior to the regatta.

But both athletes had attended anti-doping training earlier that same year, and Grant had not checked on an anti-doping website to see if what he was taking was banned. So whilst he did not receive the maximum four-year ban, he also did receive a two-year penalty. He did return to rowing after serving the ban, although not with Brookes or at international level again. Hoogland's subsequent rowing career (or indeed any career) is unknown.

'We learnt who our friends were,' says Spratley, remembering some who were sympathetic and some who were less so. Clearly, it wasn't great publicity for Brookes, as well as being difficult for the men involved, but the fact the drugs were not performance-enhancing in terms of rowing

Brookes athletes selected for 2015 U23 world championships – L to R Annie Withers, Ben Reeves, Henry Swarbrick, Jamie Copus, Rory Gibbs, cox Harry Brightmore, Morgan Bolding, Will Hall, Joel Cassells, and coach Henry Bailhache-Webb (*Brookes archive*)

The ecstasy and the agony (2013–15)

mitigated the criticism somewhat. And 2016 was going to prove an excellent antidote to those unfortunate events.

However, there was good news too for Brookes in 2015 with a record nine athletes selected to represent GB at the World U23 championships. That cohort included first GB appearances for Rory Gibbs, Morgan Bolding and cox Harry Brightmore, who would hit the headlines together some nine years later at the Paris Olympics.

But before we pick up again on the Brookes timeline and achievements at Henley, and after another race report, let's move our focus to the Head of the River race in London, often known as the Tideway Head. It is a remarkable event, and it has been another key element in the Brookes story.

Oxford Brookes

Henley Royal Regatta, 11.20 am, 7 July 2024

Race report – The 2024 Grand Challenge Cup Final

Now our race reports have jumped ahead to the 2024 Henley Royal Regatta and Finals Day, 7 July. Because of the weather forecast (thunder, lightning, plagues of frogs, you know the sort of thing) the start of racing has been brought forward from 11 am to 9.30 am. The highlight of the morning is the final of the Grand Challenge Cup for 'open' (elite) men's eights, now scheduled for 11.20 am.

But as that time arrives, the video we are watching in the grandstand shows only the University of Washington by the start, with Brookes paddling around nearby. Gradually the news emerges that the Washington crew has suffered a problem. According to Rachel Quarrell writing for *Row360*,[23] 'A blue foam grip came loose on a Husky blade-handle before the start, prompting a rain-drenched equipment delay, during which Brookes head coach Henry Bailhache-Webb and director of rowing Richard Spratley, nervous about their doubling-up athletes, had to watch as the next four races including two of their other crews, went off the start.'

Later on, speaking to Richard Spratley by the boat tents, he was not too impressed by this. 'I was down here at 7.30 this morning checking every oar, every boat.' he says. 'And Washington only had one to worry about!'

Replacement equipment has to be found. There isn't time for the crews to come back to the tents and start again, as it were, so Brookes end up paddling around for over 40 minutes until Washington get sorted. And the weather is not kind. Biblical rainstorms are sweeping Henley, and both crews suffer during the wait. Eventually, at 12.10 pm , after the scheduled last race of the morning, The Grand can commence.

The 2024 Grand Challenge Cup Final

Washington is unbeaten this season and won the top US universities event. The boat is generally considered the fastest in the United States outside the Olympic eight, although it is not exactly an all-American crew, containing as it does a British cox, three other British oarsmen, two Norwegians, an Italian and just one lonely American! But we instantly see how good they are as both boats roar away from the start, rating almost 50 stokes a minute. Remember, the Brookes boat beat the Dutch Olympic eight recently, but off the start, and indeed for the first two minutes, there is nothing in it here. At the Barrier, Brookes has a lead, but it is minuscule, just a few feet.

Beyond the Barrier, we have the one part of the course where, because of the slight bend in the river, the Bucks bank is closer to the course than the Berkshire. That means the Bucks station has the advantage of less stream for a few hundred metres, and crews want to be as close to the Bucks side as possible. But not too close …

Brookes appears to be edging slightly further ahead when disaster strikes Washington, just before halfway. The cox is perhaps too ambitious, or maybe there was a freak gust of wind. Whatever the reason, the 2-man's oar on bow side clips a post securing the booms marking the course. He stops rowing and then the stroke loses his oar and has to recover.

That effectively ends the race. Washington get going but are now a good two lengths down. Brookes carry on and indeed stretch out their lead to almost four lengths despite Washington's best efforts.

We'll never know what might have happened of course. Brookes was ahead, and had the advantage of the better station for most of the rest of the race, and indeed pulled away even after Washington got going again. We know how physically strong the crew is, and although I'm biased, I think it is very likely that Brookes would have triumphed anyway. Spratley and Bailhache-Webb rated Washington highly, but

Oxford Brookes

felt Leander in the semi-final yesterday was their bigger challenge, a race that Brookes won by one length.

A win is a win, and the trophy and records will simply say that Brookes has won the Grand. Aside from the rather odd 2021 event (see page 208), this is the first time a true Brookes 'club' crew rather than a composite GB squad crew has won the Grand, against serious opposition, which is quite an achievement. But this was a disappointing race for the crowd, looking forward to a tight finish. However, after lunch Brookes would compensate by providing more excitement and indeed more UK versus US thrills!

Chapter 14

The Head of the River

'It is not a race, it is merely a means of getting crews to do long rows.'
(Steve Fairbairn)

Bumps, Heads and Regattas

Other quirky formats such as bumping races exist, but the vast majority of competitive rowing falls into three core formats.

The first is *six (or eight)-lane racing*, generally reserved for international, Olympic and the very biggest regatta events globally. Boats race on a straight course side by side, usually over 2,000 metres, the lanes marked out by buoys, ropes, booms or some similar means. Clearly you need a very wide river, a lake (natural or constructed) or sometimes even the open sea to make this format work. For major competitions, there may be heats and repechages (a second chance for crews who don't win their heat), ending up in a final. Obviously there can be separate categories for different types of boat, levels of experience, men, women, lightweights, universities or juniors at various age groups.

Regattas, usually on narrower rivers and waterways, again have different categories but use side-by-side racing, often with two boats at a time, but sometimes three. The race distance varies, often depending on what is feasible on the stretch of river. Some 'sprint' regattas can be held over courses as short as just 500 metres. I found those to be very exciting, although frankly there wasn't a lot of time for the cox to do much (other than shout a bit) when the race lasts less than two minutes.

The rowing lanes may be marked out – or they may not be. Marlow Regatta, before it moved to the six-lane Dorney Lake in 2001, was held on the Thames, up the road from Henley, two weeks before the Royal Regatta, with three boats racing side by side. It could be somewhat chaotic in bad weather, and my Lady Margaret crew sank there one year I competed. That day, if you were drawn in the lane furthest away from the spectators, you stood about a 50 per cent chance of sinking because of the wind and stream. Several boats succumbed, including mine. Despite a degree of panic, I managed to get us within a few yards of the bank before we went under.

Finally, there is *head racing*. This is 'processional', so boats set off at timed intervals on a river or very large lake, then row the course with every boat being timed individually to the finish. Unsurprisingly, the fastest boat wins, although there are often multiple prizes, based on the different categories of competitor.

The Head of the River race in London on the Thames is one of the oldest rowing races in the world. The race was founded by legendary oarsman and coach Steve Fairbairn (1862–1938), who was a great believer in crews training over long distances through the winter to build stamina and strength. He thought a race would be a good idea, and captains of the various London rowing clubs received the idea positively, although supposedly Fairbairn said, 'It is not a race, it is merely a means of getting crews to do long rows.'

Rather controversially, the first race was held on a Sunday. On 12 December 1926, twenty-three crews took to the river and raced from Mortlake to Putney, which is the Boat Race course in reverse. London Rowing Club triumphed. After that first year, the race switched to March and a Saturday, and by 1939, entries had grown to 154 crews.

Crews row with the tide, with an average winning time of around 17 to 18 minutes, but that depends heavily on the stream, the wind and the calmness (or otherwise) of the water. Even before the two years of Covid cancellation, three races between 2013 and 2017 were cancelled because of bad weather. The 2014 race was famously abandoned after

The Head of the River

75 boats had already finished, because of the dangerous conditions mainly around the finishing line, where several boats became submarines for a while.

Queen's Tower, the Imperial College alumni club, won three times around the millennium, but before 2016, you had to go back to 1963 and University of London to find a university crew winning. Tideway Scullers dominated in the mid-sixties to the mid-seventies, and the GB national squad or Leander (often including squad rowers) won most of the races between the mid-seventies and 2015, interspersed with the odd victory by huge German or Czech international eights. This has always been an event which only the very best crews stood any chance of winning.

'You must be joking …'
So, given the illustrious history of the event, when Bailhache-Webb told Richard Spratley that he thought Brookes could win the Head, Spratley took some convincing. That was in 2010, not long after Bailhache-Webb had taken over as head coach, at a time when Brookes was doing fine, but not really progressing to a higher level.

It was one thing to win university events at Henley, and occasional fours, but going up against Leander, international squad boats, as well as the top clubs such as Molesey or Thames … it all seemed a little unlikely to Spratley. But Bailhache-Webb had confidence in his own coaching ability and saw that year-on-year improvements in training, combined with attracting better athletes through the door, was developing a stronger squad every season. So the Head of the River stayed as a personal objective.

Given the length of the race, and the March timing, training for the Head is based around stamina, strength and the ability to row effectively for a long time at a not-too-high stroke rate. You don't need a particularly fast start or a crazy 'burn' over the last 20 strokes to perform well. That actually suited the Brookes winter training programme, which works its athletes hard in the gym, and had always used long, steady-state pieces of work on the river. So Bailhache-Webb genuinely believed victory was a real target.

From 2010 onwards, Brookes established itself as a regular top-ten finisher, which a few years earlier would have been seen as an incredible achievement. By 2015, not only did the first boat finish third, but the Brookes second eight finished fourth, demonstrating that growing strength in depth which the coaches saw as a critical success factor.

2016 was an Olympic year, so the top national crews were not going to compete on the Tideway on 19 March. However, Leander had a boat full of current internationals, and past rivals Imperial, as well as top club crews from Thames, Moseley and Tideway Scullers, had to be overcome. The Brookes crew was largely the oarsmen who had failed to win the Temple at Henley nine months earlier, and every athlete was a current student – no alumni or ringers here. But by March 2016, Bailhache-Webb could see how well the boat was going, with the talent of several future GB rowers shining through.

On that Saturday, Brookes started third in decent weather, behind Leander, winners in 2015, and Molesey. Crews start approximately 10 seconds apart, although the gap is often wider for the first boats to go off. Whilst starting positions are based on previous year performance, as you move down the field of 420 boats, matters get more chaotic. Some boats that didn't row in the previous year prove to be very fast, and spend their whole race trying to overtake slower crews.

At times, there may be four or five boats in close proximity, overtaking or being overtaken, all jockeying to stay in the fastest part of the river given the tidal conditions. It is great fun to watch and to row in as long as you aren't worrying too much about your final position. But at the front of the race, Brookes didn't have to worry about many other crews, and certainly no-one was going to catch them today.

The Head of the River

The Molesey boat was steadily hunted down and caught towards the finishing line at Putney. By the end, Brookes was 25 seconds faster than Molesey, and in fact the Brookes second boat narrowly pipped that club too. The Leander lead boat had started at least 20 seconds ahead of Brookes, so was a good target in terms of pacing the race. Of course the Brookes crew could not see Leander, but the cox could, and saw that Brookes was making steady progress towards closing the gap. Leander had started too far ahead to be caught, but at the end, it was clear. Brookes had won the Head of the River for the first time in their history, by some nine seconds, joining the University of London, Imperial College London, Goldie (Cambridge) and Jesus College Cambridge as the only university crews to have ever triumphed.

That was the start of a remarkable run for Brookes at the event. The 2017 race was cancelled because of bad weather, but Brookes was back in 2018 to compete in what turned out to be the only dead-heat in the history of the race, sharing the trophy with Leander. To see a dead-heat after 17 minutes 27.7 seconds of racing was incredible.

But in 2019, Brookes did not have to share the victory. The margin was only 3 seconds over Leander, but the Brookes 'B' boat was only 0.1 seconds further back in third place, and the 'C' boat was up to third. Unfortunately, there was no race in 2020 or 2021 because of Covid and the various rules around socialising. Then in 2022, Brookes benefitted from some of the rowers who had attached themselves to the club because of the Covid situation, but who were not current Brookes students or even alumni. That perhaps explained why the margin jumped to a very comfortable 15 seconds over the perennial rivals, Leander.

But it was back to a close-run thing in 2023, with the lead just two seconds over Leander. Brookes 'B' sat in their, by now traditional, third place, but the 'C' boat was up to fourth, the 'D' boat was seventh, the

Oxford Brookes

'E' boat eleventh and the 'F' boat seventeenth! No crew had ever had 6 boats in the top 20, another remarkable achievement for the club.

In some ways, that achievement is more impressive than Henley trophies, as it demonstrates a strength in depth that probably no other rowing club in the world could emulate. The top US universities certainly have several strong boats, but I don't believe that even Washington or Harvard would have six boats that could perform quite so strongly at that level. Wouldn't it be amazing if there was a head-to-head, multi-boat event between Brookes and one of those US clubs?

In any case, if Richard Spratley had his doubts years earlier about whether Brookes could win the Head, he would once have thought the idea that the club might have 6 boats in the top 20 pretty outlandish. But that progress is testament to the coaching and management regime that Spratley, Bailhache-Webb and the team have built over the last two decades.

Chapter 15

Coxing

'So what does the cox actually do?' (Everybody I ever told that I was a cox …)

It looks easy, doesn't it?
Brookes has produced a succession of top-level international coxes in the last decades, from Rowley Douglas, who coxed the GB eight to gold at the Sydney Olympics in 2000, to Harry Brightmore in the GB 2024 Olympic men's eight. Clearly, Brookes knows how to develop excellent coxes as well as top rowers.

That video recommended earlier, showing Rory Copus coxing the victorious 2014 Brookes Temple crew, provides a good understanding of the job. But when I coxed back in my university days, before YouTube existed, the general view of most of my friends was, 'It can't be that difficult, can it? I mean, you have to be small, then just sit in the end of the boat and shout at the guys doing all the work.'

Others would ask how it felt to be thrown in the river after every race, or look at me and say, 'I thought you had to be really thin to be a cox?' To be fair, I tended to get that once I stopped competitive coxing and put on five kilos to help my football performance. More polite folk would just ask, 'So what do you actually do?' My answer was that coxes play four key roles in the boat. We:

- steer the boat
- act as 'the coach in the boat', and indeed out of the boat at times
- motivate the crew to row themselves to the point of collapse
- play a key role in tactics during the race.

All of that, and we have to watch our weight, which is usually easier for a 1.60 metre female cox than a 1.75 metre man, hence the growth in the number of women coxing men's boats in recent years.

Starting with the basics, the cox steers the boat, using a small rudder underneath the stern in modern boats. Now, in some environments, that is not exactly an onerous task. At the top level, races are usually held on natural or man-made lakes, with six lanes marked out clearly. Once the race starts, the cox should really not touch the rudder at all assuming the crew is well-balanced.

But other races are very different. Henley might be only two boats racing side by side, and the two boundaries on the course are marked with wooden booms through most of the distance, but there is no central lane marker and, within that allowed space, there is a fair bit of jockeying for position, to minimise the effect of the current and the wind, or even to intimidate the other crew. Clever coxes try to position their boat when they are in the lead so the 'wash' from their oars, the rough water, is hitting the losing crew's oars in the worst possible point to disturb that crew's rowers.

Coxing on tidal rivers, or even in the sea, is even more challenging from a steering point of view, and the annual Oxford versus Cambridge Boat Race is often a great example of that, even though there are only two boats to worry about.

The most important people in The Boat Race

Well, I say there are only two boats to worry about, but in 2004 the Cambridge cox managed to hit a large, stationary barge during the warm-up before the race, which then had to be postponed 24 hours. I don't know how that happened. Coxes do have eight large rowers blocking their view of the river ahead, but even so, I never hit even a canoe, let alone a huge barge. Oxford won on the following day.

Coxing

Barges aside, this race is a notable example of a two-boat race where coxing is critical. Here, the coxes need to combine effective steering with a strong tactical sense. Although the two boats are supposed to stay on their 'station' (an imaginary lane on the river), at least until one is clearly ahead, each cox aims to row in the best water in terms of current and wind, and tries to push the opposition out of the position they would like to be in. We have seen many examples of crews' blades clashing, although the only disqualification in the main race came in 1849 (Cambridge lost).

Back in 2012, The Boat Race was famously disrupted by a swimming protester who almost got decapitated by the Cambridge oars. The race was stopped, but the drama continued when the umpires re-started it some minutes later. The Oxford cox, Zoe de Toledo, a slight young woman who looked like butter wouldn't melt in her mouth, was actually an incredibly aggressive cox. With Oxford trailing slightly, she steered a very aggressive line that brought the boats together. Blades clashed, and the end result was that one of the Oxford crew actually damaged his oar. Cambridge pulled away to win.

Oxford challenged the result, but the umpire was not taking any nonsense. In his opinion, the clash was largely Oxford's fault, so it was just bad luck they came off worse. There is a fine line between great, aggressive coxing and disaster. There was a similar incident in the 2024 women's Boat Race, where the Oxford cox appeared to deliberately bump into the Cambridge boat. Oxford were losing by a length, so he thought he might get Cambridge disqualified if the umpire felt Cambridge were rowing 'in Oxford's water'. His tactic was bold, but the umpire was not convinced, and the loss in rhythm for Oxford meant they fell further behind and lost heavily.

The positive side of Boat Race coxing was seen in 2023. Because of the strength of the tide and the currents, boats tend to stay near the centre of the river where the current is fastest. That's why you don't see the boats taking what would seem to be the most direct route around bends. Cutting the corner is not clever if you are losing up to five kilometres an hour of river speed.

But in 2023, Jasper Parish of Cambridge broke all the rules. Oxford were the strong odds-on favourites and, off the start, the crews came together and blades almost clashed. Oxford looked good though and took a lead of more than half a length. But after about two minutes, with the water getting rougher in the middle of the river, Parish made a bold move. Instead of sticking to the centre, and staying in the stream, he headed off towards the river bank underneath the Fulham football stadium.

He was looking for smoother, calmer water for his crew to row in, but risked losing the benefit of the stream. What on earth was he doing, the commentators asked? 'I'm not sure that the water really warrants this kind of move,' said one, sounding very disapproving. 'It's slack water, it's not fast water,' said another BBC expert.[24]

But it proved to be a masterstroke, perhaps the most brilliant piece of coxing I have ever seen. The conditions were rough, because of wind, but the current was actually not that strong. Moving towards the bank took Cambridge into smoother water, and they quickly moved half a length ahead of Oxford. Staying close to the bank also cut the corner, and it also confused the hell out of Oxford. Watch the video and you can see their cox wondering whether to follow Parish, or stay on the normal path. In the end she did neither really, and Cambridge went on to win a hard-fought race in rough conditions by a couple of lengths.

In a head race, such as the Head of the River on the Thames, understanding the current, the wind and the peculiarities of the stretch of water can be critical. On the Cam in Cambridge, however, the issue is the bends and the narrowness of the river. That is why the main races are in the bumps format. Boats start at an equal distance apart, then you have to catch and physically hit the crew ahead of you before you get caught by the boat behind. It is great fun to watch but challenging to cox. It's also fun if you are the one doing the bumping! But don't go for the boat ahead just as you are going into a bend, miss their stern as you try and hit them, find you are now too late to steer around the bend and hit the opposite bank. That has happened many times.

My Cambridge college, St John's, rows as Lady Margaret Boat Club, which was founded in 1825, and historically has been one of the very best colleges for rowing. The story goes that in a very early bumps race, the St John's boat aggressively smashed into the boat they were chasing and, tragically, the sharpened bow went straight through the other boat's cox, killing him stone dead. St John's Boat Club was immediately banned from the river, forever. But days later, a 'new' club, Lady Margaret, had been formed, and was back on the river, rowing with blood-red oars in memory of their victim. (Lady Margaret Beaufort, King Henry VIII's grandmother, was the founder of St John's.)

It is a great story, used by every Cambridge tour guide, but it suffers from one small but unfortunate problem – it is total nonsense. The boat club was named after the college's benefactor when it was founded. However, the word 'blazer' for a casually cut gentleman's jacket worn without matching trousers did come from observations of LMBC's flame-red boat club jackets. They make club members stand out at Henley every year, even though the club has sadly not won an event at the regatta since 1966, although a composite with Trinity College did win the Prince Philip at HRR in 1974.

Shouting, steering, coaching, motivating …

For most regatta races, the cox's job is more about motivation, coaching and tactics than steering. They will be reminding the crew of what worked in training, or picking up on any little flaws creeping into the technique as the crew gets tired. You can't change someone's technique mid-race, but you might just remind them of something. Or it might be as basic as shouting 'you're late, number 3'. Something I shouted many times at a very good friend of mine back in our college days.

Tactically, the cox also often decides when to go with a 'push' or take the rate up. That may well be planned in advance, but the cox, often with input from the stroke (who is sitting only inches away), might decide to change the plan depending on what is happening in the race.

Motivation is harder to define, but a good cox will make the crew feel positive, reinforce their desire to win, yet know how to keep the crew calm if things start going awry. They understand the personalities in the boat and may even direct comments at individuals. Of course rowers should be self-motivated, and they must be if they're rowing at a good level, but the cox will still be looking for something to be said that can lift the crew when everything is really starting to hurt in the final stages of tough race.

In the early days of Brookes, Richard Spratley saw the cox as a useful ally in the boat, but there was little specific coaching for that role. In a coxed four, with the cox lying down in the front of the boat, they can contribute less to coaching and motivation as they cannot see the crew. 'Steering straight and being light are probably the key attributes here,' Spratley says.

However, over the years, the club has become more professional and realised just how much a cox can contribute in terms of tactics, the psychology of racing and coaching, particularly in an eight. In that Copus video, you can see and hear how he is reminding the crew of technical issues, and deciding when to 'push' harder, probably based on pre-agreed plans. But a good cox has to be flexible, and change the approach if the race is not going so well. So it may seem surprising, but quick thinking is a key part of the role.

Alex Partridge saw the coxes' role as vital, particularly in the Brookes set-up. 'Because Brookes often has many boats rowing at the same time in training, but not many coaches supervising, there is a lot of

Coxing

responsibility delegated to the coxes.' Coxes are thoroughly briefed early in the season and remain 'essential members of the programme'.

Temple and Ladies' Plate winner Matt Hnatiw remembers the young Harry Brightmore, future Olympian, as a strong 'coach in the boat' and says, 'A really good cox is invaluable. There is a reason why there are nine people in the boat!'

Competition between coxes at Brookes is just as intense as between the rowers. That was the first point that current top coxes Tom Bryce and Bakang Zondi made when I asked them what it was like to be a Brookes cox. "We all get on, but you know that there are always other excellent coxes who aspire to the top boats", said Bryce, the first eight cox.

Zondi won in the Prince Albert at Henley in 2023, and he says ultimately coxing is 'all about making the boat go faster'. Coxes do have an effect – 'If the coaches see when they move coxes around that you consistently make crews perform better, then that's what matters.' That is how you end up in the top boats, winning medals. It is also vital that trust is built between coaches and coxes. 'So don't do anything stupid, that's also pretty vital.'

Brookes has a mix of male and female coxes in the squad, and Alexandra (Allie) Bohenko was the Temple crew cox for Henley 2024. She studied at Marist College in the US before coming to Brookes to do her Master's in Education, and cox. 'There are pros and cons being a woman coxing a men's boat, but I'm loving my time here,' she says. How does the UK scene compare to the US, I asked? 'I think coxing is maybe a little more aggressive here! You don't want to break the rules, but you can push it at times.'

Henry Bailhache-Webb talks about one cox who came to the club with many skills, but without the required level of aggression. In one of the duels against an Oxbridge crew on the Tideway, the cox steered a very conservative line. 'We had a long chat about that,' he says,

Oxford Brookes

and the same cox later proved their worth in very impressive Henley performances.

Brookes is now an attractive venue for capable and ambitious coxes. 'We have lots of high performing boats, so join us and you know you have a good chance of coxing a potentially medal-winning boat.' Indeed, the success of Brookes in developing coxes can be seen in the incredibly constant flow into the GB men's and women's squads, from Rachel Quarrell through Rowley Douglas, Nick Ford, Caroline O'Connor, Rory Copus, Charlie Clarke, Scott Cockle, Will Denegri and, most recently, Tom Bryce. And of course Harry Brightmore, the Paris Olympics GB men's eight cox, was a Brookes protégé. Newcomers can benefit from that embedded knowledge and experience in the club, and Brightmore himself has been an occasional coach for Brookes, keeping an eye on the next generation of coxing stars.

So if anyone reading this has a son or daughter who likes sport, has a strong personality, can think on their feet, enjoys shouting and is on the small side, do suggest that they might try coxing. I thoroughly enjoyed it, and it proved a great topic to talk about at job interviews too. Explaining how I motivated eight guys who were all twice my size seemed to convince the Mars Group that I might be worth a place on their excellent graduate trainee scheme!

Chapter 16

Recruitment

'People are not your most important asset. The right people are.' (Jim Collins, business guru and author of From Good to Great*)*

Attracting the best

The story of Brookes shows how success breeds success. As the club started winning and becoming a stronger presence on the rowing scene, understandably more young athletes wanted to join. Whilst Brookes does a lot to develop the talent that turns up at the university, you need good raw materials. In the case of rowing, that means in particular youngsters who have learnt to row already at schools or clubs, or at other universities, if they join as post-graduates.

In recent years, the top rowing schools for boys in the UK have arguably been Eton, St Paul's, Abingdon, St Edward's (Oxford), Shiplake (near Henley), Westminster and Radley. Hampton, Pangbourne and Shrewsbury might lay claim to a place on a slightly longer list too. Some different names feature in girls rowing – Headington, Lady Eleanor Holles, Wycliffe, Surbiton High School, as well as the St Paul's Girls and co-educational St Edward's and Shiplake. What they all have in common is that they are expensive private schools, and they are on or very close to the Thames, with the exception of Shrewsbury on the Severn. These schools have both the money and the practical feasibility to pursue rowing seriously.

Successful initiatives in recent years have encouraged kids from state schools into the sport. Getting teenagers on rowing machines is one successful route, not least in discovering Mo Shibi at a state comprehensive in Surbiton. When the rowing show came to town, the tall, strong, basketball- and football-playing young man was persuaded to sit down and give it a go. The coaches saw Shibi's immediately impressive times on the machine and within six months he was British under-15 indoor rowing champion, and within a few more years he won a gold medal in the GB Olympic eight.

Clubs such as Tideway Scullers and Thames Tradesmen in London, as befits their name, have a long history of working-class participation. More recently, Hinksey Sculling School, a community club in Oxford, has brought rowing to hundreds of kids from all backgrounds and the club is now making its mark at Henley in the junior sculling events. Actually, sculling seems stronger in the state education system, with Windsor Boys School a top sculling school for years now. Clubs including Marlow and Henley have strong junior sections, and a special mention for state grammar school Sir William Borlase's School in Marlow (Richard Spratley's old school), whose girls have recently performed strongly.

But there is no getting away from the fact that at junior level rowing events, top private schools are strong. So, you might expect Brookes would be finding its intake of potential star rowers from these institutions. Surprisingly, this is not the case. Very few have joined Brookes from the schools mentioned above in recent years, and today Brookes takes in fewer youngsters from Eton and those top rowing schools than ever.

That may seem odd given the reputation Brookes now enjoys. Well, go back 30 years and it was almost unheard of for a British 18-year-old to go off to a US university, for any reason. But the introduction of fees in the UK, the general globalisation of education, and the ease with which universities can market themselves internationally has changed that. Now, for the brightest academically inclined UK 18-year-olds, Harvard, MIT or Berkeley may be a better proposition than even Oxbridge, Imperial or St Andrews. The same cachet is there, but in addition some US institutions offer very generous scholarships to tempt the brightest and best.

And the same applies in the sporting arena. Whether it is tennis, golf, soccer, athletics or rowing, the top US universities now recruit globally. A 16-year-old can send their erg times, maybe a video of themselves on the river, and their GCSE results to a US university, and within days get an offer of a scholarship worth $50k a year.

'We just can't compete with that,' Spratley says. For the youngster and parents, it is a case of avoiding the £100k that a UK course plus living costs requires, funded through loans, parental contribution or part time jobs. And parents are happy to tell friends that their 18-year-old is off to Berkeley or Washington on a rowing scholarship. One young, star British rower achieved better than expected A-levels, having been told that he probably wasn't up to the required level based on his previous year's exam disaster. On sending a text saying simply 'B C B' to his contact in the States, he had an expenses paid interview then a scholarship offer from a top-ten US rowing university within weeks.

'In recent years, the battle to sign up the best junior girls has got perhaps even tougher than for the boys,' says Spratley. Many US universities now have a policy that the women's boat club must have equal funding to the men's. Given that there are still fewer capable 18-year-old girls rowing than boys, the competition for those girls who have a good record at school is intense. 'There is no doubt that the US universities have had a huge impact on junior rowing around the world,' says Mike Sweeney, past Chairman of Henley Royal Regatta.

A parental prestige factor also comes into play even if the rower wants to stay in the UK. If the Etonian has a brain to match his rowing skills, as does his twin sister from St Paul's Girls, then parents might well encourage the kids towards Oxford or Cambridge University. Rowing in The Boat Race is still a feather in anyone's cap, even if in truth the rowing programme for most undergraduates at those universities is arguably not a patch on that at Brookes (or indeed Harvard). But telling your friends that James and Elise are off to Trinity to study PPE still has a more impressive ring than going to Brookes, despite the newer university's impressive rise up the academic league tables in recent years.

So Spratley and the team have had to develop different approaches to recruitment. There are around 100 private schools that row seriously, and there are individuals in their crews who are already very good or have the potential to achieve a Brookes-type level of performance. But the boat they are in is not strong enough overall perhaps to be noticed in the way Eton or St Paul's inevitably is. So this tranche of schools, as well as rowing clubs with good youth programmes, have become successful recruiting grounds for Brookes. Then it all comes down to the strength of the training programme, to turn promising school rowers into superstars.

And the Brookes coaches do look at personality as well as talent and rowing potential. Matt Hnatiw (2013–18) remembers Henry Bailhache-Webb talking about 'Radiators and Drains' in the squad, so people who 'warmed' and improved the atmosphere, rather than taking energy away from the team.

When Hnatiw started at Brookes in 2013, 'it was my university second choice, to be honest. But it turned out to be the best decision of my life.' His father had rowed against Richard Spratley decades earlier and, although Hnatiw had rowed with his local club in Wales, 'I'd never lifted a weight in my life, and I'd only sculled, never rowed sweep.' He found Brookes in the process of transitioning to a highly professional outfit, and then 'success breeds success', as he says. But he is an example of how Brookes has been incredibly successful in recruiting somewhat rough and ready youngsters and turning them into international level stars and Henley winners, like Hnatiw himself.

Recruitment

Going global

International recruitment has also become more important. That applies in terms of rowers coming from other countries to do a first undergraduate degree or a post graduate diploma, master's or even doctorate. Then there are the British students coming home after a stint elsewhere. Spratley describes the conversation that often arises, demonstrating his pragmatic approach.

'I'll get a rower we've been talking to for months from a school here, who calls and says, Richard, sorry, but I'm going to Washington. You feel like saying – well, just get lost then – but you don't. You say congratulations, if there is anything we can do to help let us know. And by the way, after three or four years in the US, come to Brookes for your master's and we'll see if we can help you into the GB squad!'

The rules governing US universities and sports do help here. US student athletes cannot compete for more than four years, so after a first degree, most will need to come back to the UK if they want to pursue both rowing and academia. That makes life a little easier for Brookes. 'The youngsters who go off to US universities generally need to come back here after their degree if they want to row at GB under-23 level,' says Mike Sweeney.

Universities are also not allowed to approach children under the age of 16, so recruiters have to be careful. But Brookes scouts junior events, and sends observers to international regattas. The challenge is that the top US universities do the same. The Yale varsity squad (as of March

---

The athletes speak

'Richard and Henry have always been good at shepherding young athletes through to the GB squad level. They've always wanted "their boys" (and now girls too) to do really well.'

(*Rachel Quarrell*, HRR winner, GB International, Boat Race winner)

2024) contained 21 athletes who went to school in the US, so probably American by birth, no less than 12 from the UK and 19 from other countries, with Australia particularly well-represented.

The top University of Washington eight that won the IRA (national university championship) in June 2024 consisted of four British athletes, two Norwegians, an Italian, a Kiwi – and one American. The Harvard Varsity crew that beat Yale in 2024 contained no less than six young British athletes, including more from St Paul's School, London than from the entire USA!

In fact, the point has been reached where some countries are struggling to put together credible under-23 crews for major events because so many of their stars are away in the States and not available for most of the year. Spratley highlights Germany where this has become a real problem, but in recent years, the GB set-up has taken a more pragmatic view, understanding that there are just too many great athletes taking the US route to ignore. However, whilst Brookes faces these recruitment challenges, so far it has managed to recruit enough young Brits to provide a steady flow into the national squad.

Many spectators at Henley probably don't realise the internationalism of many crews they are watching. Take that classic Brookes versus Washington Prince Albert 2023 final, described on page 35. The Washington crew had just one American in their boat – the cox, Casey Neumann, a young Californian woman. The four oarsmen were Jonathan Wang-Norderud, a Norwegian under-23 international; Ethan Blight, another U-23 international from New Zealand; Ryan Smith, despite his name a German gold-medal winning junior oarsman; and one Englishman, Archie Drummond, who learnt to row at Twickenham Rowing Club.

There are parallels here with the world of football. Henley has crews that look and sound on paper British (or American, or German) but in fact are often international. Just as the Premier League features teams

Recruitment

representing Manchester or Liverpool which contain few players from that city or even from England, and the same is true of Real Madrid or Paris St Germain, a top crew might well be a League of Nations of talented sportspeople.

Over 80% of the Brookes squad are British, but the club is sometimes criticised for recruiting from other countries. If it recruited more talented British students, wouldn't that help the GB national squad prospects? But as we've seen, many top juniors want to go to Washington or Harvard. We can't exactly force them to head off to Brookes. There is also the argument that the British athletes at Brookes, still a vast majority, benefit from being part of such a strong squad and successful crews.

So, the British rowers who make it into the top boats at Brookes have proved themselves to be successful already in an international context. Mike Sweeney, previously head of GB selectors and manager of the GB team, has no doubt that Brookes has been a positive influence on wider GB rowing. 'The club has been a strong training ground and successful in feeding through top rowers to the international stage,' he says.

Extending that football analogy, the Premier League has fewer English players than ever, yet the international team is the best to represent the country for decades. That's because if you can make it as an English player into the Manchester City, Arsenal or Liverpool team, you are clearly of international standard and already comfortable playing at the very top level.

So, whilst Spratley and his colleagues would like to find more Eton, Radley or St Paul's stars knocking on their door, they're not doing too badly with their current recruitment approach, as the results and the flow of athletes from Brookes into the GB squad demonstrates.

There are also a small number of athletes who row at Brookes on the GB high-performance or Olympic Pathway programmes. They are not students – although some may have been, at Brookes or elsewhere – but full-time athletes, generally looking for national selection with

GB or indeed other nations. Whilst there are only a handful of men and women in this category, they do of course strengthen those very top Brookes crews, enabling them to compete successfully in the Grand and Remenham at Henley for instance. 'I would always rather have students in my crews,' explains Richard Spratley. 'But we have to be realistic if we are serious about rowing at the very highest level.'

Come to Brookes!

Given the competition for the best people, how can Brookes continue to recruit so many very good rowers? They know the university cannot compete financially with the US institutions. But, as Bailhache-Webb says, 'We tell them that without a doubt, they will have the best possible experience of their rowing lives here.' If you are a talented 18-year-old rower deciding where to go next, just watch those videos of the training camp at Wimbleball, or the athletes at work in the gym, or rowing on a misty and beautiful Thames at Cholsey, and imagine that is you in a few months' time.

Brookes expects coaches to spend a considerable amount of their time on recruitment – 'Around 25 per cent,' one ex-coach told me. There are 'taster days' for prospective student athletes and the material on the website and various social media platforms promoting the club is very impressive and persuasive these days.

The university is no academic backwater these days either. Whilst at Brookes, Michael Glover won three times at Henley, twice at the Head of the River, and won 11 British University gold medals! He went on to represent GB at under-23 and senior levels too, and on the Brookes website he points out that he also 'attained a BSc and an MSc along the way, and I don't believe any programme in the world would allow me to combine these opportunities.'

As well as getting a good degree, those recruits will also stand a good chance of winning some of the most prestigious events in rowing and,

Recruitment

> **The athletes speak**
> 'Brookes' success has been all about routine and consistency of approach. So now young rowers can look at Brookes and know exactly what they're going to get if they go there.'
> (*David Peill*, member of first OBUBC HRR winning crew)

if they are good enough, Brookes will prepare them and help them in terms of national selection. There are also issues of pastoral care. Whilst this is not a scientific observation, there are a number of stories of young GB stars not thriving at US universities.

'It's very competitive – unless you are the coach's favourite,' one such oarsman told me. Selection did not appear to be as objective as it is at Brookes. He was struggling with his academic work at one of the top rowing universities, also a very academic place, and when he went to have a chat with the chief rowing coach, he was simply told to 'get over it'. He returned to the UK shortly after that.

The Brookes marketing approach has also been clever. Watch the YouTube videos and I challenge you not to feel moved and inspired. A 40-minute video made by Will Denegri, cox of the 2023 Temple crew is similarly motivational.[25] The training looks tough, but my goodness, the whole experience looks like fun too! Finally, this comment is at the heart of the Brookes offer to prospective student athletes. You will hear it from Spratley, Bailhache-Webb and the whole coaching team.

'We will help you become the best athlete you can possibly be.'

Despite the growth in the Brookes programme, 120 people now, the coaches have managed to retain that individual focus. And think about that concept for a moment – 'Helping you be the best that you can possibly be.' Isn't that what every coach, manager, or parent for that matter, should be thinking about in terms of their athletes, staff or kids?

Oxford Brookes

Henley Royal Regatta, 2.30 pm, 7 July 2024

Race report – The 2024 Remenham Challenge Cup Final
Just like the Grand, the elite women's eights is Brookes versus the Americans. There is some blue sky now, so better conditions than for many of the morning races. The Brookes boat contains five women stepping up to the elite event from last year's Island winning crew at Henley (Grace Richards, Arianna Forde, Brenna Randall, Martha Birtles and Rhianna Sumpter). They are joined by Nicole Cusack and McKenna Simpson, post-graduates recruited from Canada, Irish international and MSc student Claire Feerick and cox Beatrice Argyle.

The women are rowing in the boat named after Keith Kelly, the university's sporting Director who sadly passed away a few months ago, and the crew has already beaten Molesey, the Canadian development squad and Leander/Imperial, a GB development eight, to get to the final. Brookes, for some reason, wasn't seeded, so has had one race more than the Americans, and the mystery in this event, actually, is the poor performance of what was supposedly the German full national eight, who lost to the Leander/Imperial crew in the quarter final.

The US crew is Princeton Training Center and Advanced Rowing Initiative of the Northeast, USA (ARION). This is a US national squad 'development crew', so mainly under-23 athletes who are being lined up as potential Olympians in 2028. Some are professional squad athletes already, others have been rowing in the very best US university crews.

Off they both go at 47 strokes per minute, but Brookes goes faster. 'This is an absolutely sensational start from the British crew, how have they managed to do that to the Americans in the first 300 metres?! Outpowered, outpaced, out-rowed in that first part of the race!' The legendary Martin Cross on commentary sounds genuinely shocked as Brookes takes an immediate lead of a canvas after just a minute or so.

The 2024 Remenham Challenge Cup Final

At the Barrier the lead is half a length, but the Americans aren't going away. Slowly, steadily they creep up on Brookes in the middle part of the race and are only a canvas down at Fawley. Fergus Mainland on commentary thinks 'the Americans could win this' and, watching on the TV screens in the enclosure grandstands, I am beginning to think the same.

With two minutes to go, the US crew is almost level. But remember, Brookes boats just don't let the opposition past. Now we can see that the US boat is no longer gaining on Brookes. In fact, the initiative has been taken again by the British boat. As the crews reach the enclosures and the wall of noise hits them (nothing like a close UK/US race to get the volume up to danger level), Brookes hits the accelerator. Perhaps the greater coherence of the crew who have rowed together all year comes into play, because suddenly Brookes has half a length. The crowd is going mad. Brookes are warned for their steering, but the women hold on past the (mainly) ecstatic crowd, winning by half a length.

The celebrations are intense, but both crews are shattered after a genuinely classic Henley final. There appears to be a bit of vomiting from one Brookes rower, but she and her crewmates really won't mind. This is the first Remenham win for a wholly Brookes crew, rather than some sort of composite, and it marks another major step forward in the Brookes story. 'This crew were brilliant, they just had that ability to raise their game when they needed to,' said a delighted Henry Bailhache-Webb.

Chapter 17

Onwards and upwards (2016–19)

'We should be aiming to win the Ladies' Plate at Henley, not just the Temple.'
(Henry Bailhache-Webb, 2010)

A crew full of stars

After the first Head of the River success in 2016, it was back to training at Cholsey and looking ahead to the early summer regattas in preparation for Henley. In retrospect this was a truly great crew. Swarbrick, Aldridge, Gibbs, Bolding, Glover, Stanhope and cox Brightmore were still there from 2015, supplemented by postgraduate and GB under-23 international Robbie Massey, plus a young Norwegian, 19-year-old Ask Tjom. His Brookes career was relatively short, but he has gone on to compete at international level, and represented Norway in the 2024 Olympics.

The next big event was the British Universities championship in early May, where Brookes won in both the men's and the women's eights, the first time the club had achieved that double. Then it was off to Ghent for a significant match-up against the Dutch Nereus crew that had piped Brookes at Henley in 2015. This time, Brookes came out on top, beating Nereus by a length. But in early June, Nereus had their revenge, beating Brookes by over a length at the Holland Beker event, although the Brookes crew was missing a couple of the regular crew members.

Henley came around again, with tricky conditions. Strong headwinds made life tough for the crews, whilst wellies were de rigueur for some in the Stewards' Enclosure for the first days of the event. This year, Brookes did not have to worry about Nereus. Having won the Temple the year before, Nereus had to row in the Ladies', where they lost to

Onwards and upwards (2016–19)

Leander in one of Henley's most controversial finals. Nereus crossed the line first, by just three feet, but after much debate and viewing of videos by the umpires, Nereus was disqualified because their coach, sitting in the Umpire's launch following the boats, had signalled to his crew – not allowed, said the Stewards.

Nereus pushed their luck for much of the race, rowing towards the middle of the course rather than in their lane (not marked out of course). Arguably, they obstructed Leander, and many spectators at Henley and on YouTube felt that would have been worthy of disqualification. Ironically, their coach said he was signalling to tell them to move over! It was tough on the crew, in any case.

Back to the Temple, and Brookes almost came unstuck against another Dutch crew in the first round. Perhaps under-estimating Koninklijke Studenten Roeivereeniging Njord, Netherlands (a test for the Henley announcers), they got through a slightly uncomfortable race. The weather was pretty awful, and Harry Brightmore, the Brookes cox, pushed his luck by trying to edge into his opponent's lane to get better water conditions. He was repeatedly warned by the umpire and, after taking an early comfortable lead, the Dutch pulled back and got close to Brookes again. However, Brookes had something to spare and pulled away again, then relaxed at the end, dropping their rating, to win by three-quarters of a length.

The races actually got somewhat easier on Thursday and Friday, with Newcastle and Columbia of the US beaten by a couple of lengths each. The semi-finals saw Brookes the only UK boat left, with Yale, Harvard and Berkeley from the US also still in it. Brookes beat Yale by almost two lengths in the semis, and rowed brilliantly in the final, thrashing Harvard by over three lengths. Having lost to Harvard in two Henley Temple Cup finals in 2001 and 2002, Bailhache-Webb took particular pleasure in that result.

Starting again

That win in 2016 meant Brookes would have to produce a totally new crew to defend the Temple title in 2017, given the regatta rules. There were a couple of rowers from the Prince Albert coxed four who could be part of the crew, but in the main, the Temple boat would be new to Brookes that year. However, the recruitment pipeline that Bailhache-Webb and Spratley had worked on for several years now was paying dividends, and talented 'freshers' (undergraduate and postgraduate) were joining the club. Chris Tebb, Chris Zahn, Will Hall, Robin Stirling, Sam Nunn, Gareth Syphas, Brendan Edwards, Matthew Hnatiw and cox Charlie Clarke were ready to take on the Temple.

Meanwhile, the 2016 Temple crew would step up this year and attempt to realise the aspiration of winning the Ladies' Challenge Plate at Henley 2017, the goal Bailhache-Webb had first discussed with Spratley several years earlier. By now, some of the rowers were no longer students, so the boat raced as 'Oxford Brookes and Taurus boat club'.

Indeed, several of the athletes were now part of the GB Olympic Pathway Programme too, and the only change from the 2016 Temple-winning crew was Josh Bugajski of Oxford University, who was drafted in to replace the Norwegian, Ask Tjom. Bugajski didn't take up rowing until he was 20, but won two Boat Races with Oxford, then joined the high-performance programme at Brookes.

In the Marlow regatta, two weeks before Henley, the Brookes crew won in an amazing time of 5:30. That was top international crew pace, and must have struck fear into other entrants for the Ladies' Plate. On the Friday of the regatta, Brookes was up against Elizabethan Boat Club in the quarter final, their first race. I remember at the time as a spectator wondering who or what Elizabethan might be – turns out they were the alumni club associated with Westminster School, mainly now studying and rowing at US universities.

Onwards and upwards (2016–19)

Indeed, the Elizabethan Boat Club claims to be the oldest in the world, with records dating back to 1813, and rather than having a club tie, as most boat clubs do, members can wear a belt. It is hand-beaded in Kenya by the Maasai people, using 6,000 beads per belt, and is available for a mere £85 (at time of writing) from the Manyatta website![26]

Back to the race, and although the verdict says that Brookes won by two-thirds of a length, the crew was well ahead by halfway and treated the second half as a training row really. The commentator on the video observed that he would have liked to see Brookes up against the GB national eight and Yale, the fastest university crew in the US. But it was not to be.

The semi-final was a trickier race, with Brookes beating Bayer Leverkusen of Germany, a top club crew including several international oarsmen, by three-quarters of a length. This was close initially, but around halfway Brookes pushed hard and opened up a two lengths lead. Again, there was a touch of relaxation towards the end, allowing the German crew to come back a little, but it was a confident win. 'This is the fastest crew Henry Bailhache-Webb has ever coached,' said Martin Cross during the Henley video commentary.[27]

In the final, Brookes was up against a Leander and Moseley composite crew, which was in effect a GB under-23 crew. The commentators thought this would be a close and exciting race. But that crew hadn't been together for long, as most of the athletes were Brits at US universities. And that showed. Within a minute, Brookes had almost a length's lead. The under-23 crew hung on, and came back in the middle of the race.

Indeed, the gap was a slightly worrying half a length as the crews approached the Enclosure. At that point, cox Brightmore steered slightly out into the middle of the course to make sure the puddles from his boat were hitting the under-23 blades. And just as the crowd started to get excited, anticipating a close finish, Brookes moved away again and won by three quarters of a length. The time was an exceedingly rapid 6:01, the fastest time clocked in the entire regatta, four seconds faster than the final of the Grand, won by the German national squad boat.

Maybe Brookes could have won the Grand that year. But winning the Ladies' was a significant achievement, and Brookes became only the fourth British university to achieve that since the Ladies' became an intermediate event in 1985.

In the Temple, the results suggest the first three rounds were fairly close for Brookes. But in truth, the crew raced hard to about halfway, then reduced the rate a little and cruised home in each race against the University of the West of England, Nereus, the old rivals with their lightweight crew, and Groningen, also from the Netherlands. California Berkeley looked like a tougher proposition in the semi-final, but we saw the same pattern. Brookes were two lengths ahead before easing off a little again towards the end to win by one and a quarter lengths.

However, the final was a different matter. The University of London crew saw off Harvard in a tremendous semi-final, coming through to win after being behind for much of the race. And UL showed their toughness again in the final, not letting Brookes get away. There was never more than a length in it, but equally the London boat could never get any closer than about three-quarters of a length, which was the verdict at the end. Another Temple win for Brookes, and this was the first time a club had won both the Temple and Ladies' in the same year since Imperial College in 1992 – which, fittingly, had been Richard Spratley's first year at Brookes. Brookes was now unquestionably the top university rowing club in the UK and across Europe.

Onwards and upwards (2016–19)

The Huskies take Henley

The Brookes top crew for the Ladies' at Henley in 2018 was a tale of two halves. Bolding, Swarbrick, Aldridge, Gibbs and cox Brightmore were back from the previous years' crew, along with Hnatiw and Nunn, promoted from the 2017 Temple crew, Ed Grisedale from the 2017 Visitors' four, and a new face in Quentin Antognelli from Monaco. Stepping up from the Temple, Hnatiw remembers rowing with his new crew, including future Olympians. 'I could see people like Morgan Bolding just had what you might call a race mode, which was pretty impressive. I always felt we could beat anyone.'

At the Head of the River race in March, the crew had tied with a Leander crew that was in effect the GB national squad. At the Ratzenberg regatta, they set a new Brookes record time of 5:29 for 2,000 metres – incredible, international-level pace.

There were only six crews in the Ladies' this year, but there was another crew that was eight-ninths Brookes too. The entry was labelled 'Brookes and Edinburgh University', with Oli Wilkes from Edinburgh University the non-Brookes rower, although actually he had finished studying at Edinburgh that spring and was now attached to Brookes.

Then there was a mix of Brookes athletes – some who had rowed the previous year in the Ladies', the Temple and the Visitors' at Henley, plus a couple of new faces. As well as Wilkes, James Snowball, Brendan Edwards, Gareth Syphas, Tim Grant, Michael Glover, Jamie Axon, Joel Cassells and cox Alex Wenyon wanted to show that they were a 'B' crew only in name.

Brookes had a bye to the semi-final, where they dealt with Berliner Ruderclub pretty comfortably. Brookes and Edinburgh beat Cantabrigian comfortably, then had what looked like a tough semi-final against Leander. The Leander crew included guys from the top US universities, Boat Race rowers, and GB squad members. But they never led Brookes and Edinburgh. Wenyon coxed aggressively, looking to minimise the effect of the stream, and gradually took it away from Leander. It was a length by halfway up the course and three-quarters of a length at the finish.

So the final was Brookes versus Brookes, with just a touch of Edinburgh. The wholly Brookes crew went off quickly and seemed to just get faster and faster. It was never a race really, but what was unusual was to see a crew leading by several lengths and yet busting a gut in the last ten strokes. That was because Brookes had a secondary motive, as well as winning. They wanted to become the first crew in the Ladies' to break the six-minute barrier. Coming to the finishing line, the crew was straining every muscle, the stroke rate rising and rising – and they did it. A new record to the Barrier of 1:43, equalling the record of 2:54 to Fawley, and then 5:58 to the finish.

That was part one of the double Brookes had achieved in 2017, but part two was not going to be easy. Again, Brookes had to find a new crew for the Temple, the rowers from 2016 now being ineligible. So a bunch of in the main 19- and 20-year-olds, Luke Hillier, Seb Newman, Oli Ayres, Ben Witting, Matt Newman, Alfie Heath, Matt Rowe, Henry Bloise-Brooke and cox Gavin McWilliams took on the challenge.

But this was now in effect the Brookes third boat, up against very tough opposition. Syracuse University in the quarter final was the first real test, and Brookes came through by one length. But looking at the times in other races, it was clear there were two other star crews still around – the fastest Newcastle University crew for many years, and the Huskies from the University of Washington.

The semi-final against Newcastle was another classic Brookes race. For the first two minutes there was nothing in it, with the crews pretty much level at the Barrier. Then as often seems to happen, Brookes moved ahead in the middle part of the race, but only by half a length or so. But by the time the crews reached the enclosures, Brookes seemed to

Onwards and upwards (2016–19)

have it the bag with a one length lead. But Newcastle threw everything into it and Brookes had to hold on to win by half a length.

So Brookes versus Washington in the final, probably the two strongest university rowing programmes in the world. Brookes got a good start but, after about one minute, Washington moved ahead. They were rating slightly higher than Brookes, which in a tail wind is often a good strategy – execute lots of strokes and tap the boat along in the wind. After two minutes, Brookes seemed to be hit by a gust of wind and the boat changed course rather dramatically, which always slows you down. But then Washington was warned for straying into the middle of the course too.

Suddenly it was a length in favour of Washington. Brookes wasn't familiar with losing at this stage, and the crew came back strongly in the middle of the race. But they could not get back on terms, and the course record was broken to both the Barrier and to Fawley. The Washington boat was coxed strongly, as they hogged the middle of the course to send dirty water down to Brookes. But with a huge effort, Brookes fought back to half a length. They hit the blast of sound from the Enclosures crowd, wondering if Brookes could pull off a great fight-back. But it was too much. The experienced Washington crew came through by a length.

This was a really impressive Washington crew. It was made up of a combination of first, second and third boat rowers, with junior world champions from various countries. But to beat the Temple course record as they did by five seconds was very impressive. It also shows how close races generate fast times, not surprisingly.

Meanwhile, Matt Tarrant added another Henley medal in the GB squad boat in the Grand. There were Brookes fours in the Visitors' and the Prince Albert too. In the Visitors', the crew lost in one of the closest races ever, losing by three feet to a New Zealand crew in the quarter final. Being a four without a cox, the steering was dodgy to say the least and the NZ crew were warned for their steering within seconds of the start.

But around halfway, the Kiwi boat showed their experience and power and took a small lead. That was extended to almost a length at one stage, but approaching the Enclosure it was down to half a length. Brookes continued to gain, and the crowd certainly wasn't sure who had won – but it was the Kiwis. Another two strokes and maybe it would have been different. In the Prince Albert it was the Goldie crew from Cambridge University that proved Brookes' nemesis, as not even Brookes could spread their talent across too many events. Or not at this stage anyway.

2019 – the double double

The 2019 crew for the Ladies' at Henley saw Antognelli, Aldrige, Nunn, Swarbrick and cox Brightmore all returning from the winning 2018 crew. Glover, Wilkes, now labelled as Brookes rather than Edinburgh, Edwards and Axon stepped up from the previous year's 'B' boat. Meanwhile Rory Gibbs from the 2018 winning crew was now rowing in the GB squad four, which won the Stewards' comfortably. Old boys Matt Tarrant and Josh Bugajski rowed in the GB squad Grand eight that lost by over a length to the New Zealand national crew in the final.

The Brookes Ladies' crew was another absolutely top boat, winning the Head of the River race in March, and almost beating the German national eight at Duisburg regatta, coming within one second of the Germans. But the Ladies' was a high-quality event this year.

Hollandia Roeiclub, Netherlands a crew of young Dutch international and potential international oarsmen, broke the course record to Fawley and equalled the overall record in their semi-final, winning narrowly over Leander. That time was two seconds faster than Brookes in their semi-final, who pipped a GB under-23 crew (labelled Newcastle University and Cambridge University) by one length in another tough race, during which Brookes broke the record to the Barrier.

Onwards and upwards (2016–19)

But what looked like a tough race on paper turned out to be fairly comfortable. Brookes took a one length lead in the first half of the race and never looked like being challenged. Brookes pushed on to win in another fast time, although not quite record-breaking.

The Temple crew included some of the previous year's finalists (Rowe, Bloise-Brooke, both Newmans and cox Gavin McWilliams) plus new faces in Mikey Dalton, James Snowball, Max Thompson and Sam Bannister. In the final, Brookes was up against a US university that was a less regular visitor to the finals day at Henley. But Northeastern University from Boston was and is a strong and well-established powerhouse in the US.

Indeed, the whole event was incredibly competitive. Newcastle University had three consecutive races with verdicts of less than a length, beating Edinburgh and Brown University of the US before being pipped by Northeastern in the semi-final by one third of a length in a great race. Northeastern also beat Brookes 'B' on the way to the final, so revenge was another motive for the Brookes 'A' crew.

The four Brookes rowers from the previous year's crew were determined not to experience the same disappointment. Brookes went out strongly, but Northeastern hung on until the Barrier. But then Brookes took the lead, slowly extended that in the middle part of the race, and never relinquished it. It wasn't easy, and a two-length lead at one point was narrowed to about a length at the end, but it was comfortable.

Brookes also put out a strong four in the Visitors with Chris Tebb, Temple winner in 2017, and Peter Chambers, an Olympic medallist back in 2012, returning to Brookes racing. But they met a much physically bigger Dutch crew in the semi-final and lost disappointingly by over a length.

In the Prince Albert, Brookes lost in the semi-final to Harvard by four feet after leading until literally the last two strokes. The win came

Oxford Brookes

despite terrible steering from the Harvard cox, who moved into the stronger stream and dirty water from Brookes for some unfathomable reason. Through this whole book, we have hardly ever seen Brookes pipped on the line, and Harvard went on to win the final too, in another thriller against Durham University, despite hitting a goose towards the finish, illustrating the vagaries of Henley.

Despite those disappointment in the fours events, winning the Temple and the Ladies' for the second time in three years proved that 2017 wasn't a fluke. Brookes was now established as a real rival to Leander for the title of the top British sweep rowing club – not just the best university.

Chapter 18

The Women of Brookes

'So ... we spoke to Richard Spratley who ran the men's programme and asked if he would take us under his wing. He agreed, with one proviso – that we had to train exactly as the men's squad, no questions asked.' (Clara Devlin, née Ashford, OBUBC and GB Olympic rower, interviewed on the OBUBC website)[28]

The long history of women's rowing

It is likely that women have rowed for exactly as long as men. Women's competitive rowing can be traced back to Venice in the fifteenth century, and it was popular as a gambling event (as was men's rowing) in the nineteenth century. An image of a women's double scull race made the cover of *Harper's Weekly* magazine in 1870, and the first women's Boat Race between Oxford and Cambridge was held in 1927, but was initially termed an 'exhibition event'.

But it was only in 1950 that the European rowing establishment agreed to introduce women's events at the European Rowing Championship of 1951. Shockingly, it took another 25 years before the Olympics introduced women's races in 1976, and until the 1980s those international events were held over 1,000 metres rather than the standard men's 2,000 metres.

In 1981, Henley Royal Regatta introduced two women's 'exhibition' events, over a 1,000 metre course, but the experiment lasted only two years. That distance was in line with international events, based on the old-fashioned view that women could not possibly row all of 2,000 (or indeed 2,112) metres without exhausting themselves.

Women's international races moved to 2,000 metres in 1984 at the World Championship, but it was not until 1993 that women returned to HRR for good, with a single sculls event, allowing the first women to race over the full course, a mere 154 years after the event's founding. Then in 1998 an eights event was added, the Remenham Cup, and the programme grew from there. Women had of course raced at other regattas and head races and, in 1988, Henley Women's Regatta was established. Leander Club at Henley admitted women for the first time in 1997 – a condition of the club receiving a grant from the UK Lottery sports fund. Henley Women's Regatta quickly became a success, and indeed Oxford Polytechnic had a small women's club which competed in the early days of that event.

To give the more recent HRR stewards credit, they have moved relatively quickly to make Henley a truly mixed regatta in recent years and there are now 16 events for men and boys, and 10 for women and girls, and we are probably heading to equality or something close. The Olympics has been on a similar journey and in 2024 there will be seven events for each sex.

Calling Richard Spratley ...

Jane Gandon described women's rowing at the Poly back in the 1980s in Chapter 3, and Oxford Polytechnic women actually won a major title before their men ever did. In 1992 a crew (Fiona MacDougall, Hayley Mellor, Annette Wise, Kate Moseley, cox Katie Beaumont, coached by Steve Walter and Jamie McDonald) won the 'College Coxed fours' at the Henley Women's Regatta, the first and last win for 'Oxford Polytechnic', as the institution changed its name later that year.

But that proved to be something of a one-off, and when Carla Devlin (then Carla Ashford) arrived at what was by then Brookes in 1998, there wasn't a lot of interest from the women of the university. Ashford didn't start rowing until her second year at Brookes, but quickly showed

The Women of Brookes

aptitude, and plenty of enthusiasm. After that year rowing in the novice crew, she entered the senior squad – but there were just four women interested in competing. So Ashford spoke to Richard Spratley and asked if he would take ownership of the women's group as well as his men's squad. This is from her interview for the Brookes website:

> 'Following on from an amazing novice year, when I entered the senior women's squad there were only four of us, this was due to older girls graduating, novice girls quitting, the women's coach had left and the group just crumbled. So … we spoke to Richard Spratley who ran the men's programme and asked if he would take us under his wing. He agreed, with one proviso – that we had to train exactly as the men's squad, no questions asked … men's programme on and off the water, we rowed in boats with the men's squad and even seat raced against some of the bottom end of the men's squad, it definitely made us raise our game!'

The women would train in the same way as the men, in the same gym, and the same level of commitment was expected, another example of Spratley's combination of vision and pragmatism. He claims now that mixing the crews and standardising training was simply a sensible response to lack of coaching resource and the small number of women. But at that time, not many clubs considered mixed crews (even though the idea is gaining popularity today).

By 2001, the women's coxed four won 'by miles' at Henley Women's Regatta, in a remarkably fast time – faster than the club and open coxed fours winners. The crew was now rowing at international events, winning at the Ghent regatta, a favourite for British crews.

2002 was an Olympic year, so the entry list for the Remenham Challenge Cup at Henley Royal Regatta was lacking the big international crews. By now, Carla Ashford was on the fringes of international selection, and as there wasn't a fours event for women at the regatta, she persuaded four other rowers who were in or around the GB squad, but not rowing at the Olympics, to join up with her four, under the Brookes banner. They powered through the event, winning a semi-final against a strong German crew and then comfortably beating Tideway Scullers School in the final. This was a big moment for Brookes women, their first HRR victory.

Heiki Asmuss had turned up at Brookes a couple of years earlier, after schooling in East Germany, and asked if she could join the novice crew. Of course, said Spratley. It didn't take too long before her teammates – and Spratley – noticed that she seemed rather competent, fit and strong. After some quizzing, she admitted that she had rowed in the East German junior international squad a few years earlier! But she was not sure how much of her ability she had retained after some time off.

The answer was 'a lot' and in 2002, she was one of the powerhouses of that winning Brookes crew. That crew also included Ashford, Emma Fonseca, one of the original crew that had approached Spratley, and Elizabeth Henshilwood, whose brother Alex had won the Temple and Ladies' at Henley with Brookes in the 1990s.

Building the numbers

But after this success, the women's programme struggled with a lack of numbers. Tamsin Bryant, then Tamsin Adams, came up to Brookes in 2004 and remembers the struggles on the river and off. 'I remember Peter Haining and Richard Spratley found an old school building that we converted into a gym for the women's squad – I think Peter literally knocked down a dividing wall so we could all train on the ergs together!'

That idea had come from club captain Henry Bailhache-Webb, and Haining and Spratley actually did take chainsaws to the walls (after turning off the power, of course). Bailhache-Webb also lobbied for

The Women of Brookes

The 2002 winning Remenham crew with Richard Spratley (*Brookes archive*)

Brookes women share Victor Ludorum title with
Newcastle University, BUCS 2018 (*©AllMarkOne*)

more ergo machines - which Spratley then sourced from GB rowing cast-offs.

There was no focused recruitment programme, and Brookes continued to have a small number of good female athletes rather than building a critical mass to generate winning eights. Training with the men did help some of the strongest women though. From 2007, Brookes showed up regularly on the Remenham Cup entry list at Henley, as part of composite crews. At that stage, the Remenham was the only event for women's eights, so international level crews dominated the finals. But Victoria Bryant, Rachael Jefferies and Kirsty Myles from Brookes all won medals at international level in the late noughties, and Ashford herself rowed at the 2008 Olympics, along with cox Caroline O'Connor in the women's eight.

And there was success in the Henley Women's Regatta, with Brookes picking up the elite coxless fours and intermediate coxed fours in 2007, and the elite coxed fours in 2010. Around this time, encouragement to build the women's squad came from different sources. David Tanner at GB Rowing wanted to see Brookes replicating its success on the men's side, and Janet Beer, the Brookes Vice-chancellor from 2008 to 2015, was a supporter, helping to secure additional funding for the club.

A major step forward came in 2012 when Allan French joined as the first dedicated Brookes women's coach. In 2013, a GB squad crew competing as Leander and Brookes won the Remenham, featuring Brookes alumni Katherine Douglas, Olivia Carnegie-Brown and Zoe De Toledo. Olivia Carnegie-Brown went on to compete and finish second in the GB eight at the Rio 2016 Olympics, becoming the first Brookes woman to win an Olympic medal.

Under the guidance of French, who also coached several GB level boats, Brookes started to build the numbers of women rowing, and the club attained the GB High Performance Programme status that the men's squad had held for some years. Progress was steady and positive, and Brookes won the senior eights event at Henley Women's Regatta for the first time in 2015. The new academic eights title was also won in 2018, as the Brookes women really began to build consistency and strength in depth.

At Henley Royal Regatta, the only women's eights event was still the Remenham, which tended to be won by an international crew. Brookes lost to a Czech squad crew in 2016, and to a strong Yale crew in 2018. That year was notable though for the appearance of young Esme Booth – more on her later.

The 2018 event proved to be French's swansong with the club, as he took on a role at Reading Blue Coat School, before signing up to the challenge of Oxford University's women's squad in 2023. But the development continued briefly under Dan Janes, and the first boat set a new course record for academic eights whilst winning at Henley Women's Regatta in 2019. In the Remenham Cup of 2019, Brookes beat Edinburgh University then lost to a GB squad crew. But Janes was head-hunted to go and teach the Saudis to row, so the responsibility passed to Richard Chambers, previously a star oarsman at Brookes and internationally.

After the pandemic pause, in 2021, Brookes won the championship eights for the first time at Henley Women's Regatta, and Henley Royal Regatta introduced an event for women's student eights, the Island Challenge Cup. (It would have debuted in 2020 but the regatta was cancelled because of Covid.) That is covered in more detail in Chapter 20, but cutting to the chase, Brookes became the first holders of that trophy, a final triumph for Chambers who then moved on to rivals Leander.

Hugo Gulliver joined in 2021 from London University, where he had developed a very strong women's programme. Gulliver was originally a cox but was 'too big for coxing and too small for rowing', as he puts it. He started coaching at school, then came to Brookes as a student, but managed to continue coaching professionally at his own school, Latymer Upper in London, whilst he got his degree. Clearly, that needed impressive time management and multi-tasking skills! After Brookes, he coached in New Zealand, and then with various junior crews, before a spell at Harvard.

He came back to the UK with the University of London, then was headhunted by Brookes; he is married to Henry Bailhache-Webb's sister, so he knew Brookes well. Aside from that, Gulliver was attracted by the Brookes reputation and the professionalism of the club. 'With Richard Spratley providing the management support, and good procedures in place, the coaches at Brookes have the space to get on with the job of coaching,' he says.

He also saw that although the women's programme had been successful, 'there was more to go for. The ship was going in the right direction, but I felt I could add something. I'm not sure I would have wanted to come in and take over the men's squad from Henry after he and Richard have done such an amazing job!'

In 2022, Brookes won the academic eights again at Henley women's. But at Henley Royal Regatta in 2022 Brookes narrowly lost to Brown University of the USA in the semi-final of the Island. This was another case where that race should probably have been the final, as Brookes pushed Brown harder than Yale did in the final.

The most recent years are covered in subsequent chapters, which brings the story up to date. However, towards the end of 2023, Gulliver faced a dilemma. The family business, involved in wine and hospitality industry, needed his assistance. So he agreed with Spratley that he would reduce his coaching commitment and dedicate more time to the business. But Brookes has worked on succession planning as the club has grown, so Chris Tebb, a GB under-23 international who won the Temple with Brookes in 2017 and had coached the novice programme for a couple of years, stepped up to lead the women's programme. That continuity which is so vital to Brookes success was maintained.

The Women of Brookes

Diversity, inclusion, participation ... and winning
The women's programme has enabled the club to support wider imperatives for the University. In recent years, Brookes has placed more emphasis on sporting participation and on women's sport generally. Sadly, more teenage girls in the UK give up sport than their male peers. Women in Sport has found that more than one million teenage girls who once considered themselves 'sporty', disengage from sport following primary school.[29]

So encouraging girls and young women to continue with sport, or indeed take it up, is a growing objective for universities generally. Hence university leadership has encouraged the boat club to increase numbers in the women's squad. In 2023/4, there are some 45 women rowing. 'My aim is to have equal numbers of men and women quite soon,' says Spratley. Next year there will be seven eights (boats) for the men and six for the women, so that target is getting closer.

Of course, this will bring new challenges. The capacity of the gym and the boathouse are constraints, and no-one wants to see the men's programme weakened. But equally, everyone in the club wants Brookes to succeed with women's rowing to the extent it has on the men's side. What is helping is a boom in girls rowing at schools. Whilst that is mainly private schools still, events such as the Schools' Head of the River and schools events at Henley Women's Regatta are heavily over-subscribed these days. Whilst the issue of the top US universities attracting British talent across the Atlantic applies to both sexes, the Brookes coaching team believes they can build the success of the women's squad further.

The ethos continues to be based on integration of the two squads. Everyone trains together in the gym, with identical aerobic work. You will see 40 rowers, male and female, all pulling in sync on the ergs during the long, low-rating pieces. At the Wimbleball training camps, the top women's boat will be rowing alongside men's boats, maybe not formally racing, but measuring themselves against the male crews.

Oxford Brookes

That is undoubtedly feeding into the rising standards in the women's squad, as we saw at Henley in 2023 and even more so in 2024. 'This is all about building the culture, all for one and one for all,' says Spratley.

Another goal is to produce more international level athletes, as the club has achieved with the men's squad. If Henley Royal Regatta introduces more sweep rowing events for women, they will no doubt be on Brookes' radar, and I wouldn't bet against Brookes dominating GB women's rowing in the coming years.

'We want our rivals to think that they don't want to come up against Brookes at regattas. We've had that reputation for some years on the men's side – we are beginning to see that with our women too,' says Chris Tebb. But the young women now rowing and achieving such success at Brookes still owe a lot to the early pioneers at the club, who helped to get women's rowing established at a time when that was no easy matter.

Chapter 19

Selecting the crew

'It's not a seat race, we're just going to be timing, and changing a few people around ...' (Richard Spratley)

Ruthless – but fair

Crew selection has always been important, but as the Brookes squad grew in size, selecting the right people for the right crews became absolutely critical in terms of success. It is also a vital element that contributes, positively or negatively, to the motivation and team spirit across the whole group of athletes.

It wasn't such a big deal when Richard Spratley started his involvement with Brookes in 1991, as there were only about 20 young male rowers at Brookes. That has built steadily over the years, and today there are around 120 athletes, approximately split 60/40 male and female in the elite programme. There is also now a one-year 'learn to row' programme every year that around 100 new students sign up to. When Brookes is taking in some of the top junior rowers in the world, athletes who have probably been rowing for at least five years, it is difficult for someone who has only been rowing for a year or two – or is a complete novice – to break into the main squad. But the opportunity is there.

'We make it clear this isn't a stepping stone to our elite crews. It's about having the fun of learning to row at Brookes. Maybe one or two might go through to the programme, but that is not the point,' Spratley says.

So with around 70 elite male rowers in the squad, how do Spratley and the coaching team decide on the crews that will compete competitively, and which rowers will go into which boat? These are all guys who would walk into the first boat of most UK university boats clubs.

From the beginning, Brookes has shown an intensely competitive approach, both when racing others and also in their internal training and crew selection. Rowers from the early days of Spratley's reign remember seat racing, in pairs or bigger boats, and Spratley constantly swapping round crews to find the best combination. That quote above – 'It's not a seat race, we're just going to be timing, and changing a few people around …' actually made its way onto a Brookes fridge magnet at one point, indicative of that mentality.

Spratley was originally focused on putting together a winning crew for Henley, an eight or a four, above all else. But as the squad grew in size and strength, Henry Bailhache-Webb developed a broader approach, to the point where Brookes has 6 boats in the top 20 at the Head of the River, as we've discussed. But all the way through these years, alongside competition, fairness has been the other central tenet of the approach to selection.

To retain the motivation of everyone in what is a substantial squad today, every athlete needs to understand what they need to do to progress, and that they will be judged fairly, objectively and based on data as far as is humanly possible. Not everyone can be in the top boat, but they *do* need to know why that is, and what they could do to change their situation. And the inevitable disappointment has to be handled sensitively.

'We have to be ruthless in selection, but not ruthless with how we treat people,' says Bailhache-Webb.

What would Guardiola do?

Analysing the Brookes story, it is clear how innovative Spratley and Bailhache-Webb have been in many ways. Although he rowed at a good level, Spratley was not initially a trained coach and did not come

Selecting the crew

from an 'establishment' background, attend an elite private school or Oxbridge. Perhaps because of those factors, Spratley has never been afraid to challenge the traditional way things are done.

Crew selection is a good example of that. The traditional method of selection in most clubs is to hold some sort of competitive process at the beginning of the season (or term perhaps in academic circles), then pretty much stick with those crews throughout the racing calendar for that period. That provides the benefit of consistency, and enables each particular crew to get to know how their colleague athletes row, the different styles and even personalities within the boat.

At the bigger clubs and at international level, it also means that each boat can and probably will have its own coach, who can focus entirely on their athletes. But from the beginning, Spratley had a different view of life. He was convinced that a squad approach was a better way to go. That would allow more consistency in coaching, and more flexibility when it comes to selecting boats.

Why would you want to select a crew months before a race, he asked himself. Why not leave it as late as possible? Some would point to the need for crews to become familiar with each other. But there is evidence that this need for stability is over-rated, and Brookes themselves saw evidence of this in 2002.

Brookes was facing the Harvard heavyweight freshman crew in the final of the Temple at Henley. But the stroke of that crew, Bob Kubis, fell ill the morning of the race. The coach of the crew, Bill Manning, had to make an urgent and difficult decision. He replaced Kubis at the last minute with Graham O'Donoghue, who earlier that day has stroked the Harvard 'B' coxed four to victory over Harvard 'A' in the Britannia Challenge Cup coxed four final.

He had never rowed with the Temple crew until that day, when they paddled for ten minutes down to the starting line. And wasn't he a little bit tired? The Harvard Crimson website reported on the events of the momentous day for the New England university[30]:

> 'He (Kubis) had helped the Crimson freshman eight plow through a 32-boat field with victories in each of the previous four days, leaving just his boat and Oxford Brookes in the final. But just hours before the race, he broke out in a fit of sweating, fever and vomiting. A replacement was immediately needed. There was no choice but O'Donoghue. The eight first varsity rowers who competed in the Ladies' Challenge Plate were automatically ineligible, and all the sophomore second varsity rowers were ineligible because they had raced in the Temple Cup team last year. That left O'Donoghue … as the only option. "It wasn't much of a selection process," Manning said.'

But somehow, Harvard beat Brookes by three-quarters of a length – one of the races that Bailhache-Webb brooded over for years!

So back to Spratley and selection. When I spoke with him in December 2023, he said this (obviously before City lost to Real Madrid in the quarter final):

> 'If you asked Pep Guardiola today what his team is going to be if Manchester City are in the Champions League final next June, he would think you were mad. But there has been a history of clubs selecting their crews months in advance of major events. Take Oxford and Cambridge for example – they announce the crews well in advance for the Boat Race. Doesn't that affect the motivation for those selected? What about fitness levels, maybe injuries, a loss of form or confidence?'

So Brookes retains flexibility between crews often until very late in the day. That also means they can tailor crews for the eligibility

Selecting the crew

requirements of different events. Henley (as you might have spotted by now) has pretty complex rules for various events; other regattas are often similar. So being able to say that this is the boat that is aiming for the Ladies' at Henley, but we might bring in rower A and B for the Head of the River, then swap out C and D for E and F to have two competitive boats in different events at Ghent or Amsterdam regatta … it is all about maximising your flexibility and resources, as well as maintaining the intense competitive spirit we see at Brookes.

> **The athletes speak**
> 'Our men and women push each other on every session as we all strive towards the same goals each summer – there is no other team like it.'
> (*Matt Rowe*, GB rower, from the Brookes website)

But there are other factors that come back to Spratley and Bailhache-Webb, their ethos and modus operandi, and the way they have developed the club. The principles around standardisation of equipment might be seen as a cost management strategy, but actually it is also essential if you want to be able to switch rowers easily. Having essentially a single coaching team rather than coaches dedicated to a particular boat means there is a single and clear Brookes style and approach to rowing. Everyone training together in the same gym, at the same time, means the expectation of fitness levels is common across the club.

Now this doesn't mean that crews turn up to Henley not knowing in which boat or event they're going to be competing. But this flexibility has undoubtedly helped Brookes to maximise its resources and get the most out of its squad. It also must be good for motivation, because it means that as an athlete, you never know. Work hard, get your erg times down, perform on the river in training, and you might find yourself

Oxford Brookes

'promoted' halfway through the season to a boat competing at a higher level.

The use of telemetry is another key factor in the selection process. From the beginning, Spratley was keen on seat racing, changing crews around and racing them against each other. But telemetry data has made that more sophisticated now.

Imagine a boat with Al, Ben, Chris and Dan rowing. They beat another four in a seat racing session. Now we take Ed out of the losing boat and put him in the winning boat, moving Dan in the other direction. Al, Ben, Chris and Ed now lose. Clearly, Ed is the weak link and Dan needs to come back, right?

Well, not necessarily. If this was the final tough race of the day, maybe Al, Ben and Chris took it easy in that final race and Ed was actually the most powerful man in the crew. Perhaps Dan is an inconsistent performer who can be great or merely average — is that laziness or a lack of stamina?

Only by looking at each individual's telemetry data can a coach really tell, and Spratley is dismissive of coaches who argue differently. 'You get coaches who say, I've got a good eye for it, I can tell just by looking who is moving the boat. That's rubbish.' (That attitude persists even amongst some international level coaches, apparently.)

So this focus on data and objectivity constantly feeds into selection decisions at Brookes. It might appear somewhat brutal at times — but it is hard for anyone to argue it isn't fair. It is also an essential element in developing the team spirit that means when an athlete such as Jenny Bates (see page 4) is dropped from a crew, she says, 'I knew it was for the benefit of the crew.' If fairness wasn't so evident, she might have been tempted to say, 'F*** that, I'm joining Leander!'

Chapter 20

The pandemic years (2020–22)

'I can assure you that we will keep these restrictions under constant review. We will look again in three weeks, and relax them if the evidence shows we are able to.' (Boris Johnson, UK Prime Minister, announcing the first Covid lockdown on 23 March 2020)

'It's only flu'
In the autumn term of 2019, Spratley and Bailhache-Webb looked forward with great anticipation to the season. There were several rowers from the Temple boat of Henley 2019 still around who could step up a level for the 2020 regatta, and some of the best athletes from the Henley Ladies' crew were also available – including stars such as Aldridge, Nunn, and Wilkes.

Other Henley winners had moved on, their time at Brookes come to an end. Chris Tebb, Temple winner in 2017, took up a coaching position as a teaching assistant at Bedford School. He had coached Oxford University's Jesus College whilst at Brookes and enjoyed the experience, but starting your first full-time job in the midst of the pandemic was a strange experience, to say the least.

The coaches started discussing whether 2020 would be the year that Brookes might look to win the Grand at Henley, the ultimate prize for any rowing club. As it would be an Olympic year, it was unlikely that any of the top national eights would row at Henley, just a couple of weeks before they headed off to Tokyo. That didn't mean the Grand would be easy, but it seemed feasible. The crew that won the Ladies in 2019 had only lost to the German World Champions by one second in the Duisburg Regatta of 2019, after all. That was an international level crew already, in all but name.

Over the Christmas holidays, stories hit the press about a new virus that appeared to be spreading, and then skiers started coming back from the Alps with a rather nasty bout of something that seemed worse than the usual seasonal flu. Covid-19 had arrived. Yet it took a while before its effects became obvious.

The Quintin Head race is traditionally the first Thames head race of the calendar year. And on 25 January 2020 it went ahead, with Brookes 'A' winning it by almost 30 seconds from the Brookes second boat. Brookes 'D' came third, beating Imperial 'A' into fourth with the Brookes 'C' crew in fifth! And the Brookes 'E' crew came eighth, beating the lightweights and a heavyweight squad crew from Oxford University. This indicated a strength in depth that Brookes had been building for years, but had never shown quite so dramatically.

There is also a hint here as to how Brookes keeps so many rowers motivated in what was by now a large squad. Their men's 'E' crew won the 'Open Intermediate' pennant at Quintin. That categorisation of intermediate is based on no-one in the crew having won too many major events in the past. So you could be in that crew, only the fifth best at Brookes, yet still have some impressive wins to boast about on your sporting CV. And of course many of that boat, being relatively young and inexperienced, had aspirations to move up through the Brookes hierarchy.

But Grand glory was not to be, that year at least. On 16 March, the announcement came that many were fearing. The Boat Race and the Head of the River race, in fact, all British Rowing run events up to the end of April (initially) were cancelled. On 23 March, the first national lockdown was announced, we were into the routine of briefings from the Prime Minister and our health leaders, and debate around wearing masks, wiping down surfaces and so on.

The pandemic years (2020–22)

The Brookes team moved quickly. They identified the top rowers in the club, male and female, and called them together at the gym at Headington. At that time, the club had about 40 erg machines and a similar number of static bicycles. OK, said Spratley, take these home with you and keep training. Just one each please.

Parents were called on to supply the 'man (or woman) with a van (or Volvo)' service to bring the equipment back to homes all around the country, but again Spratley and Bailhache-Webb had shown their problem-solving capability. It wasn't ideal, but they would at least try and ensure rowers did not lose too much basic fitness. In retrospect it seems like an obvious step to take, but I wonder how many clubs actually did something like this?

Of course, none of us had any idea how long Covid was going to last. We hoped it might blow over in a month or two. But the next few months proved to be a write-off. Henley Royal Regatta was cancelled for the first time since World War Two. Spratley believes that without Covid, Brookes would have won the Grand that year, without the top crews that would have been preparing for Tokyo. But we will never know.

Henley 2021 – will it or won't it?

By the time the next academic year started in September 2020, we were into the period of somewhat chaotic changing restrictions, different rules in different parts of the UK and still much uncertainty. But students were in some cases allowed back to universities. Brookes had social distancing restrictions in the gym, but they could get some crews back on the water. 'But people kept getting Covid,' Spratley remembers, meaning that every time that occurred, others would have to quarantine for days.

Henry Bailhache-Webb wanted to strengthen his coaching team, despite the uncertain Covid situation. He called Chris Tebb, and it wasn't a long phone call. 'Chris, do you want to come and join us at Brookes?' As Tebb recalls, 'Basically, it was my dream job – I didn't have to think about my answer for too long.' Initially he took on responsibility for the novices 'learn to row' programme, but he was involved in wider coaching, and indeed it wasn't long before he was involved in the GB set-up, coaching boats to medals at international under-23 level from 2022 onwards.

For Brookes, there were also advantages in having top-class rowers within the club who were associated with the national squad. Because the Olympics of 2020 had been postponed, there were a number of dilemmas for the GB squad (more on that in Chapter 22. But the top 15 or so male rowers at Brookes, some of whom were no longer students, were by then receiving some sort of national lottery funding and were generally considered part of the 'Project Paris' group, rowers who would form the core of the GB squad for the next 2024 Olympics.

Brookes, along with the Leander Club, which was very strong for scullers and female rowers, were granted special exemption by the Department of Culture, Media and Sport via Brendan Purcell (British Rowing's Director of Performance) to 'train in a bubble', to start developing those potential Olympic rowers for Paris. In addition, there were a handful of top young British oarsmen who had finished their courses at US universities and were now back in the UK looking to pursue national level careers, but not actually in the Olympic squad. Brookes offered them a good home, and through the early months of 2021, training took place pretty much as normal, but with more river-based work and less gym.

The (London) Head of the River was cancelled again in March 2021, along with many other events. Bu the Boat Race went ahead in early April on the River Ouse rather than the Thames, and actually there were two excellent races, Cambridge winning both.

The pandemic years (2020–22)

In February 2021, the Stewards announced that Henley Royal Regatta would not go ahead on the planned dates of 29 June to 4 July. However, a move to Dorney Lake would be considered, or a later event at Henley. As Covid regulations relaxed somewhat, the Stewards announced on 29 March that there would be an event at Henley, but in early August rather than the first week of July. (The Stewards managed all of this process rather impressively, I would argue.)

Back at Brookes, cox Rory Cruickshank remembers a weird time, with much uncertainty. 'As we approached the first big competition for over a year, the universities championship (BUCS) in June, we weren't sure how we would perform against our rivals,' he remembers. 'We wondered whether different lockdown rules in Scotland might have helped Edinburgh manage a lot more work together. Or maybe another uni crew had all lived together for a year so they didn't have to distance and could train!'

But actually BUCS went very well for Brookes, the squad winning multiple championships events, men's and women's, and taking the overall Victor Ludorum prize. It didn't look like any other universities had stolen a march on the club through lockdown.

However, the changed date for Henley would limit the entry for several reasons. It would be straight after the delayed Tokyo Olympics, so not many of those top boats would want to compete again. Schools might find it difficult to field strong crews in the middle of the summer holidays, and Henley would also clash with the junior world championships. There would be less infrastructure and fewer spectators too, as numbers would be limited to allow some sort of social distancing (remember that?).

In the end, the event was a success. In fact, as a spectator, I absolutely loved it. No traffic jams, loads of space for picnics in the car park, room to move in the enclosure, not as much corporate hospitality as usual, less madness on the weekend evenings from the out-of-town party people. It was almost like the old days of Henley back in the 1980s, before it became so fashionable and commercialised.

Sir Steve Redgrave, Chair of the Stewards, also made the biggest decision in the history of the event – female guests and members would be allowed to wear trousers in the Stewards' Enclosure! The world stopped spinning on its axis momentarily, then life went on as usual. And the rowing wasn't bad either despite the lack of top crews, particularly the US contingent in some events.

Almost a tragedy

Overall, Henley 2021 was a tremendous event for Brookes. But one race almost took the shine off what was a record-breaking regatta for the club. In the Friday quarter final of the Temple Cup, Brookes was up against the Dutch university crew from the Triton club. As we've seen through the years, the Netherlands has excellent university rowing clubs, with Nereus and Triton the best known, providing many world championship and Olympic rowers for the successful Dutch national teams for decades the years.

Brookes led for the whole race, but Triton would not be shaken off. As the crews rowed past the enclosures, there was still less than a length in it. I remember watching from the grandstand when suddenly we realised something was wrong (and the video shows this very dramatically from above, courtesy of the drone). The stroke of the Brookes boat, Louis Nares, in his first year at Brookes, started being late on his stroke compared to the other rowers, then he missed an entire stroke, then another. As Triton charged up alongside and then past the Brookes boat, the stroke slumped forward and stopped rowing altogether just before the finishing line.

The cheers in the grandstand turned to shocked silence. What just happened, spectators asked each other. The medical launch raced to the Brookes boat as it drifted beyond the finishing line. It was there

The pandemic years (2020–22)

within seconds, and Nares was taken out of the boat, then back to the medical tent for treatment.

Later that afternoon, news spread that he was OK. It was 'only' exhaustion. Louis Nares had literally rowed himself to a standstill, but there were no signs of anything underlying to worry about. The entire Brookes contingent and every spectator breathed a sigh of relief. 'If you're going to row yourself to a standstill then Henley Royal is a pretty good place to do it,' as Row360 website put it.[31]

The aftermath was interesting. The brother of another crew member grabbed Bailhache-Webb and suggested rather aggressively that he never wanted to see Nares in the same boat as his brother ever again. But Bailhache-Webb knew that others in the crew hadn't worked as hard as they should throughout the whole race. If they had, perhaps their stroke man would not have exhausted himself quite so completely.

'If we had eight like Louis in the boat we would have won easily, I'm sure of it, and I'm never going to be disappointed in someone for trying too hard. His type of people are special and will come out on top once they learn to master their efforts'.

Now some old-school rowing coaches would have been in the same camp as the brother. They would not have been understanding or forgiving, and the collapse would have been the end of a promising rowing career. 'Couldn't hack it when the pressure was on,' would be the comment.

But although Spratley and Bailhache-Webb are tough men in many ways, they can also be thoughtful and empathetic. And we'll pick up the Louis Nares story later, because it does have a very happy ending.

There was also a lesson there for Bailhache-Webb. Coaches often tend to train with crews practicing flat-out rows over 1,000 or 1,500 meters. The assumption seems to be that if you are behind at that point in a 2,000-metre race, you've probably lost, and equally, if you are ahead, you can probably hang on for the last 60 strokes. But sometimes that theory goes wrong, and Bailhache-Webb vowed that training from now would be focused around the full 2,000 metres, or even 2,112 metres for Henley.

So, back to 2021. Whilst the Temple was disappointing, the rest of the regatta was a triumph for Brookes. Because of a shortage of crews in top events, there was a lot of 'doubling up' from the crews. The Visitors' fours event was won by Brookes for the first time since 2012, with four of the Ladies' Plate crew (Michael Glover, Lenny Jenkins, Oscar Lindsay and Matt Aldridge) winning that event. The Visitors' four were joined by Will Stewart, Matt Rowe, Jamie Axon, Seb Newman and cox Scott Cockle in the Ladies' Plate crew, but with just six entries for the Ladies, Brookes only had two races. The semi-final was yet another close and successful race against Leander, followed by an easy final victory over Moseley and Twickenham.

The icing on the cake was the victory in the Grand, the ultimate Henley event. That was the first time the Brookes name was seen on that trophy, although this was not a crew made up solely of rowers who had been through their student years at the University. It was really a GB squad 'development crew', with several rowers who had joined the squad, some returning from US universities, but based at Brookes and coached by Henry Bailhache-Webb.

The crew did include Henry Blois-Brooke, Sam Nunn, Sam Bannister and cox Harry Brightmore who were Brookes through and through, along with David Bewicke-Copley, Tom Digby, Oli Wilkes (a Brookes adopted son by now), David Ambler and Freddie Davidson. When Henley 2020 was cancelled, Blois-Brooke had decided to run seven marathons in seven days with a friend, and they raised £10,000 for the NHS. After that, the sessions on the erg presumably were a piece of cake. Brookes old boys Tarrant and Bolding also won the Silver Goblets pairs event, and a GB squad four won the Stewards, featuring Ambler, Wilkes, Nunn and Bannister from the eight.

The pandemic years (2020–22)

And the Brookes women (Kiera Allen, Beth Dutton, Taylor Caudle, Aisling Hayes, Isy Hawes, Jordan Simper, Daisy Bellamy, Harriet Ferguson and cox Elise Sanderson) triumphed over arch-rivals University of London (UL) in the very first rowing of the Island Challenge Cup for women's university eights. That was an excellent race, with UL leading at the Barrier and Fawley, getting about a length up at one stage, but Brookes powered through in the third quarter of the race. UL made a fight of it at the end, but Brookes held on to win by half a length. That legendary Brookes fitness and toughness, seen so often in the men's events, was now being shown by the women too.

The victorious inaugural Island Cup crew, 2021 (©*AllMarkOne*)

Oxford Brookes

However, there was some embarrassment for Brookes women. In the quarter final on Friday, the Brookes 'A' crew had come up against the Brookes 'B' crew. The umpire for that race decided that the 'B' crew had not raced flat out, which was deemed to be unfair – I assume because it made life easier for their top crew. The Stewards announced this:

> 'It is the judgement of the Committee of Management that in Race 65 on Friday 13 August, a heat of the Island Challenge Cup between their 'A' and 'B' crews, Oxford Brookes University Boat Club's conduct of the race was unsporting. The crews did not compete sufficiently for the outcome or verdict. This was, as a result, a breach of General Rule 42. Accordingly, Oxford Brookes University Boat Club has been given an Official Warning for unsportsmanlike conduct, with the effect that each crew remaining in the Regatta has been deemed to have caused a false start.'

Spratley and Bailhache-Webb were upset and embarrassed by this slap across the wrists from Sir Steve Redgrave and his colleagues. Most disappointing was the damage to the reputation of the club they were working so hard to build. It took the edge off winning the inaugural event, and was a lesson for everyone in the club. As the strength in depth of Brookes means their crews are coming up against each other more often in events, they really must make sure they provide a real race!

The 2024 Temple Challenge Cup Final

Henley Royal Regatta, 3.00pm, 7 July 2024

Race report – The 2024 Temple Challenge Cup Final
The Stewards have given this race one of the prime positions in the schedule, presumably because everyone loves a US versus UK battle, and everyone expects this to be close. The top Princeton crew has already beaten Cambridge to win the Ladies' Plate today. The bookies (if there were any) have this down as too close to call, particularly as this Princeton second varsity eight has the favoured Berks station.

Princeton actually takes a small lead off the start, and both crews sprint hard for the first minute. The Brookes crew are showing great timing in very choppy water, but Princeton holds onto the tiny lead. But as the crews approach Fawley, with both crews settled into mid-race pace of 36 strokes a minute, it looks like Brookes are just getting a few inches more per stroke out of their efforts. The Brookes cox is pushing over onto the Princeton station to minimise the stream effect. 'Get apart – we do not want to see a clash!' says commentator Jessica Eddie. But within a minute or so, Brookes has opened up a lead of almost a length.

The race is never in doubt after that point. Brookes looks very strong, says Dame Katherine Grainger on the commentary. 'Oxford Brookes, you are 200 metres away from winning the Temple Challenge Cup. Keep your heads, keep that power, move the hands, squeeze away …,' she says, moving into coaching mode.

Talking of coxes, you may remember the cox I met at Marlow regatta, Allie Bohenko, telling me that coxing in the UK was more aggressive than in the US? Bohenko is a slim, 1.6 m-tall blonde with a radiant smile, but don't let that fool you. In this race, she is vicious. She bullies the Princeton crew all the way down the course. She is constantly slipping over towards their station, not just to minimise the effect of the stream, but also once Brookes is ahead, she is aiming to

Oxford Brookes

send 'dirty water' from the Brookes oars down onto the blades of the Princeton crew. She is warned several times by the umpire, but she does seem to respond when she gets those warnings, if only in a pretty minimalist manner.

At the end of the race, the Princeton cox complains to the umpire, Sarah Winckless, who raises her red flag. We have a minute or two of concern, but she discusses the race with the other officials in the boat, and decides that Brookes has not strayed too far into Princeton's water or affected the outcome of the race. Good news for Bohenko, who could have gone from hero to villain very quickly.

The Princeton cox says Brookes was 'way over into our lane' and that interfered with their rowing. To me, biased though I am, it looked like Bohenko just about stayed legal, but she did push it to the limits and Spratley and Bailhache-Webb must have been nervous for a moment. But the white flag goes up, and Brookes has won the Temple for the third successive year and for the seventh time in the last ten competitions.

Chapter 21

The gym and training

'At Brookes, every training session has a point, a purpose. Every stroke, in every outing, has a purpose.' (Hugo Gulliver, OBUBC coach)

The Hall on the Hill

If you approach Headington Hill Hall from the bustling Headington Road, two miles west of Oxford city centre, it does not appear to be in any sense on a hill. Approaching in February 2024, I turned off the congested A420 and drove to the Hall through what appeared to be a building site. In fact, it *was* a building site. Oxford Brookes University was in the middle of a major construction programme in the grounds of the Hall, which the university bought in 1993 from Oxford Council. The 'hill' is more obvious from the other side of the Hall, where the land falls away through beautiful gardens towards the north and west.

The Hall was built around 1824, by the Oxford brewer James Morrell. The family occupied it for 114 years, then it was requisitioned for use as a military hospital in 1939. After the Second World War it was used as a rehabilitation centre, then in 1953, the Morrell family sold Headington Hill Hall to Oxford City Council for £13,700: this price included 37 acres of land, as well as its four lodges and outbuildings. Apparently 'there was applause in the council chamber when the purchase was announced'. That is not surprising. £13,700 in 1953 is around £320,000 today, so that seems like a very good deal for the council.

But Headington Hall has another place in history, through another tenant. The council originally planned to demolish the Hall, but in

1959 offered it on a 21-year lease instead. And the new occupier and soon-to-be resident? Robert Maxwell, then the owner of Pergamon Press and eventually fraudster, crook and terrible father. Initially he rented the estate purely as business premises for the Press, but soon he decided the house was to his liking and he moved in with wife Betty and eight children, moving the Press offices to the old stables.

Maxwell restored the house, spending a lot of his own money – or was it his pensioners' cash? In 1962, he negotiated an incredibly favourable fixed price lease, 75 years at £4,500 a year. You might wonder whether that deal was lubricated by some favours to councillors or officials, given just how good the terms were for him.

The years rolled on, Maxwell's sons and daughters went through a strange and dysfunctional childhood, and in 1991 his body was found in the sea after an emerging scandal around use of his company's pension funds. His business empire was declared bankrupt and at the end of 1992 Headington Hill Hall was advertised for sale by the council, with 14 acres of grounds, an annexe, a stable block, the lodge, and 50,000 sq. ft, of office buildings. That is when Brookes stepped in.

Blood, sweat and cheesy Techno

Drive up to the Hall now and, if it is after 4.30 pm, you have free parking in front of the main building if you are going to use the Sports Centre on the main campus, just over the Victorian wrought-iron footbridge which saves pedestrians from instant death on the A420. But on several evenings of the week, as you get out of your car, you might hear somewhat incongruous dance, pop or cheesy techno music coming from a building just beyond the car park. The evening I visited, Richard Spratley arrived just as I did, with his tiny dog, Rocky. 'My partner had to go out, so Rocky had to come with me'. Rocky has clearly had a long experience of rowing matters and behaves impeccably, and is clearly much loved by most of the squad.

The gym and training

So we follow the noise, climb a flight of steps and there is a long, low building overlooking the Hall – nothing fancy, perhaps technically a 'prefab', as we called them in my youth. But this is possibly the best high-performance rowing gym in the world. Step inside, and in the main room, there are about 40 erg machines and a similar number of static bikes. Next door, a large weights room is well equipped with a vast number of scary looking dumbbells and weights.

The first evening I visited, it was Thursday training. Two sessions, 4–6 pm and 6–8 pm. Athletes can choose which they attend, there is no booking system, but you are expected to be there for one or the other. Most rowers will complete three or four gym sessions a week, and on Thursdays, most will work on a 20/20/20/20 basis, alternating twenty-minute spells on the erg and the bikes.

'Over the years, we introduced more work on the bikes and less on the ergs to avoid back problems,' explains Richard Spratley. Rowers are famously susceptible to back problems, not surprisingly, so this was a sensible compromise. Bikes are fine for building cardio strength and resilience, although they do not develop the upper body muscles in the way that the ergs do.

So when we walked in, I was greeted by the sight of around 20 athletes on the bikes and maybe 40 young men and women on the ergs, all rowing in complete harmony at a low stroke rating – around 20

The athletes speak

'It's almost like training at the national team to be honest. The programme at Brookes has developed so much over the past decade under Henry Bailhache-Webb. It's extremely professional, competitive and has a very good culture.'

(*Rory Gibbs*, **HRR** and GB Olympic gold medal winner, from the Brookes website) strokes per minute. Looking at the individual machines, most seemed to be working at a 500-metre pace of around 1:50. At my fittest, I could have kept up with that for about two minutes (maybe …), whilst this group were, in effect, working at that pace for 80 minutes. Mind you, they are in the main a lot bigger than me, and significantly fitter and stronger than I could ever have dreamt of being.

Walking in on a session, you would immediately notice the mixed nature of the group. Here is a young American rower, 6 foot something and 90 kilos, doing his master's at Brookes – 'He will probably be in the Temple crew this year,' says Spratley. Next to him, a really quite petite dark-haired women – 'She's an Irish junior international sculler.' Obviously, they will be pulling with different levels of power, but all in perfect synchronicity. I don't know what the signal was, but at one point, everyone starts rowing with an exaggerated lean back at the end of the stroke. It is beautiful to watch.

The music is a mix of dance, techno, and a bit of Mumford and Sons. Clearly, a strong and clear beat helps, and the athletes take it in turns to choose the playlist. Some prefer motivational lyrics ('Lose Yourself' by Eminem is apparently a top erg favourite in the rowing community, along with 'Bodies' by Drowning Pool, which is well worth checking out). Others are only interested in the beat. I guess anyone choosing 1950s Belgian jazz or the greatest hits of Steps might not be popular. Actually, I take that back, I've just listened to '5,6,7,8' by Steps and it's probably a brilliant song for a workout. Perhaps I should offer to put together a playlist?

A substantial whiteboard on the wall lists the best times posted by the athletes – data from every individual session is recorded of course for the benefit of the coaches and the rowers. Some sessions might be a flat out 'how far can you row in 30 minutes', or it might be the 'best 5,000 metres at a set stroke per minute rating' ranking. In any case, that element of competition which is one of the foundations of Brookes' success comes through again. The athletes are working hard, but there is a sense of companionship and togetherness in the room, even though everyone is focused on their own fitness and strength.

Leaving the gym, Spratley and I walk back over the footbridge to the main Brookes campus. The sports centre is at hand, with more excellent facilities for gym work, and sports such as basketball or indoor cricket – some rather rapid female bowlers were practicing that evening. There is a bar and a café, and one of the main halls of residence, Cheney, is next door. Outside the centre, the famous minibuses are lined up neatly, ready for their hard work at the weekend ferrying the crews backwards and forwards to the boathouse.

'If new students are coming to Brookes and are going to row, I advise them to apply to live in Cheney,' says Spratley. Food is provided, they are 50 yards from the sports centre and the departure point for the boathouse minibuses, and 200 yards to the gym. Everything you need at hand. Life gets tougher after the first year when most students 'live out' in rented accommodation, but you might as well make your introduction to university life as pain-free as possible. And the more time and energy students have to work on their rowing, the faster those Brookes boats are going to go.

The Ergometer – an invention of cruel genius
The rowing machine or ergometer (the 'erg' to its friends) is one of the simplest and most beautiful instruments of torture ever invented. That is how many serious rowers feel about the machine on which they spend hours of their life every week, suffering in the name of fitness and strength.

Concept2 created the modern rowing machine in 1981. The simplicity of the machine is that it responds to the user's strength without the need for any adjustment. You don't need to set the speed or inclination as you do on a treadmill, or consider the resistance of the cross-trainer, or play with weights on a bar or a resistance machine. You just sit on the erg and pull. And if you want to go faster, you pull faster and harder. But the machine sets no limits. It is not like lifting where you do get to a point where you can't move the weights, or a running machine, which is positively dangerous if you increase its pace too far.

With the erg, your limit is when you throw up, pass out, or collapse. It is also probably the single best fitness machine invented because it exercises almost every part of your body. Arms, legs, back, stomach, even neck or ankles – an enormous range of muscles, tendons and ligaments get a work-out, as well as the heart and lungs of course. That means it is easy to underestimate how hard you have been working. In my own fairly pathetic attempts at exercising on the erg, I have gone from feeling reasonably comfortable to thinking I'm going to pass out in a very short space of time. A hard session and you really know you've been through it.

The erg has also revolutionised rowing. Before the ubiquitous machine appeared in every gym and boathouse, judging the relative performance or rowers was not easy. You could put them in small boats and race them against each other. But sculling is different from single oar 'sweep' rowing, and it was a lot of hassle to do enough swapping around to really see if James was stronger than Matt, or Fiona pulled harder than Savita.

The erg appeared to sweep away that confusion. Stick your people on the machine, time them for a 2,000 metre row (or several with intervals between if you were really cruel), or see how far they could travel in 10 minutes of flat out rowing. Test all your aspiring crew members, choose the strongest eight as defined by erg times, and you have your best crew. But is it really as simple as that? No, says Richard Spratley.

'Anyone who is selecting purely on the basis of the erg times needs their heads examining,' he says.

The gym and training

Of course the times are important. As we discussed in Chapter 16, kids are being signed up for lucrative scholarships at Berkeley, Washington and other US institutions, with erg times forming a major part of that decision-making. However, 'ultimately it is about what happens in the boat that matters. We do a lot of training in pairs, we move people around in different crews, and we see how rowers react to the pressure of actual racing,' Spratley says.

Rowing in a boat requires precision in when and how you put your blade into the water, how you take it out again, and how you do that in time with your other crew members. Making those movements consistently, with smoothness, so you don't unbalance the boat, but generating real power through the water, is the secret of effective rowing. But that sort of timing and synchronisation is not important really on the erg. The technique is also different. For instance, you don't have to worry about rotating your wrists on the erg, which clearly you do in a boat.

Phil Clapp of the UK held the world record for the 500 metres erg for some years. He is 207 cm tall (6 ft 9 in) and weighs around 122 kg (19 stone). He did row as a young man, but decided to focus on the erg later. Presumably that was because his size and power meant he could really unbalance a boat if he was anything less than technically perfect.

I remember coxing a boat which included a young man who was probably the most powerful, and was certainly the fittest, in our crew. If only he could have learnt to put his blade in the water at approximately the same time as the seven others, he would have been unstoppable. (His sculling technique was interesting too, as he moved quickly but often in a somewhat circular fashion …) In fact, the stronger and bigger the rower, the greater their potential to upset the boat if they are not synchronised and co-ordinated in their movements.

So the strongest, toughest exponents of the erg are not necessarily Olympic rowers in the making. But at longer distances, the record holders include some serious professional rowers. Matthew Pinsent, Mo Sbihi and now Tom George are the monsters of GB squad erg history. But at the erg sprint distances, athletes who are super-powerful, but might be disruptive in an actual boat, can do very well. And there are examples of athletes who are not top of the erg charts but simply seem to make the boat travel faster.

However, performance on the erg is not a bad indicator of potential for rowing excellence, and it has also proved a great tool for getting youngsters interested and identifying talent. The GB rowing team has done that effectively, with future gold-medal winners such as Mo Sbihi being identified through programmes that get youngsters to try out on ergs at local or school-based events.

Brookes certainly train long and hard on the machines. Seeing 40 of their athletes working away in the gym in sync on ergs is an impressive and somewhat terrifying sight. It is an important part of the overall training programme, even more so when bad weather makes rowing on the river impossible. The Brookes winter training programme has undoubtedly given the club a squad as fit as any in the world, up there with a handful of international squads with full-time athletes.

Outside the world of serious sport, there is a movement to make indoor rowing more user-friendly. You can now row through beautiful landscapes, or compete against your friends with a similar model to Peloton for cycling. But in the world of serious rowing, it is still largely about the pain, and the outcomes, rather than enjoyment, no matter how good the background music might be.

(Not) messing about on the river

Gym training at Headington Hill Hall takes place on Monday, Tuesday and Thursday, usually one weights session and two on the machines. Training on the river takes place on Wednesday, Saturday and Sunday. It is highly structured, everything is planned and measured, and it is

The gym and training

basically pitched at a professional athlete level of intensity. Everybody follows the same programme, whichever boat you are in.

On the river, all the men's and the women's boats will usually go out together, although obviously it takes a while to get every boat launched onto the river. If there are seven men's boats rowing, they will split into two groups with a coaching launch for each. A session on the river tends to be around 90 minutes, with a mix of exercises and long-steady state pieces of work, often executed with a low rating but high power.

Both in the gym and on the river, the focus is impressive. Not a stroke is wasted, not a minute in the gym is wasted. Bailhache-Webb is not a fan of exercises that involve only half the crew (or even fewer) rowing. That was a typical start to the outing back in the days when I coxed – get the bow pair to row, then maybe half the crew and build up to the whole eight.

'Why would you do that? Waste the first ten per cent of the time you've got on the water doing something that doesn't involve everyone? Pointless,' explains Bailhache-Webb in his usual direct fashion.

There isn't a lot of shouting from the coaches during a session on the river and it's quite hard to hear coaches from the boat anyway. But telemetry provides data about every individual's performance. The cox in each boat can see minute by minute how hard each rower is working, and can identify any who are not up to their usual standard.

There is no hiding place these days. When I coxed, the size of the 'puddles' created by each rower was the only clue I had really as to how hard each individual was working. Not quite the same as real-time digital information direct from each blade. Of course, data can be analysed later as well as in real time, and individual coaching offered.

There is a lot of side-by-side rowing for the crews, often at relatively low stroke ratings but pretty much full power. It is not racing, but there is an element of competitive pressure (remember the fridge magnet)? Bailhache-Webb also has interesting and critical views on how some crews train, up to and including national-level crews. His approach is very much individual focused rather than crew based.

'Let's say you target an Olympic gold medal in the eight, and you know over 2,000 metres you need to row about a 5 minute 20 second race to do that. So you do a full practice, and it's timed at 5 minutes 18. So the temptation is to say right, that was a great row, well done, remember how you did it, let's go out and do it again.'

But that approach is flawed, he thinks. 'I don't want to know simply that the boat went fast this time. I want to focus on each individual. Maybe a couple of people had an exceptional row that they are unlikely to repeat every time. Four performed to their own target level and two were actually disappointing. I want to focus on those two, and talk about what happened and how we can address that. It's the individual focus that makes the boat go faster in the end.'

> **The athletes speak**
> 'The coaches at Brookes emphasise that they're not always going to be there to hold your hand. *You* have the power to decide how well you're going to row today.'
> (*Sam Sheppard*, HRR winner, now Brookes Assistant Coach)

And talking of the Olympics, the 2021 event highlighted some of the reasons Brookes has succeeded as it has. Unfortunately, that evidence was provided by the GB rowing squad's extremely disappointing performance at the Games.

Chapter 22

The Tokyo Olympics

'We come away from Tokyo, £27 m of investment in British Rowing, with one silver and one bronze. At a time when the national budget is under pressure from so many different areas, is that a good return on investment?' (Olympic winner James Cracknell, from The Guardian newspaper, 30 July 2021)[32]

The Olympics catches Covid

The Covid-19 pandemic turned everything upside down. It hit European countries in early 2020, with the Olympic Games due to be held in Tokyo that summer. But on March 2020, the postponement of the Games by exactly one year was announced. By that point, few were surprised, but it caused chaos for athletes, coaches and administrators. For many, their whole life was built around peaking in July 2020, but suddenly, they had to re-focus on a point a year away.

Rowing was no exception, and when the Olympic regatta did come around in July 2021, it was a disaster for the GB team. The nation went from topping the medals table in rowing at Rio 2016 to fourteenth in Tokyo, with just one silver and one bronze to show for the investment of around £30 million in the sport between the Olympics. Whilst the team was unlucky in the sense that there were six boats that finished fourth, just outside the medals, it was not a success, whichever way you looked at it.

Ch-ch-ch-ch-changes …

Much of the rowing inquest after Tokyo focused on the departure of Jürgen Grobler. The postponement of the event had caused a specific headache for British Rowing, the body that oversees the sport. Grobler, one of the most successful rowing coaches of all time, was in place as Chief Coach for the 2020 Olympics, with an understanding that he would retire after that event. But in August 2020, it was announced that he was retiring from British rowing with immediate effect. A year later he joined the French rowing federation.

As chief coach for the men's squad, and latterly for the women's as well, Grobler coached the greats of British rowing and was behind gold medal winning crews at every Olympics from 1992 to 2016. At the time of his resignation, he said this[33]:

> 'This has been a hard and difficult decision, but British Rowing has big plans for Paris 2024, and we want to organise it now to give the GB Rowing Team the best chance of success. I can't commit for the next four years so I have resigned in order to let everything start now.'

But not everybody was convinced matters were quite so simple. Let's go back and look at how exactly the story of Tokyo unfolded for British Rowing.

After the success of Rio in 2016, most of the top British rowers of both sexes retired from the sport. That allowed a range of potential excuses after the Tokyo disaster, but some comments justifying the poor results were simply not accurate. UK Sport Chief Executive Sally Munday described the rowers as 'relatively young' and 'probably the youngest' squad in the past 20 years. In fact, the squad was the second oldest of recent GB Olympic squads and older than most other national squads at Tokyo. The team was, however, relatively inexperienced at Olympic level. Whilst the talent pipeline from clubs such as Oxford Brookes and Leander was strong, results at the 2017 and 2018 world

The Tokyo Olympics

championships were not the best for GB, so there were some early warnings. But arguably, there should have been time to rebuild.

Sir David Tanner was the Performance Director for British Rowing from 1996, after a successful career as a rowing coach and a teacher. He retired in 2017, and in the recruitment process for his successor, British Rowing emphasised the need to build a 'contemporary culture'. That indicated a feeling at board level, presumably some of it coming from athletes, that the coaching ethos was leaving the organisation open to claims of bullying.

After a recruitment process, Brendan Purcell joined as Director of Performance. He had previously been in a similar role for the GB Triathlon team. His appointment raised a few eyebrows, as it wasn't clear that he knew anything much about rowing or even had any deep interest in the sport. The GB success in Triathlon had come mainly from two exceptional brothers, the Brownlees, and it was not clear how much of their success was really down to Purcell.

The logic of his appointment was that someone with skills in developing high performance in one sport could apply that to another. But rowing was a much bigger job than triathlon, with four times the budget and 41 athletes competing at Tokyo against 5 in triathlon. And, personally, it feels like having a decent understanding of the sport in question would be pretty vital.

There were also rumours that Sir Steve Redgrave and Greg Searle, multiple Olympic winners, were interested in the job. It seems that the desire to change the culture led British Rowing to the conclusion that there really needed to be a new broom, someone from outside who could take a different approach on the people side of things in particular. However, it is hard to argue now that Purcell was a good appointment. He also did not impress many of the top club coaches in their early meetings with him.

Paul Thompson coached the women's squad to great success in London and Rio, where GB topped the medals table for women's rowing. But he was a controversial figure too. A former GB athlete, Emily Taylor, accused him of being a 'massive bully' and, according to the BBC[34] she said, 'He is fantastic technically, but in terms of people-management, his skills are non-existent.' An internal review cleared Thompson, but maybe this furore was in part behind his decision to leave in late 2018.

The decision was then made to make Grobler responsible for the women's squad as well as the men's, but in a less hands-on role than he had previously taken. But this was a huge net loss of expertise and experience. British Rowing had effectively swapped Thompson and Tanner, two hugely experienced and successful rowing coaches and managers, for Purcell, who knew nothing about the sport. Other established leaders in the British Rowing set-up were also lost, either leaving or through redundancy, such as Dr Mark Hoker, Head of High-Performance Science & Medicine.

Grobler's additional responsibilities might have over-stretched even a man of his experience and ability. There is an insightful analysis from Tom Ransley (an ex-GB oarsman himself) on the Row360 website,[35] an excellent resource, and, along with Junior Rowing News, the essential websites for GB and wider rowing aficionados. Published in October 2021, Ransley's article contains interesting quotes from various athletes, and some certainly felt that Grobler was now overstretched. There were also questions about Purcell's relationship with Grobler, which was never going to be as instantly successful as the long-standing Grobler/Tanner partnership.

Culture change – it ain't easy

It seems that Purcell's attempts to change the culture did not pay off. Henry Fieldman, who coxed the men's eight at Tokyo said, 'The set up

The Tokyo Olympics

was being terraformed into something very different, but the reasoning was unclear.'

Purcell also created selection panels.[36] He said, 'The appointment of external selectors is an important step in our plan to move decision making closer to each crew by giving more autonomy to the respective lead coaches.'

But this certainly seems to take power away from the coach of each boat rather than bringing 'more autonomy'. How can someone who isn't watching the crews, day in and day out, make sensible selection decisions? Do they base it purely on the erg scores? We've already discussed Richard Spratley's views on this.

After the Tokyo Olympics, where the Chinese squad he coached outperformed the GB team, Sir Steve Redgrave said this to the Chinese press in terms of the GB disappointment: 'But if you bring in systems and selection panels that we had in the 1970s and 1980s, you must expect results like we had in the 1970s and 1980s. I'm just stating facts: we've changed our system in the last year, and suddenly we've gone from being one of the best nations to being nearer down the other end.'

Coming back to Grobler, and in the summer of 2020, it appeared that British Rowing decided they would only allow Grobler to carry on for Tokyo in 2021 if he signed up to stay on for Paris 2024. It seems extraordinary that this was just 11 months from the start of the Tokyo event. If that was a real non-negotiable position, why hadn't it been tabled much earlier?

However, just before the 2024 Olympics, Grobler was interviewed by the Daily Telegraph and suggested that wasn't the real story.[37] He talked of being demoted, being offered the role of coach of just the men's eight. 'They said we don't want to have a chief coach anymore. Every coach is now a chief coach. You know, [in] which business do you have no leader? It was a little bit funny. I feel just sorry for the athletes ... It was unclear, who was leading? Who makes the decisions? Should the coaches now fight against each other?'

All of this paints a picture of huge change in and around the rowing squad. Then, in December 2020, just seven months before the Olympics, there was another change, with the introduction of four 'lead Olympic coaches' – James Harris for women's sweep, Steve Trapmore leading men's sweep, Paul Reedy overseeing women's sculling, and Paul Stannard in the lead for men's sculling.

These were respected coaches but as an outsider, this sounds like a recipe for chaos, with coaches at boat level, lead coaches, selection panels ... In Ransley's excellent article, he reports Fieldman again saying that there were arguments between the coaches about who would use the gym and when. Clearly, squabbling individual boats and coaches is no way to run a motivated, coherent team, and is a stark contrast to how Brookes works as a single club.

Christian Felkel also stepped down around this time as the coach of the men's coxless four, a gold-medal winning boat for GB at the previous four Olympics. We don't know whether his decision was related to the new lead coach approach, but we might guess.

So, the Tokyo Olympics eventually rolled around, with limited spectators. One analysis of GB performance suggests the squad was actually successful, but desperately unlucky. Having so many boats in their finals was a good performance, and seeing no less than six crews finishing fourth in their race, just outside the medals, could be seen as just unfortunate. But only the men's eight, with a bronze medal, and the men's quad sculls, with a silver, brought home the metal.

The multiple fourth places factor is interesting. As opposed to the bad luck theory, it might suggest that crews were good enough to be competing for the medals, but somehow just lacked that final one per cent, a second or two over the course, to turn them into medal winners. It certainly looks like the performance was not optimised, or those tiny incremental gains were missed.

It is also worth saying that not everyone regretted Grobler's departure, which many observers blamed for the poor results. After Tokyo, Josh Bugajski, who had won a silver medal in the men's eight, took aim at the ex-coach. He accused him of favouritism and of causing mental and physical suffering amongst the team.[38]

'I will admit (Jurgen) is a good coach to some people, but there were people that he seemed to take a disliking to, and what he did to them was destroy them, destroy their soul, destroy everything … He had complete power. If you didn't get selected for a boat, your funding is never going to go up. I was pretty much broke for a year, my relationships suffered, my friendships suffered.'

However, Grobler in his 2024 interview described Bugajski as 'not a team player' and said, 'A team has to fit and I don't know if he really did the eight good.'

Under Purcell, there was more focus on crew well-being. But some Olympians were scathing about this. Olympic gold-winning cox and rowing commentator Gary Herbert said he didn't mind the squad 'singing Kumbaya and making daisy chains', but could they please return their millions of lottery funding to the taxpayer if that was their focus. But there is no doubt that mental health in high-performance sporting settings is an important issue, and one that is not considered enough.

Will it make the boat go faster?

Rowing is a pretty brutal sport. The best athletes push themselves to the very brink, encouraged by their coaches. Getting the balance right between that determination, gruelling hard work and pain on the one hand, and the need to remain in a positive mental and physical state, is key. Matthew Syed, ex-table tennis star and now a successful and thought-provoking writer, wrote in *The Sunday Times* in 2024 about the balance between anxiety and performance amongst athletes.[39] He felt that a certain amount of what might be seen as imperfect 'mental health' was unavoidable if you wanted top performance. Maybe the 2021 Olympic rowing squad didn't get this quite right.

Anyway, after Tokyo, Mark Davies, the chair of British Rowing, announced a review into the performance of the team. In October 2021, Andy Parkinson, Chief Executive of British Rowing resigned, followed shortly afterwards by Brendan Purcell, who stepped down, a decision made by 'mutual consent'. Purcell went off to coach GB canoeists; he was an athlete in that sport himself, so perhaps he will have a happier time there.

Deputy Director of Performance Pathways and Paralympic Programme, Louise Kingsley, took over as interim Director of Performance, and in December 2021 after an open recruitment process, she was appointed to the role permanently. Christian Felkel returned as Technical Efficiency Specialist coach in 2022.

Since then, the GB squad performance has steadily improved and world championships results have been good. Richard Spratley and Henry Bailhache-Webb are diplomatic when it comes to views on the Purcell era, but now have a good relationship with Kingsley and other coaches, including the highly regarded High Performance Coach, Steve Trapmore.

So what can we learn from the story of rowing at the GB 2021 Olympics? How about these headlines.

- Effective change management is difficult – whether it is structures, processes or people, it is just not simple, and has to be executed carefully and professionally.
- In elite sport, coaches really do matter and continuity certainly helps, as we can see from the Brookes story.

The Tokyo Olympics

- The balance between driving top performance and athletes' mental health is a tricky one. Athletes respond differently to motivational techniques, so arriving at the 'best' approach for a crew is difficult. The best coaches are flexible and learn quickly to handle different athletes in different ways.
- As in any walk of life, clarity in terms of responsibilities is key. If no-one really knows who is in charge, you have a problem.
- GB Rowing leaders should be clear whether the 'squad' is a collection of individual boats, or a genuine 'team', and set up structures and processes accordingly.

There are two other big questions. Firstly, how would Oxford Brookes have done at the Olympics? Their eight (which did include some GB squad oarsmen who had not studied at Brookes, but were training there) won the Grand at Henley in 2021, but without much serious opposition. Four of that Brookes boat went on to form the GB coxless four at the Paris Olympics. Three others rowed in the GB Paris eight. Perhaps there should have been a 'practice' at Caversham, a couple of months before the Olympics, with the Brookes crew racing against the GB squad eight. That would have been a fascinating exercise.

Secondly, how would GB have performed if Spratley or Bailhache-Webb had been in Purcell's role? Understandably, they didn't want to comment on the topic, and we will never know, but it is an interesting thought.

Chapter 23

Brookes' *annus mirabilis* (2023)

'Save some for everyone else, won't you Brookes? ... This Regatta represents one of the single greatest performances from one boat club in the history of our sport.' (Tom Morgan, founder of Junior Rowing News website, 3 July 2023)[40]

A year of rebuilding

After the heroics of Henley 2021, it was back to Headington and Cholsey for some rebuilding and searching for the next generation of Brookes stars. The final lockdown laws were rescinded in July 2021, and the club lost a number of the top rowers to the GB squad, with operations getting back to normal post-Covid. Henley in July 2022 still did not have quite the full pre-Covid contingent of US universities, but the regatta was moving back towards full strength. Corporate hospitality was back too, unfortunately, but there was plenty of excellent racing.

We've seen through this story that the Temple Challenge Cup holds particular significance for Brookes, demonstrating as it does that your pipeline of new athletes is strong. The Prince Albert Challenge Cup for coxed fours is similar, in that athletes who have already won at a high level are not eligible. Brookes had never won both in the same year, having focused mainly on the Temple and putting the best of their relatively inexperienced rowers in a Temple crew. But in 2022, the quality of the programme and resulting strength in depth the club had built really came through.

At Henley, Jack Prior, Louis Nares (who had collapsed the previous year), Blaise Ivers-Dreux, Marco Tognazzi and cox Amie Jones took the Prince Albert after beating University of California Berkeley in

Brookes' *annus mirabilis* (2023)

another of the great HRR Brookes races. The way Bailhache-Webb prepared the crew for that race demonstrated his tactical nous and ability to motivate the crew – more on that later.

If you watch the video of the race, the interview afterwards is interesting too.[41] The crew talk very sincerely about the support from other Brookes athletes and supporters along the course. 'We appreciate every single person that turned up to cheer us on, we're really grateful. This victory is for them as well.' That's the Brookes spirit showing up again.

The Temple was a totally new crew with limited Henley experience, comprising Odhran Donaghy, Matt Heywood, Toby Lassen, Ben Hinves, Connor Mcgillan, Jens Hullah, Jake Wincomb and Miles Devereux, with cox Will Denegri. They beat old rivals University of London and Triton on their way to the final, before coming up against another long-standing rival, the University of Washington. Washington led by about half a length by the Barrier, but in the third minute of the race, Brookes just moved into another gear. Over the next two minutes or so, they put in a devastating spurt, taking two lengths from the American crew. After that, the result was never in doubt, and Brookes cruised home four lengths ahead.

The presence of Brookes alumni in GB squad boats was the norm by now, and a GB crew won the blue-riband eights event, the Grand, featuring well-known names from the UBUBC hall of fame – Gibbs, Bolding, Bewicke-Copley and Digby this time. But 2022 was really notable for that achievement of the Temple and Prince Albert double, the first time that had ever been achieved by a university, and another large feather in the OBUBC cap.

Moving into the 2022/23 season, and another strong crop of freshers arrived. All though the season, results were impressive, from the Head of the River, to Duisburg, where Brookes women beat Dutch and German national 'development' crews. A trip to the San Diego Crew

Oxford Brookes

Classic in California was a first, and Brookes men lost narrowly to the Berkeley crew that had home water advantage, but beat the Canadian national eight. Dominant displays at Marlow and Met regattas and the University championships followed, and the women carried off the double at Henley Women's Regatta, winning both the championship and academic eights, the first club to ever achieve that.

That all set up the club nicely for Henley, and what turned out to be an amazing few days for Brookes.

Henley, 2023 – the Temple

Several race reports have been littered throughout this book, and Brookes had an amazing regatta, with seven crews (including two GB boats with a Brookes contingent onboard) reaching their event final.

It was however unusual to see so many obviously non-British names in Brookes boats. In the Temple crew, along with Louis Nares, Sam Sheppard, Max Mills, Marco Tognazzi, fresher Fergus Woolnough and cox Tom Bryce, there were three Dutch rowers: Pim Mattijssen, Hessel van Vilsteren, and Nykle Krijgsveld.

They were three friends from Dutch universities, but not from the rowing powerhouses of Nereus and Triton. They decided to come to Brookes to do postgraduate study 'to get the Brookes rowing experience', Spratley explains. Well, they had a pretty good experience.

It's interesting in that context to hear Spratley say that the Temple and Island are the number one objectives for Brookes every year. Why is that? There may be a touch of nostalgia, given the Temple was the first event Brookes won at HRR. Now the club has an incredible record, winning it at six of the last nine Henleys, so there is definitely a desire to keep building on that record. But most relevantly, these student events are an indicator of the current *and* future health of the club.

If you consider the crews that rowed for Brookes at HRR in 2023, the rowers in the Grand and Stewards, two of the very top events, and the Ladies' Plate, all contained men who started their Brookes journey in a Temple crew. Rory Gibbs, for instance, rowed in the winning Temple crew in 2016, moved on to winning crews in the Ladies', won the Grand with Brookes in 2022 and won it again in the GB national eight (rowing as 'Brookes and Leander') in 2023.

So the Temple crew provides the raw material for all the more 'senior' crews in the club. But that doesn't mean it is full of recent novices or first year students. Louis Nares, who stroked the 2023 crew, had already rowed at Henley four times at that point.

But there are some other more personal reasons for the focus. In terms of the Temple, the years between 1995 and 2006 were a fallow spell for Brookes in that event. Several near misses litter the record, including in 2001 and 2002. Chief coach Bailhache-Webb was a member of the Brookes Temple crew in those years, and on both occasions the crew felt they had a good chance of winning. And both years, they were beaten in the final by a Harvard Crew. 'That really didn't feel good,' he remembers clearly, even 20 years later.

A chance for revenge was provided in 2023. There was a strong entry from US universities, and in the quarter-final Brookes came up against Harvard. Now Bailhache-Webb is not the most loquacious man in the world, but at the appropriate time, he can turn it on. Sam Sheppard, who rowed in the 2 seat in the Brookes Temple boat, remembers his pre-race speech to the crew as they prepared to set off to the start.

'Harvard used to be the daddies in the Temple. I know, I lost to them. Twice. And it hurt. But they're not the best now. They're not the daddies. We're the best, we're in charge. You've got this, go out there and crush them.'

Was this really motivational, I asked Sam? 'Damn right it was! You always pay attention to anything Henry says, but this was memorable.' Even talking to Bailhache-Webb today, you can feel the passion and the frustration around those losses when he was in the boat, but he feels a

Oxford Brookes

lot better these days since several crews he coached have taken their revenge on Harvard.

In the Temple, Brookes progressed onwards, culling two other US universities (Washington and the Princeton 'B' crew) on their way to the final. Princeton 'B' was not an easy task, as it was the fastest lightweight crew in the US that year. But just for good measure, the Oxford Brookes 'B' crew, also competing in the Temple, beat Princeton 'A'. (We can assume the word 'Brookes' was not uttered too positively during Princeton's end of year boat club dinner.) Washington in the semi-final was a big threat, but the Brookes crew was magnificent – 'The best we rowed all year,' remembers Sam Sheppard. Brookes 'B' lost in a close race to Syracuse in the semi-final, so that meant no all-Brookes final, which was probably good news for spectators. Such races never really have the flavour of a real two-club tussle.

Temple winners at Henley 2023 greeted by Brookes fans! (©*AllMarkOne*)

Brookes' *annus mirabilis* (2023)

In the Brookes stroke seat was Louis Nares, the young man who collapsed within sight of the finishing line in 2021. As the crews lined up for the final of the Temple in 2023, there must have been some slight nervousness in the crew and amongst the coaches. If the race was tight again, and Syracuse really pressed, what might happen? But there were no issues this time, as Nares and his crew held firm, never looking like losing. Brookes cruised home without too much trouble. (More on that race on page 91.)

In July 2023, a month on from Henley, Louis Nares became an under-23 world champion in the GB eight that won in Plovdiv and, in June 2024, he was selected for his full international debut. (That's even before we get to Henley 2024.) It is all quite a redemption for him, and a great story for any young athlete to remember.

Henley 2023 – Brookes triumphant

Brookes also featured in the finals of the Island, the Prince Albert, the Ladies' Plate, the Visitors', and (with their alumni rowing in GB squad boats) the Grand and the Stewards'.

As well as the Temple, the exciting Island (page 119), Ladies' (page 64) and Prince Albert (page 35) races have been covered in race reports. Brookes won all seven finals, making it the best ever day for the club and one of the outstanding club performances over the 200 years of the Regatta's history.

Not all finals were close though. The Brookes crew in the Stewards' was the GB international four, World Champions and probably the fastest coxless four in the world. Although all four had historical links with Brookes, most of the year they rowed with the GB squad as professional athletes at Caversham, near Reading. But for a few major events, including Henley, Oli Wilkes, David Ambler, Matt Aldridge and Freddie Davidson could return to row as a Brookes crew.

But as you might expect, not too many other crews fancied their chances against this boat. I suspect there were behind the scenes negotiation with the Stewards, who run the Regatta, desperately trying to get someone else to enter. I can imagine Sir Steve Redgrave saying to a few other good crews, 'Come and row, you never know, Brookes might have a bad day, steer into the booms, and you could win a HRR blue-riband event.' To which the response was generally, it seems, 'Thanks, we will take our chances in the Visitors', which we might actually win!'

So Thames finally did the decent thing for the sake of the Regatta's credibility, and entered two crews in the event, making three entries in total. The Thames crews raced each other in the one and only semi-final with Brookes being given a bye to the final. Not surprisingly Thames 'A' beat Thames 'B' comfortably, so today the 'A' crew was up against Brookes. Thames are all previous Henley winners, but they are not a current peak performance crew. I suspect they got together just to come and have some fun at Henley. As expected, Brookes won comfortably.

The Visitors' is the intermediate event for coxless fours and attracts entries for clubs and universities. Brookes was up against familiar foes, Leander, here. The Leander crew was very strong, including Calvin Tarczy who was a member of the 'fastest schoolboy crew ever', the St Paul's 2018 eight. But Brookes, in the shape of Toby Lassen, Ben Hinves, Jonathon Cameron and Jack Prior, had a strong pedigree too.

Brookes held a slight lead for much of the race, but it was close. However, as the boats reached the enclosures, Leander's steering suddenly went awry, usually a sign of some tension or tiredness in the crew, and they veered towards the middle of the course. It might have been a steering issue or perhaps one rower lost power, causing the problem.

The umpire warned the Leander crew, and their steersman then over-responded, pulling on the rudder too hard, which moved them

The Brookes Henley winners, 2023 (©*AllMarkOne*)

The Brookes coaches – Hugo Gulliver, Chris Tebb,
Henry Bailhache-Webb, Richard Spratley (©*AllMarkOne*)

Oxford Brookes

away from the Brookes boat, but reduced boat speed, as hard steering always will. That was really the end of the race but the final margin of one and three-quarter lengths made it sound easier than it was.

The Grand was a similar story. The problem is that really, there are only in any given year half a dozen eights in the world who row at the very top level. More and more countries focus their attention on fewer, often smaller, boats now (pairs and fours), with the Olympics dominating the thinking. The investment needed to run a top-class programme is significant, so some countries decide that concentrating their best handful of rowers in a four or a pair might be a better bet than going for the eights, prestigious though that is.

That means there are fewer potential international entries for the Grand, and the top US universities nowadays tend to go for the Ladies' Plate, whereas they used to be regular Grand winners or at least serious contenders.

The other issue is that once a really top crew has entered, others may decide not to bother risking their reputation and interrupting training to go against them, as we saw in 2021, when international crews were either exhausted after the Tokyo Olympics or scared of their likely loss to Brookes.

Anyway, at least there were two international crews. The GB squad, pretty much half Brookes rowers (with Rory Gibbs, Morgan Bolding, Tom Digby, and cox Harry Brightmore) and half Leander, was badged, not unreasonably, as Oxford Brookes and Leander. Up against them was the Canadian national eight, not a bad crew but not really in the very top flight.

Meanwhile the GB boat set the fastest ever time by a British eight in a heat at the World Cup race in Varese on 23 June, winning by a mile (in international rowing terms). Sure enough, the GB boat won here comfortably, but ex-Brookes cox Harry Brightmore provided some excitement. Rowing on the Bucks station, furthest from the riverbank

Brookes' *annus mirabilis* (2023)

and therefore suffering from more stream working against the boat, he consistently edged over towards the Berks station.

GB was far enough ahead to avoid interfering with the Canadians, but the umpire spent half the race gesticulating that Brightmore should move back. Brightmore generally ignored him apart from a couple of token gestures, moving a few feet before slipping back to the centre of the course again. I guess that's what makes him a top international cox.

Winning both men's student events, the eights and the four, was a great achievement, but to combine that with winning the two intermediate events, the Ladies' and the Visitors', was unique in Henley's history. If the University of Washington or Harvard brought their full squad over to Henley, might they have been able to do something similar? We don't know, but that strength in depth that Brookes has developed over the last 20 years looked world-leading at Henley 2023.

It was an extraordinary day for Brookes, and we all thought that Henley 2023 would forever be remembered as 'Brookes' Year'. But of course, we didn't know what would happen in 2024 …

Chapter 24

What makes Brookes special?

*'Racing is about producing the best possible performance when under pressure.'
(Henry Bailhache-Webb)*

As we're close to the chronological end of the story (for now, anyway), let's attempt to explain just *how* Brookes has achieved this transformation. What has enabled the club to catch up and overtake all the best UK university and non-university boat clubs, with the possible exception of Leander, the only rival for the title of 'top club in the UK'? Brookes now also outperforms pretty much all the top US universities in terms of strength in depth, despite receiving only a fraction of the funding. How has this been achieved? We have discussed some aspects such as recruitment in detail already, but there are other interesting factors to consider.

Racing and winning – preparing the crew

The Brookes philosophy around getting the most out of every athlete is clear. That applies when it comes to racing too. Spratley and Bailhache-Webb both appear to get a particular kick out of occasions when a Brookes crew beats a rival that on paper looks 'better' – perhaps better erg times, or more experienced, international rowers.

Without a doubt, that is in part down to the analysis and planning that goes into each major race, and the way the Brookes crews are prepared psychologically. As Bailhache-Webb says, 'It is all about helping the crew produce the best possible performance when under pressure.' Winning seven out of seven finals at Henley 2023, and (spoiler alert) six out of

What makes Brookes special?

seven in 2024, suggests that when crews are pretty evenly matched, Brookes comes out on top more often than randomness would predict.

One of the most interesting comments from Bailhache-Webb was this. 'I tell the crews that we should be thankful for the opposition, and the better they are, the more thankful we should be – because they will make us row better.' I also heard him tell the crews before the Head of the River race in 2024 that 'it is fine to be nervous. That's good, it makes us row better.'

That is brilliant psychology. Don't be scared you are up against the best in the world. Be grateful, and a little bit nervous, because they are going to spur you on to be the best you can be (another Brookes mantra). The coaches prepare crews to stay calm and enjoy the process of rowing, and every race has a focused mindset. If it is an early round, where Brookes is the strong favourite to win, use that race to test the process, to prepare for later rounds. But keep that purpose in every stroke – don't get a two-length lead then just switch off, keep improving down the course.

Based on watching many Brookes races, it certainly appears that the crews focus on their own performance. Of course they are conscious of the opponent, but they seem to row to a plan unless something very unexpected happens. The recording of cox Rory Copus in the 2014 Temple race (see page 141) showed this perfectly. The other crew, where they are, or what they are doing, is barely mentioned by Copus.

It also looks like Brookes are masters of pacing. You rarely see them blast into a big lead then find the opposition coming back at them, until maybe right at the end if the race is clearly won and inevitably rowers ease off a touch. You often see other crews following a plan which relies on grabbing the lead then hanging on for grim death. There is a basic problem with that approach, which relates to human capability. Look at it this way.

Suppose I can run 5k in 20 minutes at a steady pace, a pretty decent 'fun runner' time. My coach has a suggestion. Why don't I do the first

2.5k in a faster pace, covering it in 8 minutes, then I can relax and take 12 minutes for the next 2.5k, achieving the same time overall?

The problem is this. Even if I can achieve that 8 minutes for the first half, I will be absolutely shattered by the end of it. It won't be a case of taking it slightly easier for the rest of the run – it will be a case of lying on the ground, struggling for breath with a heart rate of 200 bpm.

So working harder than we are capable of doing at a manageable pace will not help over the whole run, or the whole race. Crews that go out faster than they can sustain are likely to blow up later on (watch the Washington/Brookes final of the Prince Albert in 2023 for a great example). Brookes crews appear to understand this very well. They do look to increase their pace towards the end for a final spurt for the line, when they need to, but their athletes tend to look pretty comfortable until that very final section of the race.

One note of caution though. Psychologically, it is not ideal to be a long way behind after the first 30 strokes, even if you are rowing to your best theoretical profile. So Brookes tend to start strongly, without going too berserk, to put down an initial marker.

Richard Spratley also points out that a headwind and stream at Henley can make the race 30 seconds longer than in better conditions. 'The rowers have to adjust their effort to make sure they can row efficiently for maybe seven minutes rather than six and a half,' he says, and the planning takes that into account too. I'm not sure many coaches think about that factor.

My suspicion is that telemetry data has helped to inform this process, and I also suspect Bailhache-Webb in particular uses it better than any other coach today in terms of race preparation. If there is still a 'Brookes secret', it may well lie in that understanding of data and race planning.

What makes Brookes special?

Daniel Kahneman would be proud ...
Bailhache-Webb also uses priming techniques (see *Thinking Fast and Slow* by Daniel Kahneman for more on that concept).[42] He will brief the crew the evening before a race, to get plans and different scenarios into their heads, so they feel comfortable whatever might happen the next day. In the final of the Prince Albert Cup for coxed fours at Henley in 2022, Brookes was up against a fearsome and huge University of California, Berkeley crew in the final. From his analysis of the heats, Bailhache-Webb had a clear idea of what was going to happen. He sat down with his crew the night before the race.

'I've got bad news for you. Berkeley are going to lead you for threequarters of this race. They will have a length at the Barrier and maybe a touch more by Fawley. If they go any further ahead, we need to respond. But don't panic, because the good news is you're going to win. They haven't had to really race the last 500 up to now and they're not prepared for that. Stay calm, don't worry that you're down, trust the process.' Watch the race on YouTube and it was exactly as predicted. Berkeley looked superb early on, taking a lead of around a length.

'This is the first time Brookes has had to come from behind,' says the commentator. 'They will feel in an uncomfortable and unusual position to be down ...' But they weren't feeling uncomfortable, because they were expecting this. They were primed. After halfway, Brookes just steadily and slowly gained on the Americans, ultimately winning by a fairly comfortable one length.

After the 2024 Oxford versus Cambridge boat race, Olympic rower Cath Bishop wrote an article in *The Guardian* newspaper.[43] She commented that the Cambridge coach had warned the crew that they might be down at one point (Bishop must have been present for the pre-race briefing). She felt this was pretty revolutionary stuff from a coach; but that sort of honesty has been routine at Brookes for years.

The team culture that Brookes has developed is also evident when it comes to racing and events. The coaches take care to make everyone in the club feel they are part of the success and involved. After a success, 'Remember, it might be you in the winning crew next year, and it was your efforts that spurred on everyone in that crew,' Bailhache-Webb tells the squad. 'Keep pushing!'

The Brookes ethos
The technical side of rowing is obviously key to success, but the psychological aspects of the club and the athletes within it are at least as important. After observing the club and the people within it over the last months, what seems incredible and admirable is how Brookes combines two seemingly conflicting philosophies.

The first is the ethos of competition that pervades everything at Brookes. You can see that in the gym, with athletes looking to move up the leaderboard of the best times, or on the river with the long history of seat racing to select crews. As Hugo Gulliver said, 'Even the best rower in the crew, or in the club, has to keep going, every session, every day, if they want to hold their place.' When Bailhache-Webb took over as head coach, he put up the 'leaderboard' in the gym, and bought an industrial strength spotlight to illuminate everybody's results!

With such a large squad, it might be easy for those in the eighth men's boat or the fifth women's boat to stop trying quite so hard, to settle for a comfortable life. But that competitive spirit means every rower, it seems, is looking to move onwards and upwards. That is supported by the philosophy of individual attention that Henry Bailhache-Webb has instilled. He and the coaching team are looking to optimise the performance of every individual, using specific and detailed data, and one to one coaching and discussion. So within that competitive environment, athletes generally feel supported and that the coaches are there to help them get the most out of themselves. They can 'become

What makes Brookes special?

the best rower they can possibly be', perhaps the central principle of the club.

Now it should be noted that some people have left Brookes over the years feeling less than happy. Inevitable, competition means some people will be disappointed and feel that they should have been picked for crews that they were not. My observation today is that this is managed as fairly and sensitively as possible; but of course, over 30-something years, not every decision will have been welcomed by everyone.

However, it appears that the sense of perpetual competition, driving the athletes on, is accompanied by a very impressive and genuine team spirit, the 'one for all and all for one' approach. The competitiveness is positioned as benefiting the whole club and therefore every individual. Those at the bottom of the hierarchy are helping by pushing everyone upwards, so are valued just as much as the top crews.

That goes right back to Peter Lowe and the founding fathers of the modern OBUBC. Remember how Lowe reacted with fortitude and dignity to losing his seat in what turned out to be the winning Henley crew of 1993. The attitude has been reinforced by the coaches. Everybody is treated the same, as we've seen, training together, with no special treatment for the 'stars'. Personal responsibility is key, and rowers seem to buy in to the idea that they are all part of the process that leads to wins at Henley. Everybody in the club feels that they contribute to the overall success. (Interestingly, that was another feature of the Cambridge women's approach discussed by Cath Bishop in the article mentioned earlier.)

At some universities, the coaches very much feel that they are training an 'officer class' of athletes. But at Brookes, although there are plenty of private school boys and girls joining up, there are also quite a few coming from less privileged backgrounds – the 'infantrymen' (and women these days) as it were. That brings a different dynamic, perhaps, compared to some other universities, and also fits with that long-standing Brookes underdog attitude.

'We were a certain type in those crews of the early nineties, very fit, very competitive and maybe with a bit of a chip on our shoulders, with something to prove,' says Alex Henshilwood of the 1995 crew. That position is not justified today in reality, but is still remembered from the early days and colours the culture of the club, relating to when the Poly, and then Brookes, genuinely were the upstarts of the rowing world.

There is also a 'work hard and play hard' approach, which again comes up when you talk to those early rowers. Today, Wednesday evening is the club night out generally, following the session on the river. The squad is not averse to a few beers, although they know that Spratley and the coaching team these days are not over sympathetic to excess. There is another club mantra which is 'don't be a dickhead'. As Spratley says, 'I don't want any nonsense around throwing up in the Thursday gym session!'

But there are club songs and traditional forfeits and games, some of which were described to me. Unfortunately, most are not suitable for this book. The songs often hark back to when Brookes was 'just' a Poly, and X-rated comparisons with Oxford University are a regular theme of the lyrics. I'll leave that to the imagination ...

Data, linked to fairness and objectivity in selection decisions, is another central tenet of the Brookes method. Everyone knows that every session contributes to their reputation and ranking in the hierarchy. A night overdoing the beers might just cost you a place in the Henley Temple or Island crew, so most know when to stop, even on a particularly good night out. And it seems that even when rowers are dropped from a crew, as we saw with Peter Lowe thirty years ago and Jenny Bates three years ago, they generally feel it is not done unfairly. There are plenty of other athletes in other clubs who don't feel the

What makes Brookes special?

same about selection decisions that have impacted their careers, up to and including international level.

But at Brookes, even disappointed rowers in most cases seem to look at the big picture, what it means to the club, and they buckle down to their new crew and role. It would be easy in those situations to walk away, but that is not the Brookes way.

When it comes to racing, ultimately coaches have to trust the athletes in the boat. That trust is built over time, as Matt Hnatiw explains. 'As I got more experienced, I could have proper conversations with the coaches and give my views, which I knew were listened to.'

The coaches are however not afraid to provide 'tough love' when that is appropriate. An athlete who tried to cheat on their erg times to get promoted into a higher boat, going as far as to create a fake video, was called out in front of the whole team. 'This is just not how we behave,' said Bailhache-Webb. If the cheating had succeeded, a deserving athlete would have lost their place unfairly, he pointed out. This wasn't a victimless crime!

As Bailhache-Webb says, 'We can't keep doing what we've done without everyone contributing, everyone pushing all the time. That's one of the keys to our success.' Personal responsibility is always stressed, and it is not unusual for parents to thank the Brookes coaches for the change they have helped to generate in their son or daughter during their time in the club.

How does Brookes compare?

The discussions that fed into this book provided insights in terms of how other boat clubs compare to Brookes, and perhaps highlight the key success factors.

The University of London (UL) is an interesting case. Although on paper it should be the best university boat club in the UK, if not the world, purely because of its size (over 200,000 students) and location, it is nowhere close to that. It appears to have been limited in the past at least by issues of structure, governance and management.

'It might as well be called Chiswick Boat Club,' was one comment – it has no formal links with or funding from the university, so amazingly does not have the resources of Brookes, an institution a fraction of the size. That is mainly because of the odd structure of London University, a loose confederation of 17 academic institutions, each in effect a separate university in its own right, and three central academic bodies. 'Colleges' such as Imperial, King's, University, Royal Holloway, SOAS, and Queens Mary's all have their own identity and priorities.

Some row seriously, like Imperial, a club that has overall outperformed UL in rowing over the last 30 years. A talented rower at Imperial will in all likelihood stay within the Imperial system. A good rower at some 'colleges' that don't take the sport so seriously may well gravitate towards the UL club. But the governance and management is still very voluntary and amateur in nature compared to Brookes, Harvard or Washington.

Those US clubs are the closest competitors to Brookes for the title of 'best rowing university in the world', with Washington the clear US number one in 2024. They also have the huge advantage of what seems like almost limitless funding from alumni. It is not at all unusual for a benefactor to chip in a couple of million to fund another coaching position in perpetuity.

Harvard takes around 50 rowers down to Florida every year for a training camp. Travel is paid, they stay in good hotels and receive spending money. The cost must be well into six figures, all funded by benefactors. It used to be just the men's first and second boats that went, until in 2014, Bill Ackman, a billionaire who had rowed for the third boat while he was at Harvard, decided that boat should also go to Florida every year. So he gave the club $5M to support that initiative

What makes Brookes special?

over the next 25 years![44] Indeed, some US universities have a 'waiting list' of potential donors; basically more money than they know what to do with.

When Brookes go to Wimbleball, they stay in youth hostels and the equivalent, and cook for themselves. (When Rachel Quarrell went, as a slightly older athlete with a job by then, she booked her own accommodation!) Yet Brookes has overtaken Harvard, most experts would agree. Much of that is down to those cultural aspects, I suspect, such as the combination of competitiveness allied to team spirit. The coaches must take huge credit for their skill in building both technical and psychological excellence.

Other factors include recruitment and the structure of most US clubs. In the chapter on recruitment, I mentioned the limitations on how rowers can only usually compete for four years in US university sports clubs. That is an issue, and Brookes has certainly been clever in keeping athletes involved in the club, even after they finish their time studying. It is certainly not 'just' a university club any longer, although the top Brookes crew purely made up of current students still beats pretty much every other university in the world these days.

US universities also seem more traditional and fixed in their structures. New arrivals usually start in a freshman crew and generally work their way towards the 'varsity crew' in their third or fourth year. There seems to be limited flexibility in terms of moving between boats, although some US universities are now changing their internal rules, recognising that they are losing out because of their rigidity. The top Washington crew in 2024 actually demonstrated that change.

But Brookes has always had a fluid, flexible approach, where rowers are constantly competing with each other, knowing that crew selection will depend purely on performance, not how long they've been around. A brilliant 18-year-old could be rowing almost immediately in the fastest Brookes boat, whilst that would be unlikely to happen at Harvard.

Continuity and management

Another difference between Brookes and others is the continuity of those key coaches, well supported by the senior management in the wider university structure. Having had Spratley involved for 30 years, and Bailhache-Webb for 18 years, has been invaluable. Of course, continuity itself isn't enough if the coaches aren't actually capable. But clearly Brookes has had two brilliant long-term coaches, as well as the input from other key people over the years such as Haining, French and Gulliver. Young coaches like Chris Tebb and Sam Sheppard are now picking up the reins.

Other clubs have had periods of success of course. Imperial College, London was the Brookes equivalent for 20 years or so from the early 1980s to the noughties, without ever dominating in quite so strong a fashion. But the club has dropped a little in the rankings in recent years, and is no longer a GB high performance centre.

However it is not merely the long-term approach to technical coaching that Richard Spratley has brought or his inspirational qualities, but also the role he has played since Henry Bailhache-Webb took over the lead coaching responsibility. Spratley now makes sure everything else is taken care of at the club, leaving the athletes and coaches to get on with the job of creating very fast boats.

At other clubs, coaches have to get involved in many different non-rowing issues. Booking those hotels. Sorting out management issues around premises or equipment. Brookes has also put in place good support from the wider university. If there is a disciplinary issue – maybe a dispute between club members – there are processes in place and issues can be referred through a defined wider university process. Elsewhere, coaches can get caught up and distracted by off-the-water issues that take time and energy away from their core skills and core goals. Enthusiastic coaches know they can come to Brookes and concentrate on what they are good at, and that is certainly an attraction.

What makes Brookes special?

The way that continuity was maintained when Spratley handed over the head coach role was critical. Bailhache-Webb undoubtedly brought in new methods and approaches that were needed to take the club to the next level, and that brought some tension within the club at times. But generally, the change was incremental rather than disruptive or destructive, and those key individuals worked out a new way of working together, which has been the foundation of success over the last two decades. Many other sports teams, or indeed businesses, have hit a crisis when a successful and well-established leader left or handed over to a successor. Brookes handled that transition brilliantly.

Oxford Brookes

Henley Royal Regatta, 3.40 pm, 7 July 2024

Race report – The 2024 Stewards' Challenge Cup Final
This is now the last race of the day. The Stewards moved it to give the Brookes rowers more recovery time as they were part of the Grand crew which suffered the delay earlier. Wincomb, Woolnough, Ruiken and Nares have had about two hours back in the boat tent, trying to keep loose, have something to eat and relax before they are off again to take on arch-rivals Leander in the last race of Henley 2024. The rain has stopped, and Brookes have the preferred Berks station, but the Leander crew has the big advantage in that they haven't rowed already today and been out in an hour or so of deluge.

It is half a length to Leander by the end of the Island, a big lead for so early in the race. By the Barrier, the Leander lead is out to a length and the commentators are talking about how tired the Brookes athletes must be after their previous race. Dame Katherine Grainger also points out that the psychological impact of winning one race then having to come out again is tough. But the chance of getting this double (the Grand and the Stewards') is so rare, that will be overriding the pain, she says.

As the crew approach Fawley and halfway, it is clear that Leander is not increasing its lead. In fact, very slowly, centimetre by centimetre, inch by inch, the Brookes boat is coming back. But this is a GB international four in the Leander pink, and they are maintaining their composure. As the crews come alongside the enclosures, Leander has moved ahead a touch further again and still holds a lead of about three-quarters of a length. Surely the physical effects of the Grand must kick in now in that Brookes boat.

Well, something kicks in, because the four Brookes men find another extraordinary gear. In the course of 20 strokes as the crews pass the Stewards' grandstand, the Brookes athletes move the boat from half a

The 2024 Stewards' Challenge Cup Final

length down to almost a length ahead. Suddenly it looks like Leander are rowing through treacle. Brookes power on, and cross the finishing line, with the records showing a winning margin of two lengths. That makes it sound like an easy race, although Brookes only led for the last 20 strokes or so. In truth, they rowed their opposition to a standstill, and the Leander boat virtually drifts over the finishing line, the rowers totally spent.

Brookes on the other hand are experiencing the biggest surge of adrenalin imaginable. A rather rude word comes from one of the Brookes crew, which will earn them a stern warning from the umpire later. But these four young men have pulled off a quite remarkable achievement today, winning arguably the two most prestigious men's events within a few hours. It really is historic.

When I speak to Henry Bailhache Webb later, he says, 'I told the crew they would be down off the start – that would be when they experienced the biggest impact of the previous race. But as the race went on, I told them they would get stronger.' They certainly did, in what was perhaps the most remarkable of many remarkable Brookes victories at Henley.

Chapter 25

But is there a dark side?

This book is obviously positive about Brookes and what they have achieved, reflecting my views and understanding developed during the research and writing process. But for balance, it is worth considering aspects of Brookes' recent hegemony that some perceive negatively. Is this all too good to be true? It is also interesting to ask the big question – 'Can Brookes be beaten?'

The Dark Side?
Perhaps the obvious and most common complaint about OBUBC is that Brookes' success is bad for British rowing or British university rowing. It is a fair point to make. Being able to field six men's boats that finish in the top 20 at the Head of the River in London is remarkable, as was Henley in 2023 and 2024, and Brookes does now put every other university boat club in the UK in the shade.

You hear this occasionally on rowing websites or from commentators, but really, it seems unfair to 'blame' Brookes for this state of affairs. We'll discuss shortly how others might mimic Brookes. But somehow expecting Brookes to try less hard, in order to let Imperial, Durham, Newcastle or Edinburgh do better seems obtuse and unrealistic, to say the least.

It took Brookes many years and much effort to get to the point where the club can routinely take on and beat top US universities. If Brookes eased off, do we really think those other GB institutions are magically going to thrash Yale and Washington at Henley next year? And in terms of GB rowing, Brookes is providing a steady flow of absolutely top-level athletes into the GB squad in a manner that only Leander now

But is there a dark side?

emulates. Mike Sweeney, ex GB rowing and Henley Regatta supremo, was very clear about the benefits Brookes brings to the national set-up when I spoke to him.

Actually, in some ways, I suspect Spratley, Bailhache-Webb and the team would welcome more competition. Remember Bailhache-Webb telling his athletes to enjoy racing other top crews, because they would bring out the very best in their own performance. I'm sure the team wouldn't want to stop winning completely, but an intense rivalry with Imperial, Newcastle, Oxford or Cambridge (if those last two stopped focusing so single-mindedly on the Boat Races), would spur Brookes crews on further.

Anyway, the criticism of success is what we hear when a football team wins the Premiership or the Bundesliga year after year, and of course I would much rather Sunderland or Brentford won than Manchester City. But as long as City obey the rules, really it is up to others to improve and win.

The other point to make is that the Brookes dominance does not cover every aspect of rowing. Sculling in particular has never been a Brookes focus. Now that might change in the future, just as the club has become a significant power in women's rowing over the last few years. Leander, the biggest UK rivals, is still a more 'rounded' club arguably, in that it does cover junior (under-18) rowing and scullers, as well as strong men's and women's sweep boats.

The athletes speak

'Brookes is such a fun place to train. There are such great role models, people are really supportive of each other, we pull each other up, but we also keep everyone accountable.'

(Jenny Bates, HRR winner, GB trials winner & GB full international)

The second charge against Brookes is that they are 'arrogant'. I have heard this a few times, including from a coach as crews were putting their boats on the water for the Head of the River race. He felt Brookes had 'pushed in' to get on the water before his boys. But Brookes boated first because they had six fast boats which needed to start their race about 30 minutes before his crew, ranked 200! So the rules required them to get afloat in start order.

My take is that Brookes has managed to stay largely clear of the arrogance, hubris and entitlement that often goes with major success of any sort. That has come from the early underdog culture, and certainly from Richard Spratley himself, a man short on personal arrogance, who is really rather uncomfortable when the spotlight is trained on him. 'No dickheads' is a Brookes motto, and arrogance is very much seen as a dickhead trait in the club.

Indeed, one ex-Brookes international star told me that, 'It is probably good that the boys from Eton and St Paul's don't tend to go to Brookes – it isn't a club that welcomes tall poppies.' (He means individuals who believe they stand out from the crowd.)

Any other issues? Well, I was told that there are some who did not enjoy the Brookes rowing experience, which is inevitable really, although I did not find any who wanted to comment here. Logically, there must be some who did not enjoy the competitive nature of the experience, or felt they didn't get in the boat they should have, or simply didn't much like the coach at that time. But I can only repeat what I've said elsewhere. My observation is that the vast majority of the athletes have a great time at Brookes.

The final point that was made to me was that some ex-Brookes rowers have struggled somewhat with 'life' after university. But that is probably more indicative of a general issue for sports stars and others who achieve much early in life. If you have won a gold medal at the Olympics or World Championships in your early twenties, I imagine

But is there a dark side?

the rest of your life might seem a little dull or disappointing. And of course rowers don't have the financial cushion that a young footballer or pop star might accumulate in those years of success.

Now actually many Brookes alumni seem to have achieved a lot since their university days – climbing Everest, swimming the channel, successful businesses and careers. But there will always be some who struggle, and there can be many reasons for that, none of which are unique to Brookes.

Could other clubs 'do a Brookes'?
As Tom Morgan on the JRN website put it, 'How to beat this machine-like monstrosity of rhythm and aggressivity.'[45] Not sure about 'monstrosity' but I'm sure Brookes does appear a ferocious opponent to most rivals! So how might other clubs challenge Brookes?

There was some nervousness in Brookes initially about this book. Would it spill the secret sauce, and suddenly Brookes would lose to Scumbag College at Henley next year after their coach reads the book?

Well, for what it is worth, I do think it is possible for another club or university to emulate Brookes. Indeed, Leander operates at a similar level, although that club has the benefit of around 200 years of experience and a lot more money. Even here, Brookes has had the better of recent Henley head-to-head battles. So if another university or club wanted to follow the Brookes model, all they have to do is pay attention to the following guidance.

First of all, you need a great river to row on. The ability to execute long training rows, with two or even three boats rowing side by side, generates both competence and a competitive tension that can be channelled positively. Then I'd suggest at least a decade of consistent investment in the club in terms of equipment, recruitment, a decent boathouse, excellent training facilities and more. That means consistent funding and support from the right people in the university (or club) hierarchy.

A highly demanding and well-thought-out training programme is key, combining work in the boat and intense gym and weight training, supported by serious expertise in fitness and conditioning. You need to be, in effect, a professional sports club, not a bunch of friends just enjoying rowing (nothing wrong with that approach, I should stress, but it won't win you medals). Someone also needs to be a highly effective manager of 'men, materials and money', as Peter Haining said.

You must have coaches who are motivational and understand the technical side of rowing in real depth, and know how to use telemetry data. But they also need to be astute from a people point of view; master psychologists, with an understanding of rowing and rowers, and how to get the absolute best out of the crews in training and competition. 'With Brookes, the whole is greater than the sum of the parts,' says coach Chris Tebb. 'Over the years, the coaches have been successful at taking athletes, who were maybe not quite as talented as some, and getting the absolute best out of them.'

Then the whole club must commit to building a clear mission and ethos, which can generate strong team spirit, yet allied with keen competition within the club. That also means you need a certain critical mass of serious athletes, so very regular and highly professional recruitment is vital. As is continuity; none of this will work if new coaches come along too often with totally different plans and processes, as we saw with the GB 2021 Olympic team.

So if, for instance, Newcastle University really wanted to emulate Brookes, it is not impossible. But looking at that list, it would be a huge challenge, and would need at least a decade of patient work, probably more, before any club could be at a similar level to Brookes. I don't think Spratley and Bailhache-Webb need to worry too much right now.

But is there a dark side?

But there are some risks, which apply to even the most successful organisations of any type. The support of the Brookes hierarchy and top management to ensure provision of finance was mentioned earlier. OBUBC has benefited from strong support for over a decade from Keith Kelly, the university's Director of Sport. Very sadly, Kelly passed away in April 2024 after an illness, at the age of just 54. He is very much missed by everyone who knew and worked with him.

So the club will no doubt want to establish a similar relationship with his successor. But if university bosses decided Brookes rowing needed to be all about access, maybe just focusing on getting 200 novice youngsters out on the river every year, and that is where the money was going to go, the elite programme could wither quite quickly.

There is a catch-22, however, for any leader thinking that way. Novices are unlikely to be interested in learning to row at Brookes if the club is not successful at the top level. It certainly would not be the main reason for applying to the university, unlike the 50 or so new students every year who do think that way. The boat club would appear to be a positive income generator for Brookes, even without considering the wider reputational benefit.

Coaches leaving is another obvious risk, and if Spratley and Bailhache-Webb both disappeared in quick succession, there could be a potential issue. But there is some resilience now, with promising young coaches taking wider roles, and perhaps Brookes could weather the storm if one or the other disappeared.

'Coaches start by doing to their athletes what was done to them,' says Alex Henshilwood at Eton College, who has been successful rowing at Brookes and GB level and then as a coach. He credits Spratley and Sean Bowden as mentors who supported his own very successful schools coaching career. There are a number of coaches around the system now who trained with OBUBC and could be credible future Brookes head coaches too.

Oxford Brookes

Henshilwood is also impressed with the way, 'Brookes and their coaches manage so many crews and individuals at the same time', both from a logistical and a motivational perspective. That is not as easy as Spratley and Bailhache-Webb sometimes make it look, he believes. So replacing those stalwarts would be a challenge.

The athletes speak

'Richard Spratley takes the pressure off the coaches and the crews. What he does behind the scenes reduces athletes' stress levels and helps our recovery. Everything is planned and set up for us to perform – we just have to go out and do what we do.'

(*Matt Hnatiw*, 2x HRR winner, GB U-23 international)

Obviously a major scandal could derail the club, but there has been no hint of that other than the minor drugs issue in 2015. More young rowers disappearing off to the US might be a threat, but my suspicion is that may have peaked. There are stories of unhappy athletes returning home as well as those that have had a good time. I'm not convinced that the USP (unique selling proposition) of Brookes – 'having the best rowing experience of your life' – is threatened too much even by Yale or Berkeley.

My observations over the last few months certainly support that USP. The Brookes athletes really do seem to have a good time, even when it hurts ('Fun in a serious way,' as Henshilwood puts it), as well as having the best chance they will find anywhere to win and to develop into top-level rowers. Looking from outside now, Henshilwood comments that, 'Brookes is head and shoulders above other UK universities – it is the place to go if you want to compete against the top US universities. The Brookes team really are the only ones who have cracked it.'

So it won't be easy to depose Brookes.

Chapter 26

Onwards to 2024

'Rowing is almost exactly like raising kids. Both require patience, endurance, strength, and commitment. And neither allow us to see where we're going – only where we've been. I find that very reassuring, don't you?' (Bonnie Garmus, Lessons in Chemistry)

The motivation for this book was the amazing performance of Brookes at the 2023 Henley Royal Regatta. But writing this book during the winter of 2023/4, then moving towards publication through the spring and summer of 2024, life and Brookes rowing continued.

It was a mild but exceedingly wet late autumn and winter in much of the UK, and the Oxford area did not escape. For many weeks, the Thames was too high and flowing too fast for safe rowing. Athletes went a little stir crazy, working hard in the gym but unable to get out onto the water. The Wallingford Head race, traditionally the first big event of the season for Brookes, was cancelled in November, so Richard Spratley arranged at very short notice an additional training weekend at Wimbleball.

The rain subsided enough in the new year for Brookes to participate in the now annual races against the Oxford and Cambridge University Boat Race crews – men and women, first and second boats and lightweights. Brookes came out on top in every event, showing again that the Oxford and Cambridge Boat Races are really a competition to decide the second best rowing university in the UK.

The Head of the River
At the women's Head of the River race in early March, Brookes came a close second to Leander, just 3.8 seconds (one boat's length) behind over four and a half miles. That was a good result, the best ever for Brookes, but also an indication that winning the Remenham Cup for the top women's crews at Henley in July wasn't going to be easy. The second eight improved on the 2022 by finishing in fifth place. This crew beat Cambridge University's Blue Boat (that later went on to beat Oxford at the Boat Race) and was the highest-ranking second boat at the race.

The third boat came home in eleventh place, beating all other universities except London and Newcastle. The fourth boat finished in thirty-third place, and the fifth boat finished in eighty-third place after finishing two hundredth overall in 2023. The strength in depth that the men's squad developed was now being seen in the women's group too.

I watched the men's Head race in late March live for the first time since I competed in it some 30 years ago. Brookes entered eight boats, which all take to the water from the Barn Elms boathouse as they have done for many years. It is certainly not one of the most luxurious boathouses on the river, but it has a homely charm, befitting its purpose to encourage a wide range of Londoners to try rowing. Andrew Hall – 'Big Ted' to his friends – coaches at Barns Elms and is in charge here on the day as the various crews use the facilities.

He has obvious admiration for Brookes and the coaches, Richard Spratley in particular. 'Loyalty and patience – you don't see that very often these days, but that's how Brookes has got to where they are today,' he explains. When the juniors he coaches are having a bad day, he thinks of Brookes – 'Keep at it, be persistent, don't expect overnight success! But you can have fun on the journey too.' Hall enjoys hosting Brookes. Spratley is always 'relaxed, down to earth and pleasant to

Onwards to 2024

everybody – but also very focused'. He has also offered to host the Barns Elms juniors for a day up at Wallingford.

But Richard Spratley didn't choose Barns Elms randomly or because Hall is one of life's good guys. The boathouse is near the finish, so only a short row 'home' for tired athletes after the race. You can get boat trailers right up to the boathouse on the playing fields behind, although the final few yards is a hairy journey. Crews lift their boat up a short, steep slope, through and over a narrow gate flanked by barbed wire-topped fencing, then down another steep slope, sharp right turn, try not to hit any passing cyclists or knock a pedestrian into the river … and you're on the towpath.

This year there is additional spice to the event. Three men who would probably have been in the Brookes first boat today moved to Leander, the arch-rivals, at the beginning of this season. Their reasons were more logistical than sporting, it seemed. No longer students, Leander in Henley was a more convenient training location for them than Wallingford and Oxford. Maybe there was an element of wanting a new challenge too. But Matt Rowe and Sam Bannister (Ladies' Plate Henley winners in 2023), who became part of the Leander 'A' crew, and Jack Prior (Visitors' winner in 2023), who graced Leander 'B', were a big loss to Brookes. That means the Brookes 'A' crew is probably a little less experienced and younger on average than Leander.

As I arrive at the river, two hours before the race starts, the Brookes athletes are taking the boat sections from the trailers, assembling them and fitting the riggers. They then go off to get changed. Henry Bailhache-Webb gets out a cloth and a spray can and polishes the underside of all eight boats. I'm not sure how many Head Coaches do this themselves, but the humility and lack of big egos that keeps cropping up is on show again today.

Then is the team talk, with 72 athletes crowded into the changing room – which also has a rowing tank in the centre. (See this brilliant

Pathe News clip from 1968 featuring the tank!)[46] I'm very worried someone is going to fall into the tank, but everyone keeps their balance. Some of Bailhache-Webb's remarks are pure logistics, but even here, 'incremental gains' come into play. Spratley will drive up to the start and collect track suit tops from the crews, which minimises the weight in the boat. 'If you can pull in to the pontoon, do that, if not, put your kit in the bin bag and fling it onto the bank for Richard to collect!'

The motivational element of the talk is low key but intense. Remember how hard you have trained – you are the fittest group we've ever seen. The conditions are fast, that will suit good oarsmen. We're good oarsmen. Keep focused, remember the key elements of a good technical stroke. When Bailhache-Webb is finished, there is a call of one … two … three … and then a single shout of 'Brookes'. In a fairly small room, with 72 people giving it their all, it is deafening.

I watch the race from the Barn Elms boathouse. At the start, Spratley times the gap between Brookes, the lead boat, and Leander, going off second. He sends a text to Bailhache-Webb and me. Brookes started 32 seconds before Leander – a bigger gap than the organisers like to see. At Hammersmith Bridge, coach Chris Tebb measures the gap at 31 seconds.

By the time the two crews come into my sight, just past the half-way mark, they are taking quite different courses down the river. Brookes is closer to the Fulham bank, maybe mimicking the line Cambridge took last year (see page 158). Leander is more central. Big Ted sounds worried. 'He wants to be closer to that buoy,' he says, pointing to a small marker well across the river from where Brookes are steering.

I take the times as the boats pass a marker on the opposite bank. I make it a 27-second gap now. Leander has rowed the middle part of the course around four seconds faster than Brookes. It doesn't look good, but there is still about four minutes' rowing left. Can they pull it back?

Onwards to 2024

At the finish line, Bailhache-Webb waits anxiously. But Brookes has not made an incredible final push, and it looks like Leander has made up around five seconds over the course. As the official results come in, that is confirmed with a margin of 5.1 seconds. Brookes held on over those last minutes, but could not narrow the gap. The Leander crew has also broken the course record, with a time of 16:26.7, not surprising with a strong crew, a strong stream and a tailwind.

The good news is that Brookes 'B', the second boat, has finished third, just behind Brookes 'A', and has beaten Leander 'B'. The Brookes 'C' boat is sixth, winning the 'Bernard Churcher Trophy' for crews that are 100 per cent current students. The 'D' crew is eighth too, only five seconds behind the 'C' boat, so there is going to be intense and healthy competition for seats in the Henley Temple and Prince Albert crews this summer. The top 6 boats finish in the top 20, and the Brookes seventh and eight boats finish thirty-second and thirty-eighth, still very respectable positions. (As a comparison, my old college came ninety-eighth and the fastest Cambridge college crew was Downing in seventy-eighth place.)

The mood is mixed as the crews disassemble the boats again. It is all a little quiet, as you might expect given the physical exhaustion and losing the Head for the first time since 2015. The top crew is, of course, disappointed, although a 5-second gap over 16 minutes is not a lot. It gives them something to aim for over the rest of the season, to turn a loss into motivation. But there is no time for much discussion now. It is the annual boat club dinner tonight back in Henley, so it is all about getting packed up and on the road again.

The Dinner

The Brookes team has kindly invited my wife and me to the club dinner, which means a quick escape from the river. A couple of hours later, as we drive to Phyllis Court in Henley, Jane asks me, 'Do you think it will be a bit of a subdued evening?' I don't know, I reply. I mean, the other Brookes boats did pretty well and the top boat losing to a more experienced crew by five seconds is no disgrace.

We enter the drinks reception, and a wall of excited noise hits us viscerally. I think we can safely say that the mood is *not* subdued! The evening can be best described as riotous, but generally in a controlled manner. Peter Lowe has turned up just for the pre-dinner drinks because he is rowing in the Veterans' Head on the Thames the next day. James Symington from the victorious 1993 crew and around a dozen coaches and guests like us are present, and I get to meet the legendary Tim Levy for the first time, plus around 120 or so athletes.

It continues to be loud, but no-one oversteps the mark. Everyone looks like they have read coach Chris Tebb's lengthy missive to everyone before the event, which includes classics such as 'no drink to be brought into the dinner' and 'there will be a £1,000 fine for anyone throwing up on the coach back to Oxford'! As Spratley says, 'We want everyone to have a great time. But remember – no dickheads. That's the rule.'

The guest speaker is Lizzie Cottrell, now captain of Thames Club. She reminds us of the time when the women's side of the club was a lot less powerful than it is now, and talks about how friendships made now will last a lifetime. Then there are some short speeches from the coaches and half a dozen prizes given for achievement and contribution to the club, including to Louis Nares, Sam Sheppard, Beth Dutton and Arianna Forde, one of the current Brookes GB under-23 squad members.

Jake Wincomb was also rewarded. This is a man who has won the Temple and the Ladies' at Henley, and won back-to-back gold medals in the world under-23 championships in 2022 and 2023. A touch of arrogance and swagger would be well deserved, but there was not a hint of it in his demeanour or his speech. 'I had three sets of goals in mind when I started here,' he said. 'A basic set, what I thought was a realistic set, and then my dream. But I've gone way beyond my dream, and that's all down to this place, the club, the people I've rowed with, the coaches.'

Must have been some dust in my eyes at that point, I think. Just let me get a tissue …

The coaches talk about the trust that rowing generates with your colleagues in the boat – 'You won't lose that as you move through life.' The emphasis is always on the club, the team, not the individual. And between the prizes, there was an increasing clamour from a couple of the tables, with cries of 'Sam Clarke' echoing round the room. Who was this hero, I wondered?

Well, Clarke is currently one of the less powerful athletes in the club, and rows near the bottom of the Brookes hierarchy (although remember the Brookes sixth boat is better than virtually any other UK university's top boat). But despite having had some bad luck this year, as he told me, his spirit, attitude, and personality has won him the hearts of his clubmates.

He *is* a hero, and typifies the Brookes spirit. 'I've got two more years, so I'm hoping to move up,' he explained. But even now he is an example of the club's cohesion and the way the rowers in 'lower' boats push hard from below, raising the standard for everyone. And the big surprise for my wife, having not been exposed to the club as I have over recent months, was 'the lack of ego on display'. She pointed out that 'given their accomplishments and success, a bit of arrogance would be quite understandable. But I just don't see it,' she said.

Personal egos seem to be subsumed into an overarching celebration of club success. That has definitely flowed down from Richard Spratley over the years, a man who is not comfortable in the spotlight. He did make a short speech, but he is clearly not at his happiest on stage. But the loudest cheer of the night came as one of the speakers finished their remarks with two simple but unforgettable words. *"F**k Leander!"*

It then became de rigueur for everyone else who spoke to do the same and finish in that manner. Maybe that would have been a better title for this book – how about *F**k Leander – and no Dickheads*? I'm not sure Waterstones would be too keen on that though.

The third fastest boat in the world?
The weather continued to be a nuisance in 2024, with crews at the Cholsey boathouse in April wading through a pond to get to the actual river, with the coxes begging a piggy-back from a friendly rower to avoid getting soaked. Brookes athletes disappeared off for the final GB national trials in the same month, where Jenny Bates cemented her reputation as one of the most promising young female rowers in the country, winning the sculling trials.

So the season moved on through various regattas, with Brookes dominating the eights races at the British Universities championship, despite the absence of their post-student athletes, of course. Brookes finished first and second in the Open Championship men's eights, and first, second and third in the 'Intermediate' men's event, with the Brookes 'D' boat pipping the 'C' boat in that Intermediate final. And do you remember the young athlete being feted at the dinner for his spirit and attitude? Yes, victory for the 'D' boat meant young Sam Clarke is now the proud owner of a BUCS gold medal! The women's eight won the championship eights by two lengths from Durham, with the Brookes second and third boats achieving a one/two in the Intermediate classification too. Brookes women are beginning to achieve the same dominance in university sweep rowing as their men have held for some years.

In early May, Brookes took over 100 athletes to the international Ghent regatta. Here, the women were dominant, thrashing Leander and everyone else. But Leander had some revenge in the top men's event, beating Brookes by tiny margins on both days, certainly with the

Henry Bailhache-Webb paddling (!) back to the boathouse at Cholsey in early 2024 (©*Peter Smith*)

advantage of a better lane on Sunday given the wind conditions. That same crosswind led to the Brookes women's second boat beating the first boat on the Sunday, and Brookes continued to make crew changes as the coaches searched for the optimum combinations for future events, with the Brookes/Leander rivalry for Henley building up nicely.

Brookes beats the Olympians

There was more success at the international Amsterdam Beker regatta in early June. Rather embarrassingly, the men's open eights on Saturday saw a final between five Brookes boats after the only Dutch crew to make the final withdrew! On Saturday, Brookes women focused on the fours, which they duly won, but on Sunday their first eight comfortably beat the Dutch national squad 'next generation' development crew.

But the men surpassed even this. On Sunday, the Dutch Olympic eight joined the competition, as it was the Dutch national championship day. But in a brilliant race, Brookes, including Thijs Ruiken, originally from the Njord club in the Netherlands, but now studying at Brookes, took a lead early on and never relinquished it, despite a storming

Oxford Brookes

finish from the Dutch eight, with the final margin just 0.25 seconds (about three feet or one metre). The same Dutch crew won bronze at the Lucerne world championship event just two weeks earlier. So that makes Brookes the third fastest eight in the world, presumably?

Henry Bailhache-Webb described it as 'one of the very best Brookes performances, ever', which seemed a reasonable assessment. Ruiken, now doing his medical research at Brookes, spoke to the Dutch rowing website (nlroei.nl) after the race.[47] He highlighted one of those critical success factors discussed earlier.

'They put the best together in the boat. You have to work very hard for it. And you always have to realise that someone ends up behind you, and also someone above you. It's hard, but also stimulating, and no one is left out. If you're dangling at the bottom, there's almost always a team in which you can compete in Henley.' (With thanks to Google Translate.)

But it wasn't all good news this month for Brookes, Spratley and Bailhache-Webb. Harry Brightmore, Brookes alumnus and cox of the GB Olympic eight, was lined up to join the coaching staff post-Olympics. But instead, Oxford University announced his appointment as Assistant Coach, with Mark Fangen-Hall taking over from Sean Bowden as Head Coach after the disastrous 2024 boat races (Cambridge 6, Oxford 0). There were mutterings about money being injected into OUBC, perhaps by the Winklevoss twins of Facebook fame, but good luck to Brightmore, and perhaps he will be back at Brookes one day.

The GB Olympians were not selected for the final World Cup regatta of the year at Poznan in June, giving a chance for the next generation, and Jake Wincomb, Louis Nares, James Doran, Matt Heywood, alumnus Martha Birtles and our friend Jenny Bates, now rowing in a double scull with Freya Keto of Thames Rowing Club, all got their first full international selection. So did Bannister and Rowe, the Brookes pair who had moved to Leander.

Chapter 27

Henley (and Paris …) 2024

'Once again, this was a magnificent Regatta for a program who are simply the best pound-for-pound boat club on the planet.' (Tom Morgan, JRN, July 2024)[48]

Preparing for Henley

From the Head of the River (HoR) event onwards, Spratley thought that Brookes would enter the first eight into the Ladies' Plate at Henley. Losing to Leander at the HoR and Ghent supported the view that being favourite for the Ladies' was preferable to being a longer shot for the blue-riband Grand, assuming Leander entered that top event. Bailhache-Webb was more bullish however, feeling that Brookes could beat Leander by the time Henley arrived. He also felt that Regatta chair Sir Steve Redgrave might push Brookes up to the Grand anyway.

A few days before entries for Henley closed, a crew meeting agreed on the Ladies' approach. But on Monday 17 June, the crew enjoyed an excellent training session at Cholsey. Back in the boathouse, several crew members spoke up. 'Let's go for the Grand', was the message. Are you sure, Spratley asked the crew. We don't even know who might show up in the Grand, a top Olympic crew might throw their hat in the ring and their oars in the Thames.

We know, was the response. But if we don't try, we'll never know. So at 11.53 am, seven minutes before entries closed, Bailhache-Webb called Redgrave and Brookes entered the Grand. Redgrave was delighted, and Brookes found themselves up against not just Leander but two international development crews from the USA and Canada, as well as the University of Washington Varsity boat, the fastest student boat in the USA in 2024. That meant what had been the Brookes 'C' (or third) boat was now going to be the Ladies' Plate entry, and the 'B' (second) boat would stay in the Temple as planned, because of the eligibility issues.

Marlow Regatta, two weeks before Henley, is the last chance for crews to impress the Henley Stewards in terms of seeding and qualification without having to qualify. Sam Nunn (named 'spare man' for the GB team) was released from the Olympic squad, so came back to the Brookes top boat, although the standard is such that it was by no means certain he would win a place back in that crew.

But Leander's top eight didn't show up, maybe a sign of weakness, and the Brookes first eight, with Nunn on board, duly won the Championship eights in a very fast time, the second fastest ever recorded by a Brookes crew, although maybe with less margin over an excellent London Rowing Club crew than expected. That London boat pipped Brookes 'C' (now the Ladies' crew) for second place and Harvard in fourth place beat Brookes 'B' (the Temple crew). So winning all three of those events at HRR was starting to look unlikely, and even two might be a stretch.

A Brookes and Taurus coxless four, featuring the legendary almost-veteran Jamie Copus, beat Leander in that event to take the victory, and in the coxed fours, Brookes dominated with the first two places. So the Visitors' and Prince Albert events at Henley looked like reasonable bets for Brookes anyway.

Henley 2024 arrives

So Henley approached, which means it is time for a quick discussion on the two 'stations' at Henley – the notional lanes that the crews must row within. There has been much discussion over the years about the relative advantages of each. Henley used to publish in the racing programme a comment along the lines of 'since 1945, the proportion of races won for the Bucks station is 48.18 per cent, from the Berkshire, 51.82 per cent'. That comes from the 2003 programme, but the number is no longer published. That couple of percent difference doesn't sound like a lot, but over 2,000+ metres it certainly can be significant. It only really matters when the crews are closely matched, but by the time we get to the later stages of the events, coaches do consider this factor.

The Bucks station is nearer the centre of the river for most (but not all) of the course, so it must suffer a little if there is any significant 'stream' flowing against the direction of rowing. It is also more prone to the water being disturbed by boats going up and down the river the other side of the booms. The wind is another factor, but there is a view that the Bucks station has a small advantage if the prevailing south-westerly wind is blowing.

As soon as the initial draw is made, you can see the profile in terms of which station you will be on for every round. So on the Saturday before Henley week, Richard Spratley was delighted by the draw for the Grand which put Brookes on Berks for both semi-final and final if they made it; less so with the Ladies' Plate draw which was likely to see Brookes on the 'wrong' station for a tussle with Cambridge in the semi-final, and again if the crew reached the final. But knowing how close the Brookes and Leander crews had been this year, that Grand draw seemed important.

But before the event started, a sickness bug struck the club. Notices about handwashing went up in the boathouse, but Bailhache-Webb was worried they weren't being heeded. He got the whole squad together at the boathouse. 'Two of you will not be rowing at Henley,' he told them. There was immediate consternation – who had been dropped? 'That's because, based on recent events, two of you are going to be sick. More if you don't take every precaution.'

The Brookes Henley squad 2024 (©*AllMarkOne*)

This was one of the strongest Henley fields ever, despite the lack of almost all Olympic crews. A record 771 crews entered from 27 countries, with 217 overseas crews, another record. The qualifying races before the main event reduced that number by almost half, and there were 409 races in the Regatta itself. It was also a Henley where the weather took many headlines. Sun, wind, rain, mist, more rain, and biblical downpours that left the local roads and pathways flooded. If you turned up in a nice summer dress and heels or ballet pumps you were in real trouble as areas within the enclosure and car parks turned into mud pits. (I wore serious walking boots and a raincoat on Sunday and felt very smug.)

In the Temple for student men's eights, Brookes 'C' and 'D' both came through the qualifying race to join their 'A' and 'B' crews. That made 15 Brookes boats in total, including Jenny Bates in the women's double sculls with her non-Brookes partner.

Bailhache-Webb's sickness projection proved correct, and some changes had to be made during the week, including in the highly fancied Visitors' crew. But as the week progressed, generally Brookes crews lived up to expectation. The Temple 'B' crew got as far as the semi-final, losing to Princeton. The women's Town four lost to Leander in the semi-final, and the Ladies' Plate boat was pipped by Cambridge in an excellent semi-final, with Brookes rowing from the 'wrong' station. That left nine Brookes crews in the finals.

On the eve of final's day, the Brookes Facebook page led with the message we keep hearing about the whole club ethos.

'Every current and ex-athlete has had an influence on where this club is now and has helped create the biggest day in the club's history tomorrow. Please do your bit and arrive to boat bay F, 60 minutes before race time and be ready to empty your lungs.'

Finals Day 2024
It is 10 am at the Regatta boat tents, where Brookes women's squad coaches Hugo Gulliver and Chris Tebb are waiting for the Island crew minibus to arrive from Oxford. Richard Spratley is 'off moving some trailers around', they tell me. Typical for him to be focusing on practical details. Brookes will face Newcastle in the Island final. 'They're one of the clubs that has responded well to Brookes success,' Gulliver says, 'while some others just moan!'

The first race today with a Brookes interest, though, is the Stonor Challenge Trophy. Now the Jenny Bates story through the book has focused on her overcoming challenges and triumphing. But this Sunday, in the final of the women's double sculls, it is not to be. She and her partner, Freya Keto, row in probably the heaviest downpour of the whole event, with very choppy water on the Bucks station. We can barely see the race from the Grandstand through the curtain of hammering rain. She and Keto battle, but it must have been miserable as they are overpowered by an experienced German pair, Wibberenz and Gutfleisch, who missed Olympic qualification this summer by just one place.

Next for Brookes should be the Grand at 11.20 am. But it is delayed by some 50 minutes because of Washington's equipment issue (more on page 146), so we get two more Brookes tussles before that showdown. At 11.30 am, Brookes takes on the old enemy, Leander, in the Visitors' Cup, the intermediate coxless fours event. The station matters today, and unfortunately Brookes has the 'wrong' side. Having beaten the same opposition at Marlow, the crew of veteran Jamie Copus, Alex Nichol, Odhran Donaghy (replacing the ill Max Mills) and Tom Horncastle hang on to Leander the whole way, but never quite look like winning, going down by one length.

As the final of the Island (for women's student crews) approaches at 11.30 am, the weather is wild. The race starts in bright sunshine and by halfway, the crews are dealing with biblical rain. But the Brookes rowers are inexorable. Against Newcastle University, they hammer off the start, lead by over a length by Fawley and steadily pull away. Newcastle's sprint finish that did for Durham and London Universities is nowhere to be seen as cox Sofia Bernal, Olivia Hill, Amelia Carpenter, Anna Bloomer, Emilia Regan, Aida Cosijn Diez, Shelby Kolbeck, Aggie Burt and Lindsey Morrissett triumph.

Finally, the Grand is ready to go. The extraordinary final is covered on page 146, and Brookes wins again, although maybe not in the way they imagined or would have liked, as Washington literally crash out. That means Matt Heywood and Jake Wincomb have completed what might be a unique treble at Henley, winning the Temple, the Ladies' and then the Grand in three successive years, an incredible achievement.

Henley (and Paris …) 2024

As the victorious Brookes rowers (Heywood, Ruiken, Nunn, Doran, Wincomb, Woolnough, Lassen, Nares and cox Bryce) are cheered back into the boat tent, I talk to the delighted mother of Fergus Woolnough, one of the undergrads in the Brookes crew. A couple of minutes later, Fergus himself emerges. My chance for an exclusive interview. How was it, I ask? 'Cold,' he says. 'Freezing. Especially as we had to paddle around for ages in the rain waiting for them to get sorted out.'

But time is limited for celebration now, as Fergus is also rowing later in the Stewards'. He's shaking a little now, whether that is the cold, adrenalin or both. He only has two hours till he's off again, and there are no hot showers at Henley.

So is Richard Spratley receiving the plaudits of the Brookes supporters? No, here he is, soaked to the skin, carrying the Grand crew's oars back to the boathouse. He's wet but delighted too, of course. 'I thought we had it under control. We were happy for it to be close, just stay in control, then we would have gone from the beginning of the enclosures,' he says. 'But a win's a win.'

I eat my lunchtime sandwich in the car, in the rain, then go back for a quick pint before the afternoon races. The Bridge Bar (next to the Real Ale kiosk) is most unusually empty, understandably since sitting out on the lawn with a Pimm's has not been a sensible option today!

At 2.30 pm, we witness one of the races of the day, the final of the Remenham for the top women's eights. If you have read the report on page 172, you will know that this was a superb triumph for Brookes. Indeed, you might argue that this was the most impressive Brookes victory of the day. The event included several international-level crews, and Brookes (somewhat inexplicably) weren't even one of four seeded crews. This was Brookes women reaching the very peak of the rowing world, and a culmination of years of hard work by athletes and coaches to get the programme to this exalted level.

Later, Richard Spratley tells me that he is as proud of what Brookes women did today as of anything achieved over his 30-year tenure.

'When I saw those 18 young women getting their medals ...' He's not an emotional man, but he was clearly affected by the successes.

Then at 3 pm, with the Brookes boats coming thick and *very* fast, we see the Temple and another victory over an American crew. Earlier, Princeton first eight has taken out Cambridge University in the Ladies' Plate final, but their second boat stood no chance against the Brookes crew of cox Allie Bohenko, Blaise Ivers-Dreux, Travis O'Neil, Callum Gilbey, Dominiko Arnerich, Ben Newton, Edward Lemanowicz, Jack Cooper and Marine Arnerich (more on page 211).

What should have been the last race of the day is the Prince Albert. Here it is Brookes 'A' versus ... Brookes 'B'! Yes, the two best student coxed fours in the event are both from Brookes, even though the story this year has been that some other universities, including London and Edinburgh, were putting their best oarsmen into this event.

That is an 'unbelievably impressive feat', says Fraser Innes on the JRN website.[49] The Umpire tells the crews he will call them 'DeSilva' and 'Thompson', the surnames of the respective coxes. Better than shouting 'A' and 'B' the whole way, I guess. So who won? Yes, despite a fast start from the 'B' crew, Brookes 'A' (cox Samuel DeSilva, Richard Hawes, Kai Schlottmann, Shay Bradley and Charlie Chick) ran out comfortable winners.

The final of the Stewards' is moved from 3.20 pm to 3.40 pm, making it the last race of the day. The Brookes crew comprises of four rowers from the winning Grand crew, so the timing change is to give them a little more recovery time as the Grand final was delayed earlier. (The Stewards do try and achieve racing that is as fair as possible.)

But this is still quite a task for Fergus and his three crewmates, Louis Nares, Thijs Ruiken and Jake Wincomb. They will have to row just three hours after their previous race, and remember they had to paddle about for around an hour in the rain before that race because of the Washington equipment issue. Up against them, four Leander men who

Henley (and Paris ...) 2024

were in the eight which lost to Brookes yesterday in the Grand, which means they haven't had to race already today.

There was some extra spice in that two of the Leander crew are Bannister and Rowe, who decamped from Brookes to Leander at the beginning of the season. The Leander four had also been selected to row for GB at the World Cup regatta in Poznan the previous month, and some were already talking about them as probables for the Los Angeles 2028 Olympics.

Well, the report is on page 254 and the GB selectors might be thinking again. It is a shame rowing does not get more general media coverage, because this win for Brookes, coming from behind in the last thirty strokes, should be heralded as one of the decades' great sporting achievements. At the boat tents, after the crews return, stroke Louis Nares is bouncing around, adrenalin in full flow. 'I want to do it again! Can we have another race?' he shouts. Fergus is beaming. 'We just weren't going to let them get away. I was shouting at Thijs (*sitting in front of Fergus in the boat*), just keep it going, we can do it.'

There might have been an odd F-word in that remark, and the crew was reprimanded for an 'audible obscenity' as they crossed the winning line. It's not surprising recently. To win two of the most prestigious Henley events in the space of three hours, as a genuine club rather than an international squad, beating your biggest rival and a full GB international crew to boot – my goodness, I think we might forgive them the odd expletive!

The athletes speak

'Brookes taught me how to be tough trainer and race a tough race, to race until there are no strokes left, to create a result from nothing.'

(*Alex Partridge*, Multiple HRR winner, 2 x GB Olympic medal winner, 3x World Champion)

Brookes men win the Grand Challenge Cup (*photograph courtesy AllMarkOne*)

Brookes women win the Remenham Challenge Cup (©*AllMarkOne*)

Henley (and Paris …) 2024

This victory was at least as much about the club ethos, psychology and the sheer will to win that Spratley and Bailhache-Webb have instilled in their athletes as it was about technical rowing skill. It was a great testament to their methods, as well as to the skill and determination of those four athletes.

So after thinking Henley 2023 was as good as it could get for Brookes, Henley 2024 was arguably even better. Six wins, all genuinely the club rather than GB squad boats badged as 'Brookes'. The first British club to win the top men's and women's eights events in the same year. The first to win the two women's eights events in the same year. All three student events, again. That very rare Grand and Stewards' double. It was another amazing day for OBUBC.

Paris 2024

After Henley, there was more to celebrate as a record number of Brookes athletes, six men and four women, were selected for the GB U23 team to compete in the World Championships in August 24. Sam Sheppard and Chris Tebb were both appointed as coaches to the squad too – not bad for Sheppard at the end of just his first full year of coaching.

Back now to the GB Olympic squad, and the results running up to the Paris Olympics were mixed. Through the season, the woman's crews had generally met or exceeded expectation, and the men's eight and pair were fine. The men's four of Oli Wilkes, David Ambler, Matthew Aldridge and Freddie Davidson had rowed as Brookes at Henley in 2023 and trained at the club before that, and Wilkes had a longer association with the club. But after dominating world championship events in 2023, they lost at Lucerne in May to the USA and New Zealand.

The Olympics was greeted by torrential rain then plenty of heat. I won't provide a blow-by-blow account of every GB race, but the GB women's quad sculls kicked off the finals by giving us a huge adrenalin rush, winning with quite literally the last stroke of the race. The women's lightweight double, strong favourites, also cruised to gold, meaning Emily Craig and Imogen Grant will probably be forever champions as lightweight rowing disappears from the Olympics. The new women's double achieved an unexpected and brilliant bronze.

Brookes alumnus Esme Booth in the GB coxless four that was a strong favourite (and also included the legendary Helen Glover) missed Olympic gold by an agonising one-foot margin against the Dutch. As favourites, GB were disappointed, whilst the GB women's eight won bronze, probably meeting expectations. But the Romanians looked very powerful out in front.

Rory Cruickshank, ex-Brookes cox, now a top rowing photographer, also pointed out how the Brookes influence is spreading globally. The winning Dutch women's coxless four in that great race included Tinka Offereins, who rowed for a year with Brookes. (Perhaps she 'learnt to win' at OBUBC, as many athletes have said.) Evan Olson, part of the brilliant Brookes Ladies' crew of 2023 that beat Leander at Henley, was in the US men's eight that won bronze.

Quentin Antognelli, another Ladies' winner for Brookes in 2018, competed for Monaco in the single sculls, making the quarterfinals, and Ask Tjom, Temple winner in 2017, competed for Norway in the lightweight double sculls. He and his partner, Lars Benske, impressed by making the final in a very competitive field, where they fought hard but finished sixth. As Cruickshank said, 'Brookes is all about the power of the programme, not just individual stars. That is being recognised now by athletes from different countries who want to come and turbo-charge their careers.'

So two golds, a silver and two bronze for GB women. The picture was also positive if variable on the men's side. The coxless four finished third, after a terrible start which saw them almost a length down after 20 strokes. That crew's dominance in 2023 seemed a distant memory. After the event, stories that the crew had suffered 'illness and injury' this year started surfacing. James Cracknell speaking on Eurosport said that stroke Freddie Davidson 'had a couple of back injections', which might explain the slow start and a tactical race to ensure they won bronze.

In the men's pair, favourites Tom George and Ollie Wynne-Griffith were leading with just three strokes to go when a mistake took pace off their boat and the legendary Croatian Sinkovic brothers slipped through to win the third gold of their careers. Maybe there was some tactical naivety there, or perhaps it was simply bad luck for the GB pair.

But in the men's eight, the GB crew was magnificent, drawing away from the USA and Netherlands to win relatively comfortably. Rory Gibbs, Morgan Bolding and cox Harry Brightmore, all Brookes through and through, and Tom Digby, who came to the club after Yale University, stood together with their crewmates on the podium to receive their medals. Gibbs, who arrived at Brookes with limited rowing experience back in 2014, was a source of great pride for Spratley and Bailhache-Webb, as they had seen him develop from a raw teenager to the world's best.

In April 2024, Richard Spratley and I discussed the GB selection for the first World Cup event of the year in Varese. He was a little surprised that there were no changes in the men's sweep crews (the eight, coxless four and pair) from the 2023 season. Was it likely that, over a year or more, no-one had come through to stake a claim, no-one had maybe dropped off the pace a little, or had an injury that might affect performance? Remember Spratley's comment that Pep Guardiola wouldn't select a Cup Final team months before the match.

At Brookes, that large squad, with others ready to step up, provides flexibility, as we've discussed. It is unfair to be too critical when the crew did win medals, but the performance of the GB four raised questions after their dominance in 2023. Perhaps there should have been changes if illness and injury were issues, but the GB squad does not have half a dozen instantly ready replacements to hand, as Brookes usually does, and it is difficult to make changes at the last minute when individuals and crews have worked towards the Olympics for years.

That ability to change crews successfully close to competition has been at the heart of the Brookes' success story, so maybe that is something for the national leadership to look at before Los Angeles in 2028.

However, eight medals for GB, including three golds, was a very strong performance, certainly in a different league to Tokyo, and Brookes played its own part in that success. And never forget how much all those athletes went through just to make it to Paris. Rowing hurts. The men's eight made it look reasonably comfortable in their final, but there was a great quote from Jacob Dawson from that boat, asked in the post-race press conference whether it was a hard race. 'You go numb, your brain turns to liquid and dribbles out of your ears,' was all he said. That sums up top-level rowing pretty well.

Los Angeles 2028 beckons?
The under-23 world Championships in Canada completed the 2023/24 season in August 2024 with yet more glory for Brookes. No less than ten OBUBC athletes won gold medals as GB topped the medal table. Jake Wincomb became the first Brookes athlete to win three consecutive U23 golds stroking the coxless four, with Fergus Woolnough in the crew becoming a two-time gold medallist. Louis Nares stroked the eight to victory with crewmates Toby Lassen and cox Tom Bryce. Nares, Lassen and Bryce became double gold medallists too.

Grace Richards and Arianna Forde in the winning coxless four on the women's side also set a world record time, whilst Rhianna Sumpter and Olivia Hill won in the eight, with Hill stroking the boat brilliantly. Brookes coaches Sam Sheppard and Chris Tebb were chosen to coach crews, and Tebb completed an amazing season leading the Brookes women's squad by coaching the gold-medal men's eight. He has very quickly established himself now as one of the very best young coaches in the UK. The prognosis for the GB squad and for that Brookes contribution to it looks promising in terms of the Los Angeles Olympics in 2028.

Chapter 28

Learning from Brookes

'The Brookes culture is to train hard every day and to push forwards every year. And hard work beats talent every time.' (Chris Tebb, Brookes Women's Head Coach)

This is a book about a sports club and its development. I considered trying to make it a business and leadership book, not least because the potential market might be larger! But it would be forcing the story to fit a certain template to achieve that.

However, Brookes provides many lessons for other organisations, including sports clubs of all types, but also businesses and public bodies. At an individual level, anyone who wants to encourage high performance from their people can learn something. So here are a dozen suggested lessons extracted from the Brookes story. Perhaps they will have wider application in your organisation, whatever that may be.

Patience and loyalty – of course, most commercial organisations don't have much patience, but Brookes success has been built on 30 years of improvement, much of it incremental, with occasional positive step-changes and frequent minor setbacks too. Spratley and Bailhache-Webb in particular have been patient and loyal and the Brookes university authorities have reciprocated with their support. The message for other organisations (which they may not want to hear) is that it usually takes time to achieve real, embedded success.

Learning from Brookes

Continuity and careful recruitment of leaders – Richard Spratley was the driving force in the early days, then the glue and facilitator as the club expanded and he stepped back somewhat from front-line coaching. Recruiting from within Brookes (including Bailhache-Webb, Tebb and Sheppard) helped to cement the culture, but Spratley's pragmatic approach means also being open when an opportunity arises to get someone top-class from outside (Haining and Gulliver). We often see leaders who don't know when to let go, or to bring in outside help, but Spratley's management of the transition to Bailhache-Webb taking over as head coach was exemplary. There are not many people who can look at someone else and say 'yeah, he might actually be better than me at that', even though they have done the 'that' very successfully for 15 years. Which leads us nicely onto the next point.

Humility – central to the Brookes culture is a lack of personal arrogance and ego. Some who don't know Brookes well may perceive the club as 'arrogant', but my feeling is what they mean is 'they keep winning stuff'. From the inside, it certainly appears that the organisation comes first, not the individual. 'One for all and all for one' truly is the belief system. The success of the organisation and every victory is down to everybody, from the top to the bottom. This is easy to say and harder to put into practice, but it has really worked for Brookes. The almost egalitarian ethos (unlike how many other clubs work), treating everyone the same from gold medal winners to novices, training together, wearing the same kit, has played a major role in building that humility *and* team ethos.

Confidence and challenging targets – but humility does not mean you should not aim high. Brookes went to continental regattas when they were unknown as a club beyond the Thames. They wanted to win the Head of the River, and beat the US university giants, which seemed impossible dreams, but they achieved those goals. They went for the Grand at Henley 2024 rather than settling for (almost certainly) winning the Ladies' Plate. Avoid the arrogance of thinking you have the right to beat anyone, but equally, aim to be the best, and set yourself challenging targets.

Intense internal competitiveness – the most notable aspect of the Brookes culture may well be how the club has combined intense internal competitiveness alongside strong club spirit. Every training session and race feeds into the relative ranking and hierarchy of athletes within the club, and crew selection for major events is made late in the day. So everyone is trying to push themselves up the ranking into a better crew. (Except those at the top, who simply want to hang on to what they have got!) That 'push' from below drives everybody onwards and upwards.

Strong team culture – yet this competitiveness does not appear to have led to an unfriendly or unpleasant atmosphere, quite the opposite. The team spirit is very visible, and rowers really seem to buy into the philosophy that everybody contributes to the club's success, informing behaviours and attitudes. Brookes and the long-standing coaches in particular have also used their 'creation story' of the underdog club to build a particular spirit which has persevered long beyond their true underdog status. (cf. Alec Ferguson's 'everybody hates us' approach at Manchester United!) In the corporate world, if you are running a sales team, for instance, how could you instil that duality of competitiveness *and* team spirit?

Learning from Brookes

Fairness, respect, openness and honesty – these core values also contribute strongly to that culture. As the coaches say, 'We aim to make every individual as good as he or she possibly can be.' Tough decisions such as on crew selection are made as fairly as possible, based strongly on objective data. Coaches are honest with athletes and explain if they aren't going as far as they hoped in the club, but they treat people with respect even if they're disappointing them. This trait is certainly something leaders can emulate in any organisation.

Personal responsibility – if there is an expectation that coaches will behave with consideration for the athletes, there is reciprocation too. Everybody in the club is expected to take responsibility for themselves and to contribute more widely to the success of the whole entity. Examples of this such as crews cleaning their own boats and doing minor repairs or adjustments (unlike at US universities) have cropped up earlier. The logistics of rowing from a location 16 miles from Oxford has meant just getting 120 athletes to and from the river is a military operation. So everyone must take responsibility for their own actions and behaviours, a philosophy that can and should be widely applied.

Recruitment is key – everybody would agree with that statement, but not every organisation acts on that principle. If you don't get the right people in, you won't succeed, no matter how good the coaching might be. Brookes only moved to the higher level of performance once the leaders realised this and took action to be more attractive to potential recruits and more proactive in their approach.

Incremental improvement pays off – often linked to *data and measurement* at Brookes. Telemetry means the coaches understand each rower in detail, how they are performing, the 'shape' of their stroke, how their power output varies over a race and more. That might not be possible in business life, but the concept of always looking for those data-driven marginal and incremental gains applies everywhere. Richard Spratley is the master of 'men, materials and money', and the team constantly look for improvement and advantage in every detail. Other sports coaches such as Dave Brailsford in cycling have been lauded for this in recent years; arguably, Spratley was there first. Matt Hnatiw, who rowed for five years at Brookes says, 'Every season, Richard and Henry were looking to step on. They would reflect on any loss and make little changes through the year.'

Standardisation brings benefits – the way Brookes standardised on boats, other equipment and indeed on coaching, training and racing approaches means the club has great flexibility in terms of their athletes, as well as lower costs. There is something in that for most organisations to consider. (I know from my early career that you could walk into a Mars factory or office anywhere in the world and feel instantly at home – one of the reasons for that firm's huge success.)

The athletes speak

'There is a clarity of purpose at Brookes, based on hard work and competition – but athletes have fun too, in a serious way!'

(*Alex Henshilwood*, HRR winner and GB International)

Learning from Brookes

Clarity, hard work and structure – finally, we should acknowledge that it is hard to succeed in anything without working hard, unless you are very, very lucky or a genius. (And most geniuses work hard too.) Brookes started on their journey with Spratley telling rowers that if they trained twice as hard as established rivals, they stood half a chance. That work has to be carefully structured and monitored, but there is no short cut to faster erg times, faster rowing and winning races. To some extent, Brookes and its athletes have just wanted it more than any other rowing club in the world over the last thirty years. 'Every stroke matters; every training session matters,' as the Brookes coaches say.

The clarity of purpose at Brookes means don't waste time, stay focused, work hard, trust the process. It is hard to do that day after day in most organisations, when you don't have the equivalent of sporting competition to drive you on. But every action, every decision, every day *does* actually matter. Maintain that attitude and improvement and success will come.

Chapter 29

The Future

'I'm sure the most important factor has just been sheer hard work over many years, from coaches and many hundreds of athletes.' (Richard Spratley, 2024)

Where next for Brookes?
Where does Brookes go from here? Are there more mountains to be climbed, or will it be enough of a challenge to maintain the current level of success? And what will happen if and when key people move on?

GB Olympic rowing in Paris was back to the top of the medals table, with a strong Brookes influence on the men's side very evident. Continuing to provide a steady flow of rowers at that international level is a key Brookes objective, as is continuing the dominance of university events at Henley and in other regattas. Winning back the Head of the River title in 2025 is high on the agenda too.

Richard Spratley has no intention of retiring yet from his Director of Rowing role, and the difficult transition we often see when a star coach moves on (think Sir Alex Ferguson and Manchester United) has already been managed successfully at Brookes with Bailhache-Webb now established as quite probably the world's top rowing coach. Chris Tebb, Hugo Gulliver and Sam Sheppard also play key roles now.

Mike Sweeney, one of the most knowledgeable and central figures in British rowing over the last 50 years, describes Brookes as 'a machine that is rolling well, they offer a good education alongside the rowing, and are so well organised. At the moment, the system Richard Spratley developed, and Henry Bailhache-Webb took further, looks unstoppable, and of course success breeds success.'

The Future

But there are cycles. Sweeney remembers the days when Imperial and University of London had spells at the top of GB rowing, but their positions were not maintained. You can never be sure. For example, if and when Spratley does step back, there is the question of who will pick up his team management responsibilities. His mastery of 'men, materials and money' can often make his role look quite straightforward, but it is not. As Chris Tebb puts it, 'Getting everything right around the rowing means less stress, and lets the athletes and coaches make the hard work as simple as possible.' Much of what Spratley does is invisible, but vital. I spoke to people who think Brookes will be fine when he eventually retires, whilst others were not so sure.

Bailhache-Webb is the other central individual here, providing Brookes with unparalleled coaching skills and understanding of how to win big races. He would clearly be a huge loss, and if he was offered the top coaching job by GB Rowing, he might be tempted (although the 'politics' of working at that level might frustrate him, I suspect).

But Spratley and Bailhache-Webb still talk about new challenges. Can Brookes produce a crew to break the course record in the Grand at Henley? There are targets in terms of the Head of the River and other regattas for the women to aim for, and there is a desire to see more Brookes women going through to national selection, which surely must happen after this year's performance. For Brookes women, as well as men, Olympic gold medals in 2028 must be on the cards.

At the other end of the experience scale, can Brookes develop the 'learn to row' programme and win Novice events at major regattas? Brookes has never focused on sculling, in the main because, as Spratley points out, there are generally more events for 'sweep' rowing than for sculling. However, there are still Olympic and Henley sculling events, and it is strong and popular at junior level, so there could be an appeal in terms of student interest. So maybe that is an area where Brookes could develop a new focus. Capacity is an issue for either more novice effort or sculling, but Spratley is nothing if not resourceful, as we've seen many times.

The future of Brookes is inextricably linked of course to the wider future of rowing. The sport is reasonably strong at grassroots level, although more clubs are focusing on smaller boats because of the cost of buying and running an eight and the challenge of finding eight reasonably well-matched rowers.

But as a major international sport, it is less healthy. It is highly dependent on the Olympics and the funding from that event, so the IOC (International Olympic Committee) has considerable power – witness the effect on lightweight rowing when it was reduced then withdrawn (after Paris) from the event. Instead, we will see coastal rowing in the form of 'beach sprints' as an Olympic sport in 2028. Will this be a successful addition, as ski cross racing, for example, has certainly been to that sport, despite the initial doubts of many skiing fans? Henry Bailhache-Webb always wanted to be a surfer, so perhaps this new discipline will attract his attention! Olympic rowing in 2028 will also be over 1,500 metres rather than 2,000, which is not seen as a positive step by many in the sport.

And unfortunately, outside the Olympics, there is limited general interest in major domestic or international competition. Henley and the Boat Race, and the big US university events, arguably all draw more interest than the World Championships, and the Head of the River gets barely a mention in the UK media other than a couple of specialist websites. And as we have seen, the leading US universities hoover up young rowing talent from around the world. That benefits their own performance, and keeps their millionaire alumni donors happy, but personally I'm far from clear it is to the benefit of the sport globally.

But whatever happens in the future, the story of Brookes over the last 30 years or so has been an extraordinary one. The club has transformed

The Future

from a small polytechnic boat club in the shadow of Oxford University, sharing a boathouse, then rowing out of a 'cowshed', to the best university rowing club in the world, and one of the very best clubs of any kind.

Whatever happens next, Oxford Brookes University Boat Club has in some sense achieved a sporting miracle over the last 30 years or so. However, the word 'miracle' suggests something supernatural, lucky or unearned, and that is certainly not the case here. This success has been based on consistency, talent and effort from everyone involved. Henley winner Matt Hnatiw puts it like this: 'There is no secret, just consistent effort, turn up every day, do the work, follow the programme.'

Richard Spratley says, 'I'm sure the most important factor has just been sheer hard work over many years, from coaches and many hundreds of athletes.' And the end result has been positive for many hundreds of young athletes. Henry Bailhache-Webb speaks of his pride that 'we've helped to develop super-confident people, who know how to perform under pressure, and can use the lessons they learnt rowing at Brookes to help in their future lives'.

The Brookes story deserves more recognition as one of the great British sports stories of the last 30 years. Commentating at Henley in 2024, as the women's first boat demolished the Canadian national development crew, rowing guru Martin Cross was spot on when he said this[50]:

> 'I don't think enough people in the UK know that Brookes is a sensational rowing university. They still think that Oxford and Cambridge are the best and I think the wider public needs to know that Brookes is a phenomenal success story.'

But this isn't a sporting 'miracle'. Richard Spratley, through the whole period, and Henry Bailhache-Webb, during the last 20 years, deserve

Oxford Brookes

huge credit for what they have achieved. Indeed, everyone involved with Oxford Brookes University Boat Club during that period, from the men and women who were early pioneers at 'the Poly', to the youngsters signing up last year, from Olympic winners to sixth-boat strivers, should feel proud of themselves. They have all contributed to a great sporting story of hard work, innovation, and achievement, and the building of a truly great club.

References

1. Website which quotes Ashleigh Teitel https://10morestrokes.wordpress.com/about/
2. The history of Falcon Boat Club https://falconboatclub.org.uk/sites/default/files/page/Falcon%20History.pdf
3. Photographs of the Isis Boathouse opening, 1990 https://radar.brookes.ac.uk/radar/items/2217f724-9f3a-1187-1da2-b1b98a9bd23a/1/
4. The Isis Boathouse for sale, property details in 2024 https://www.pennyandsinclair.co.uk/properties/18235320/sales#/
5. Brookes training at Wimbleball Lake https://www.youtube.com/watch?v=2_ziiEC_Pbs
6. HRR video of the Brookes versus Washington Prince Albert Final, 2023 https://www.youtube.com/watch?v=K9bWgySmCeQ
7. Henley Royal Regatta YouTube channel with every race since 2016 https://www.youtube.com/user/henleyroyalregatta
8. Yale Men's Rowing video https://www.youtube.com/watch?v=2k1nUIi6dis
9. Mike Reynaud in Gladiators, 1995 https://www.youtube.com/watch?v=ER0OL0UuqFg
10. YouTube video of the Henley Royal Regatta 1993 Temple final, the first ever Brookes victory at the regatta https://www.youtube.com/watch?v=-lYZeaHgA8o
11. Oxford Mail reports on Brookes beating Oxford University https://www.oxfordmail.co.uk/sport/14303274.rowing-talented-oxford-brookes-defeat-dark-blues-boat-race-warm-up/
12. Brown University rowing club website reporting on the 1994 crew https://brownbears.com/honors/hall-of-fame/1994-mens-crew-team/601
13. My late father in law's book on submarine design https://www.amazon.co.uk/stores/Roy%20Burcher/author/B001KDUEAC
14. An interesting paper looking at the history of debate around rowing technique – *'It was a fearful stroke, but they made their old boat hum' – A Social and Technical History of Rowing in England and the United States* by Stewart Stokes, 2000 https://web.colby.edu/crew/files/2010/06/It-Was-A-Fearful-Stroke-Stews-Thesis.pdf
15. Olympic coxless four rowing final, 2004 https://www.youtube.com/watch?v=h2WoTnCto5I

16. Peter Haining wins the world championship in 1993 https://www.youtube.com/watch?v=Of3YwwfNoUI
17. Daniel Topolski in *The Observer* covering Peter Haining at Henley 2001 https://www.theguardian.com/observer/sport/story/0,6903,518566,00.html
18. Oxford Mail newspaper reports on new sponsored Brookes boat, June 13th 2001 https://www.oxfordmail.co.uk/news/6614592.gallery-owner-backs-rowing-crew/
19. *Four Men in a Boat* by Tim Foster and Rory Ross, published by Orion in June 2004 https://www.amazon.co.uk/Four-Men-Boat-Tim-Foster/dp/0297847252
20. Crossy's Corner, with Martin Cross interviewing Richard Spratley https://www.youtube.com/watch?v=bmlwY5zKqws
21. Brilliant video of Rory Copus coxing Brookes to victory in 2014 https://www.youtube.com/watch?app=desktop&v=RDFsB7XwCzY
22. Brookes versus Nereus, day 3 at Henley 2015 https://www.youtube.com/watch?v=owYmzaqQ6-s
23. https://row-360.com/henley-royal-regatta-sunday-report-2024/
24. BBC video of the 2023 Oxford/Cambridge Boat Race, with brilliant coxing on display https://www.youtube.com/watch?v=EqqFNWK-Hbs
25. The 2022 Brookes Temple crew video – 'Double or Nothing' – from Will Denegri https://www.youtube.com/watch?v=sLR2GR4Mq2E
26. Manyatta website and the Elizabethan Boat Club belt https://manyatta.co.uk/products/elizabethan-boat-club-old-westminsters?_pos=1&_sid=a4e881691&_ss=r
27. Henley Royal Regatta video, Brookes and Bayer Leverkusen in the Ladies' Plate 2017 semi-final https://www.youtube.com/watch?v=rm8HR1zO4eQ
28. Brookes website interview with Carla Devlin https://brookesrowing.org.uk/carla-devlin-to-speak-at-this-years-taurus-dinner/
29. Article from Women in Sport concerning participation of teenage girls https://womeninsport.org/news/more-than-1-million-teenage-girls-fall-out-of-love-with-sport/
30. The Harvard Crimson website on a momentous win for the university https://www.thecrimson.com/article/2002/7/12/m-crew-wins-three-henley-titles/
31. Row360 website article from Rachel Quarrell https://row-360.com/medical-alerts-at-henley-royal/
32. The Guardian analyses the GB rowing performance at the Tokyo Olympics, 30 July 2021 https://www.theguardian.com/sport/2021/jul/30/team-gb-win-bronze-in-mens-eight-as-inquest-starts-into-poor-olympic-regatta
33. The British rowing website reports the resignation of Jurgen Grobler https://www.britishrowing.org/2020/08/jurgen-grobler-steps-down-as-chief-coach-of-the-gb-rowing-team/
34. BBC article on bullying claims in GB women's rowing squad, 17 June 2016 https://www.bbc.co.uk/sport/rowing/36565587

References

35. Excellent and insightful article from Tom Ransley on the Row360 website, analysing GB Tokyo Olympic rowing failure https://row-360.com/let-down-by-management/
36. British Rowing announces selection panels for rowing squad https://www.britishrowing.org/2021/02/british-rowing-announces-seven-new-external-selectors-for-the-gb-rowing-team/
37. Jurgen Grobler interview in *The Daily Telegraph*, 25 July 2024 https://www.telegraph.co.uk/olympics/2024/07/25/jurgen-grobler-interview-team-gb-rowing-paris-olympics-2024/
38. Josh Bugajski quoted in the *Manchester Evening News*, speaking about ex-GB coach Jurgen Grobler https://www.manchestereveningnews.co.uk/sport/bugajski-stockport-rowing-olympics-21187092
39. Mathew Syed in *The Sunday Times*, May 2024, writing about anxiety and performance in high-level sport https://www.thetimes.com/sport/olympics/article/anxiety-elite-sport-success-matthew-syed-m7ngpx6sc
40. Junior Rowing News website with Tom Morgan reporting on Henley results, 3 July 2023 https://juniorrowingnews.com/henley-royal-regatta-2023-view-from-the-press-box/
41. Henley Royal Regatta video, Brookes versus California Berkeley in the 2022 Prince Albert final https://www.youtube.com/watch?v=7gyPyKw1fRU
42. Wikipedia entry for *Thinking Fast and Slow* by Daniel Kahneman https://en.wikipedia.org/wiki/Thinking,_Fast_and_Slow
43. *The Guardian* article by Cath Bishop commenting on the Cambridge women's boat race preparation https://www.theguardian.com/sport/blog/2024/apr/03/cambridge-women-boat-race-culture-sport-cath-bishop-rowing
44. Report on donations at Harvard to support rowing https://pershingsquarefoundation.org/2014/04/13/donor-of-the-day-giving-for-learning-and-for-rowing/
45. Tom Morgan's Henley 24 recap on JRN website https://juniorrowingnews.com/henley-royal-regatta-2024-view-from-the-press-box/
46. Pathe News film of the Barn Elms rowing tank https://www.britishpathe.com/asset/88770/)
47. Thijs Ruiken talks about Brookes beating the Dutch Olympic eight at Amsterdam Beker, June 2024 https://nlroei.nl/een-hollander-verslaat-de-holland-acht-thijs-ruiken-komt-bij-oxford-brookes-in-recordtijd-tot-bloei/
48. JRN website, 8 July 2024 https://juniorrowingnews.com/henley-royal-regatta-2024-view-from-the-press-box/
49. Fraser Innes summing up the student events at Henley 2024 https://juniorrowingnews.com/henley-royal-regatta-2024-sunday-briefing-the-student-finals/
50. Brookes paddling three-quarter pressure crush Rowing Canada in the Remenham Cup, Friday 5 July 2024 https://www.youtube.com/watch?v=75wUfVNvIrI

Index of people

Abraham, Chris 125
Ackman, Bill 250
Akers, Matt ix, 39–60
Aldridge, Matt 142, 174, 179, 201, 208, 237, 283
Allen, David 84, 87
Allen, Kiera 209
Alvis, Pete 49, 53, 133
Ambler, David 208, 237, 283
Antognelli, Quentin 179, 182, 284
Argyle, Beatrice 172
Armstrong, Brian 85
Arnerich, Dominiko 37, 280
Arnerich, Marine 37, 280
Ashley-Carter, Piers 28
Asmuss, Heiki 188
Axon, Jamie 179, 182, 208
Ayres, Oli 180

Baker, Phil 61, 84, 108
Bailhache-Webb, Henry ix, xiv, 3, 6, 9, 78, 101, 102–118, 122–9, 132, 138–42, 144, 146–7, 151–4, 161, 166, 170, 171, 173, 175–7, 188, 192, 196, 198, 199, 201, 203, 207–10, 212, 215, 221, 230–1, 233, 235, 238, 242 –6, 249, 252, 253, 255, 257, 260–2, 265–7, 271–2, 273–7, 283, 285, 288–9, 294–7
Bannister, Sam 64, 183, 208, 265, 272, 281
Bates, Christopher 110
Bates, Jenny ix, 1-9, 120, 200, 248, 257, 270, 272, 277
Beaumont, Katie 186
Bellamy, Daisy 209
Bernal, Sofia 278

Bewicke-Copley, David 208, 233
Birtles, Martha 120, 172, 272
Bird, Max x
Bishop, Cath 245, 247
Blight, Ethan 168
Bloise-Brooke, Henry 208
Bloomer, Anna 278
Blyth, Chay 49
Bohenko, Allie 161, 211-2, 280
Bolding, Morgan 142, 144–5, 174, 179, 208, 233, 240, 285
Bowden, Sean 261, 272
Bowers, Jasmine 120
Bradley, Shay 280
Brailsford, Dave 292
Brightmore, Harry 139, 142, 144–5, 155, 161, 162, 174, 175, 177 179, 182, 208, 240–1, 272, 285
Broughton, Tim 138
Brown, James 49, 107
Brownlee brothers 225
Bryant, Tasmin (ne Adams) ix, 130, 188
Bryce, Tom 161, 162, 234, 279, 286
Bugajski, Josh 176, 182, 229
Burt, Aggie 278
Burton, Tom 103, 106, 108, 109
Bushnell, David 84

Cameron, Jonathon 238
Capello, Fabio 115
Carlson, Jack 138
Carnegie-Brown, Olivia 139, 190
Carpenter, Amelia 278
Carson, Toby 86

Casey Neumann 168
Cassells, Joel 140, 144, 179
Caudle, Taylor 209
Chambers, Peter 126, 183
Chambers, Richard 4, 115, 125, 191
Chick, Charlie 280
Clapp, Phil 219
Clarke, Charlie 162, 176
Clarke, Mark 88, 90
Clarke, Sam 269, 270
Clewes, Hannah 126
Cockle, Scott 162, 208
Coe, Seb 51
Coni, Peter 32
Coode, Ed 109
Cook, David 15
Cook, Russell ix, 15
Cooper, Jack 37, 208
Cooper, John 49, 52, 53
Copus, Jamie 64, 140, 141, 144, 274, 278
Copus, Rory 138, 140, 141, 156, 160, 162, 243
Corry, Gareth 88, 106
Cosijn Diez, Aida 278
Cottrell, Lizzie 268
Couldwell, Clive ix, 9, 15, 16
Cracknell, James 106, 109, 135, 223, 285
Craig, Emily 284
Cross, Martin x, 139, 172, 177, 297
Cruickshank, Rory x, 205, 284
Curry, Gareth 86, 87
Cusack, Nicole 172

Dalton, Mikey 183
Davidson, Freddie 208, 237, 283, 285

Index of people

Davies, Alasdair 15
Davies, Mark 230
Davies, Ryan 116
de Toledo, Zoe 157, 190
Denegri, Will 64, 162, 171, 233
Dennis, Simon 90
DeSilva, Samuel 280
Devereux, Miles 233
Devlin, Carla (ne Ashford) 75, 125, 185–188, 190
Devlin, Jonno 88, 103, 106, 108, 110
Digby, Tom 208, 233, 240, 285
Donaghy, Odhran 233, 278
Doran, James 64, 279
Douglas, Katherine 139, 190
Douglas, Rowley 82, 88, 103, 155, 162
Drummond, Archie 168
Durant, Mason 130, 138
Durant, Scott 125, 130, 138
Durgan Martin 15
Dutton, Beth 209, 268

Edwards, Brendan 176, 179, 182

Facy, Errol 71
Fairbairn, Steve 94, 97, 149, 150
Falstrup-Fisker, Evan 37
Fangen-Hall, Mark 272
Feerick, Claire 188
Felkel, Christian 228, 230
Ferguson, Sir Alex 290, 294
Ferguson, Harriet 209
Fieldman, Henry 226, 228
Fitt, Prof. Alistair 137
Fonseca, Emma 188
Ford, Nick 162
Forde, Arianna 8, 120, 172, 268, 286
Foster, Tim 135
French, Allan 190, 191, 252

Gandon, Alex ix, 17, 18
Gandon, Jane (ne MacMillan) ix, 17, 18, 186
Garmus, Bonnie 264

George, Tom 285
Gibbs, Rory 139, 142, 144, 145, 174, 179, 182, 215, 233, 235, 240, 285
Gilbey, Callum 280
Gillard, Dave 108
Glover, Helen 1, 284
Glover, Michael 142, 170, 174, 179, 182, 208
Grainger, Dame Katherine xv, 211, 254
Grant, Imogen 284
Grant, Tim 140, 143, 144
Grisedale, Ed 140, 179
Grobler, Jurgen 102–103, 223–9
Guardiola, Pep 196, 198, 285
Gulliver, Hugo ix, 5, 6, 120, 191, 192, 213, 239, 246, 252, 277, 289, 294

Haining, Peter ix, 89, 90, 102, 110–8, 122, 188, 252, 260, 289
Hall, Andrew ix, 264
Hall, Will 242, 244
Harris, James 228
Hawes, Isy 209
Hawes, Richard 280
Hawkins, Richard 140
Hayes, Aisling 209
Heath, Alfie 180
Heathcote, Alastair 125
Henshilwood, Alex ix, 49, 55, 58, 61, 84, 101, 248, 261, 262, 292
Henshilwood, Elizabeth 188
Hepworth, Jeremy 49
Herbert, Gary 109, 229
Heywood, Matt 31, 64, 233, 272, 278, 279
Hill, Olivia 278, 287
Hillier, Luke 180
Hinves, Ben 233, 238
Hnatiw, Matt x, 161, 166, 176, 179, 249, 262, 292, 297
Hoffstot, Henry 138
Hoker, Dr Mark 228
Hoodless, Alex 49

Hoogland, Sybren 138, 140, 143, 144
Horncastle, Tom 278
Hudspith, Chris 125
Hullah, Jens 233
Hunt-Davis, Ben 104
Hynes, Lewis 13

Innes, Fraser 280
Ivers-Dreux, Blaise 233, 280

James, Tom 124
Janes, Dan ix, 191
Jenkins, Lenny 208
Jenkins, Oliver 61
Johnson, Boris 201
Jonathan Wang-Norderud 168
Jones, Amie 233
Jones, Callum 140
Jordan (Katie Price) 133, 134

Kelly, Keith x, 172, 261
Keto, Freya 272, 277, 278
Kingsley, Louise 230
Kirchhoff, Dietlef 112
Kolbeck, Shelby 278
Krijgsveld, Nykle 234
Kubis, Bob 197, 198

Lassen, Toby 43, 233, 238, 279, 286
Lemanowicz, Edward 280
Levy, Tim 22–4, 26, 27, 48, 52, 268
Lindsay, Oscar 208
Louloudis, Constantine 136
Lowe, Peter ix, 18–24, 28, 29, 32, 47–9, 247, 248, 268
Lucy, Tom 124

McDougall, Alan 113
MacDougall, Fiona 186
Magee, Tim ix, 16
Mainland, Fergus 173
Manning, Bill 197, 198
Marett, Dan 90, 103, 108, 109
Martyn Smith, James 140
Massey, Robert 174
Mattijssen, Pim 234

Maxwell, Robert 214
McDonald, Jamie 186
Mcgillan, Connor 233
McWilliams, Gavin 180, 183
McWilliams, Kevin 103, 110
Mellor, Hayley 186
Menevia, the Emeritus Bishop of xv
Miller, Lottie 45
Moffatt, Cameron 115
Morgan, Tom 232, 259, 273
Morrell, James 213
Morris, Hayden ix, 15, 17
Morris, Kevin ix
Morrissett, Lindsey 278
Moseley, Kate 186

Nares, Louis 206, 207, 232, 234, 235, 237, 254, 268, 272, 279, 280, 281, 286
Nash, Elle 3
Newman, Matt 180, 183
Newman, Seb 183, 208
Newton, Ben 280
Nichol, Alex 278
Nunn, Sam 64, 176, 179, 182, 201, 208, 274, 279

O'Connor, Caroline 125, 130, 162, 190
O'Donoghue, Graham 197, 198
O'Neill, Travis 280
Olson, Evan 64, 284
Ovett, Steve 51

Parish, Jasper 158
Parkinson, Andy 230
Partridge, Alex x, 104, 106–110, 124, 130, 160, 281
Peill, David ix, 41, 42, 47, 49, 60, 68, 71–74, 171
Phelps, Richard xv
Pinsent, Sir Matthew 106, 109, 112, 135–7, 220
Prior, Jack 232
Prior-Reeves, Frances x
Purcell, Brendan 204, 225–7, 229, 230

Quarrell, Rachel x, 81–84, 106, 146, 162, 167, 251

Randall, Brenna 120, 172
Rankov, Boris 16, 18
Ransley, Tom 226, 228
Redgrave, Sir Steve xiii, xv, 87, 107, 108, 112, 135–7, 206, 210, 225, 227, 238, 273
Reed, Ludo 31
Reed, Pete 110
Reedy, Paul 227
Regan, Emilia 278
Reggiani, Ruben 115
Reynaud, Mike 46–50, 60
Richards, Grace 120, 172, 286
Robinson, W 116
Rosen, Lionel 52
Ross, Alistair 84
Ross, Robert 56
Ross, Rory 135
Rowe, Matt 64, 180, 199, 208, 265
Ruiken, Thijs 275, 280, 281
Russell, Mark 49
Ryan, Nick 15

Saban, Nick 52
Sanderson, Elise 209
Sapstead, Nicole 143
Sbihi, Mo xv, 66, 220
Scarlett, Fred 55, 61, 86, 88, 102, 103, 136
Schlottmann, Kai 280
Searle, Greg 110, 225
Sens, Robert 112
Sheppard, Sam ix, 2–9, 222, 234–6, 252, 268, 283, 287, 289, 294
Silk, Roger 78
Simms, Raymond 110
Simper, Jordan 5, 209
Simpson, McKenna 172
Smeding, Orren 120
Smith, Ryan 168
Smith, Sheena 10
Snowball, James 179, 183
Spratley, Jeremy 23

Spratley, Richard 22–4, 25–33, 38, 39–54, 55–63, 66, 68–79, 80–7, 102–118, 122–130, 131–7, 139–142, 144, 146–7, 151, 154, 160, 164–171, 176, 178, 185–193, 195–200, 203, 207, 210, 214–9, 227, 230, 231, 234, 244, 248, 253, 257–262, 264–9, 272, 273, 275, 277, 279, 283, 285, 288, 289, 292, 293, 294–7
Stanhope, James 142, 174
Stannard, Paul 228
Stanning, Heather xv
Stewart, Will 208
Stimpson, Charles 15
Stirling, Robin 176
Strange, Nick 112
Stubbs, Andrew 109
Sumpter, Rhianna 120, 172, 286
Swarbrick, Henry 142, 144, 174, 179, 182
Sweeney, Mike (CBE) ix, 61, 62, 129, 165, 167, 169, 257, 294–5
Symington, James ix, 28, 268
Syphas, Gareth 176

Tanner, Sir David 190, 225, 226
Tarczy, Calvin 238
Tarrant, Matthew 125, 130, 138, 142, 181, 182, 208
Taylor, Emily 226
Tebb, Chris ix, 176, 183, 192, 194, 201, 203, 204, 239, 252, 260, 266, 277, 283, 286, 288, 289, 294, 295
Teitel, Ashleigh 10–12
Telling, David 42
Thompson, Max 183
Thompson, Paul 226
Tjom, Ask 174, 176, 284
Tognazzi, Marco 232, 234
Topolski, Daniel 112
Trapmore, Steve 228, 230
Tredell, Lance 138

Index of people

Triggs-Hodge, Andrew 110, 124
Tucker, M 116

van Vilsteren, Hessel 234
Von Maltzahn, Jo 88, 103, 106

Wallace, Bill 26
Walter, Steve 186

Watchhorn, John 61
Webb, Ben 84
Wenyon, Alex 179
Wettach, Brian 138
Wilkes, Oli 179, 182, 201, 208, 237, 283
Williams, Steve 60, 61, 86, 88, 90, 102–4, 109, 110, 124, 136
Winckless, Sarah 212

Wincomb, Jake 64, 233, 254, 268, 272, 278–80, 286
Winklevoss twins 272
Wise, Annette 186
Witting, Ben 180

Zahn, Chris 176
Zondi, Bakang 38, 161

General index

10 more strokes website 10

academic
  eights (Henley women's regatta event) 191, 192, 234
  studies 104–5, 143, 171
  institutions 18, 250
  leadership 80
  reputation 166, 170
accountability 9, 257
Advanced Rowing Initiative of the Northeast, USA (ARION) 172
aerodynamics 95
A level results 165
Alps, the 202
alumni (inc. clubs) 151, 176, 296
  Brookes ix, 49, 52, 76, 87, 103, 130, 138, 190, 233, 237, 259
  Harvard 133, 250
  Yale 133
Army of the Union of the Soviet Socialist Republics xvi
Aston 24
Atlantic rowing 49
Arsenal 169
Auriol Kensington Rowing Club 40
Australia 41, 50
  rowing / rowers 90, 168

balance 45, 51, 229–31, 266
  of the boat 96–9
Barn Elms 264, 266
Barrier, the (Henley course timing point) 36, 62, 65, 119, 142, 147, 173, 181–3, 209, 233, 245, 254
Bayer Leverkusen 177
BBC, the 158, 226
Bedford School 43, 49, 201
Benson Lock 73
Berkeley, University of California 164, 165, 178, 232
Berkshire / Berks station (Henley course) 36, 147, 211, 241, 254, 275
Berliner Ruderclub 179
Bernard Churcher Trophy 267
best rowing experience 262
bicycle(s) 62–3, 203
blazers xiv, 159
boat (general)
  buying 77
  cleaning 78, 291
  maintenance 18, 78
  manufacturer 77
Boat Races, the (Oxford versus Cambridge) 131
  competitors 11, 18, 64, 81, 136, 165, 176, 179, 198
  course 156, 50, 156
  coxing and steering 46, 157–8
  disqualification 157
  practice races against Brookes 56–8, 263
  races xiii, 101, 202, 204, 257, 264, 272, 296
  women's race 185, 245
  youngest ever competitor 56
boat (types of)
  coxless four 32, 84, 86 –7, 89, 90, 109, 116, 125, 130, 135, 190, 228, 231, 237, 238, 274, 278, 284–6
  coxed four vii, 4, 31, 35, 84, 86, 87, 103, 104, 118, 125, 138, 141, 160, 176, 186, 187, 190, 197, 232, 245, 280
  double scull 90, 185, 272, 277, 284
  eights 4, 5, 18, 25–6, 30, 31, 40, 46, 61, 64, 65, 70, 84, 91, 101, 108, 116, 120, 124–5, 129, 146, 151, 172, 174, 186, 190–3, 209, 233–4, 240, 241, 270–1, 274, 276, 279, 283
  pair 3, 26, 41, 84, 88, 90, 110, 112, 221, 240, 272, 278, 283, 285
  quad sculls xvi, 89. 228, 283
  single scull 2, 7, 111, 186, 284
boathouse
  Barn Elms 264–6
  Cholsey (Brookes) 3, 11, 68–79, 81, 87, 104, 122, 131, 193, 2217, 259, 270, 273, 275, 279, 297
  Isis 20–1, 25, 69
  Yale 43, 133
boatman 26, 78–9
body, the 11, 89, 95–8, 214, 215, 218
Bootswerft Empacher 77
Bowbridge 70, 71, 77, 86–7
Brakspear's brewery 51
Brentford Football Club 257
Bristol Head race 5

General index

British Polytechnic Sports Association 17
British Rowing (governing body) 117, 137, 202, 204, 223, 227–230
British Universities (BUCS) regatta 3–4, 5, 8, 9, 189, 205, 270
Brown University 59, 103, 129, 140, 183, 192
Bucks station (Henley course) 36, 65, 106, 120, 147, 240, 275, 277
bumping races 13, 16, 149, 159
Bundesliga, the 257

California 50, 234
Cam, the 42, 158
Cambridge colleges
  St. Johns (see also Lady Margaret Boat Club) vii, xiv
  Downing 267
  Jesus 153
Cambridge University / University of Cambridge 87, 165
Cambridge University rowing xiii, 30, 33, 43, 78, 116, 131, 153, 182, 211, 257
  blue boat (1st boat) 11, 56–8, 64, 101, 156–8, 185, 198, 204, 263, 268, 272, 275, 277, 280, 297
  college rowing 13, 31, 42, 51, 76
  Goldie (2nd boat) 56, 58, 153, 182
  lightweights vii, 88, 90
  women's boats 245, 247, 264
Canada 140, 172
  geese 65
  national rowing squad 109, 273, 286
Cantabrigian Rowing Club 179
catch, the 94, 100
Caversham (GB training centre) 136, 231, 237
champagne 119, 121, 136
Champions League 198
Cheney Hall of Residence 217
Chinese rowing 227
Cholsey 3, 20, 70, 72, 79, 170, 174, 232, 270–1, 273
City of Oxford Rowing Club 15, 16
cleaning / cleanliness 78, 291
Cleeve Lock 50, 73
coaches see *"People Index"*
coaching (*key references only*) 7, 18, 33, 53, 61, 82, 100, 101, 117, 118, 127, 132, 159–160, 192, 197, 199, 211, 221, 246, 295
Colgate University 117
collapsing crews / athletes 11, 37, 93, 155, 206–7, 218, 232, 237, 255
Columbia University 175
Concept2 217
construction and building 23, 26, 72, 75, 77, 102–3, 122, 125, 132, 213
Cornell University 115, 140, 142
course length xv, 11, 13, 89, 95, 115, 149, 179, 185–6, 207, 208, 218, 222, 275
covid 2–5, 150, 153, 191, 202–5, 223, 232
cowshed, the (first boathouse at Cholsey) 70–5, 297
coxing and coxes (*see also "People Index" for individual coxes*) vii, 46
  Brookes approach 160, 162
  coaching 47, 155
  motivation 155, 159–1622
  race steering 147, 156–9, 161, 173, 184, 211
  recordings and videos 141, 155, 243
  responsibilities 155–162
Crabtree Boat Club 87
Crossy's Corner x, 139
crowds 35, 37, 63
culture 133
  in GB rowing team 225–6

see also Oxford Brookes
cycling 220
Czech rowing 151, 191

Darwin, Charles 39
data 4, 29, 41, 44, 63, 100, 101, 196, 200, 221, 221, 244, 248, 260, 291–2
degree(s) 20, 40, 105, 107, 118, 167, 170, 192
Department of Culture, Media and Sport 204
Devizes to Westminster kayak race 49
dickhead, don't be a 248, 259, 268, 270
dirty water 181, 184, 212
diversity 193
donors 250, 291
Dorney Lake 149, 205
Drowning Pool (rock band) 216
drugs
  Benzoylecgonine 143
  Modafinil 143
  Modalert 143
DSR Proteus-Eretes 115, 143
Duisburg Regatta 182, 202, 223
Durham University 5, 29, 59, 120, 140, 184, 256, 270, 278

Eastern Sprints (US event) 140
East Germany 188
Edinburgh University 20, 29, 119, 179, 180, 182, 183, 191, 205, 256, 280
egalitarianism 43, 134, 289
elitism 197
Elizabethan Boat club 176–7
Eminem 216
Encouragement, French rowing club 46
English Channel, swimming of 49, 259
English Orthodox (rowing style) 97
Ergos (rowing machine) 13, 69, 70, 190, 203, 217–220
  Ergo sessions 123, 130, 141, 208, 215–6

Ergo times 2, 3, 7, 48, 115, 139, 165, 199, 219, 227, 242, 249, 293
Estates Management 71
Eton College 39, 101, 136, 163–6, 169, 258, 261
Everest 259
Evesham regatta 84
Exmoor 27

Facy department store, Henley 71
Fawley (Henley course timing point) 36, 62, 65, 92, 119, 121, 142, 173, 180, 181, 182, 209, 211, 245, 254, 278
finance and money
  funding of OBUBC 128, 133, 137, 190, 260
  student fees 131–2, 164
Fine Art 105–6
Florida 250
Flower Pot Hotel, Aston 24
fluid dynamics 95, 99
fours head race 82
France, national rowing squad 30
friction 95–6, 98
frogs, plague of 71, 146
f**k Leander! 269–70
Fulham
  football ground 158
  side of the Thames 266
fun 1, 5, 132, 136, 152, 159, 238
  fun at Brookes 9, 79, 107, 171, 195, 257, 262, 264
Further and Higher Education Act of 1992 25

GB Rowing 295
  high-performance programme 102, 190
  influence of Brookes 137, 169, 256–7
  relationship with clubs 85–6
  trials 7, 23, 43, 48, 270
  World Class start programme 1, 220

see also Olympics, world championships
GCSE results 165
German national rowing xvi, 30, 109, 151, 168, 172, 178, 182, 201, 233
  see also individual clubs
Ghent regatta 20, 30, 143, 174, 187, 199, 270, 273
Goldie (Cambridge University reserve crew) 56, 58, 153, 182
grandstands (at Henley) 37, 121, 146, 173, 206, 254, 278
Guardian newspaper 223, 245

Hampton school 163
Hartpury University & College 1–4
Harvard University 8, 33, 62, 91, 93, 106, 111, 119, 133, 138, 139, 141, 154, 164, 166, 168–9, 175, 178, 183–4, 192, 197–8, 235–6, 241, 250–1, 274
Head races/racing 11, 82, 158, 186, 202, 263
  Head of the River (London Tideway head) 9, 20, 29, 45, 58, 61, 65, 83, 84, 112, 145, 149–154, 158, 170, 174, 179, 182, 193, 196, 199, 202, 204, 233, 243, 256, 258, 264, 273, 290, 294–6
Headington 50, 213
  Gym at Headington 203, 220, 232
  Headington Hill Hall 213–4
  Headington School 163
Heidelberg 77
Henley Rowing Club 22
Henley Royal Regatta
  boat tents 52, 63, 146, 254, 277, 279, 281
  Bridge Bar 22, 279
  Chair of the Stewards xv, 61, 87, 129, 165, 206, 273
  commentators 66, 97, 100, 158, 177, 254, 256
  Committee of Management 210

course xiv, xv, 14, 36, 106, 147, 185–6
eligibility & qualification rules 61, 84, 87, 91, 232, 274
2023 Finals Day 35, 64, 91, 119, 234–241
2024 Finals Day 146, 172, 211, 254, 273–283
History xiv, xvi, 64
intermediate events 61, 64, 178, 238, 241, 278
open events 90, 140, 146
race videos x, 36, 53, 62, 141, 146, 155, 158, 160, 177, 206, 233
Regatta Enclosure 36, 66
Stewards xiv, xv, 62, 63, 64, 87, 175, 238, 254, 274, 280
Stewards' Enclosure vii, xiv, xv, 13, 22, 37, 65, 119, 121, 174, 206
Henley Royal Regatta events
  Britannia Challenge Cup 83–4, 86, 87, 90, 106, 138, 140, 197
  Grand Challenge Cup 31, 61, 64, 91, 116, 146–8, 170, 178, 181–2, 201–3, 208, 231, 233–5, 237, 240, 254, 273, 273, 275, 278–283, 290, 295
  Henley Prize 20, 25, 31
  Island Challenge Cup 4–5, 8–9, 119–121, 172, 191–2, 209–210, 234, 237, 248, 277–8
  Ladies' Challenge Plate 7, 59, 61, 64–67, 84, 85, 88, 91, 107, 116–7, 121, 126, 128, 142, 161, 174–184, 188, 198, 199, 201, 208, 211, 235, 237, 240–1, 265, 268, 273–277, 278, 280, 284, 290
  Prince Albert Challenge Cup 4, 35–8, 64, 125, 141–2, 161, 168, 176, 181–3, 232–3, 237, 244, 245, 267, 274, 280

General index

Prince Philip Challenge Cup 106, 108, 159
Remenham Challenge Cup 75, 108, 139, 170, 172–3, 186–191, 264, 279, 282
Silver Goblets & Nickalls' Challenge Cup 90, 208
Stewards' Challenge Cup 254–5
Stonor Challenge Trophy 277–8
Temple Challenge Cup 5–9, 25, 31–4, 45–54, 55, 60–3, 64, 84, 91–93, 103, 106–7, 114–8, 120, 122, 125–9, 133, 138–143, 152, 155, 161, 171, 174–184, 188, 192, 197, 198, 201, 206, 208, 211–2, 216, 232–7, 243, 248, 267, 274, 276–280, 284
Thames Challenge Cup 17, 40, 59, 61, 84
Town Challenge Cup 277
Visitors' Challenge Cup 86, 90, 103, 106–9, 114, 116, 130, 179, 181, 183, 208, 237, 238, 241, 265, 274, 277, 278
Wyfold Challenge Cup 86–7
Henley Women's Regatta 2, 5, 8, 31, 108, 118, 186, 187, 190–3
Henley-on-Thames (the town) 3, 22, 24
Hinksey Sculling School 164
Holland Beker Regatta 174, 271
Hollandia Roeiclub 182
humility & lack of ego 128, 265, 269, 289

illness and injury 5, 124, 261, 275, 284–5
Imperial College, London 5, 20, 22, 30, 33, 45–6, 59, 61, 87, 90, 107, 151–153, 164,
172, 178, 202, 250, 252, 256–7, 295
India 90, 143
indoor rowing and championships 2, 43, 164, 220
infrastructure 129, 209
integration at Brookes (men and women) 187, 193
Internet, the 4, 50, 127
IOC (International Olympic Committee) 90, 296
Isis (Oxford University reserve crew) 56, 58

Japan 89, 90
Japanese crews 20, 88, 126
Junior rowing 21, 43, 47, 50, 55, 65, 78, 80, 89, 101, 109, 120, 130, 140, 164–8, 181, 195, 205, 257, 295
Junior Rowing News (JRN) x, 226, 232

K.S.R.V. Njord 175, 271

Lady Eleanor Holles School 163
Lady Margaret Beaufort 159
Lady Margaret Boat Club vii, xiv, 13, 59, 78, 150, 159
Lake Windermere 49
lane racing 149
Latymer Upper School 192
leaderboard (in the Brookes gym) 246
leadership 80, 128, 193, 286, 288
League of Nations 169
Leander Club 3, 104
  club 3, 23, 81, 184, 191, 200, 204, 224, 242, 256–9
  crews and races 8, 64–5, 84, 148, 151–3, 172, 175, 177, 179, 180, 182, 190, 235, 238, 240, 254–5, 264–7, 270–2, 273–281, 284
  history 65, 186, 259
leg drive 95

Lightweight rowing 149
  at the Olympics 284, 296
  Brookes athletes 23, 47–8, 107, 115–6, 125, 130, 140
  crews 178, 202, 236
  Cambridge / Oxford University Lightweights vii, 58, 88, 263
  GB squads 59, 61, 84–6
  history and decline of 88–90
  world championships 111–2
  see also Peter Haining (Index of people)
Liverpool FC 169
Loch Lomond Rowing Club 110
lockdown (Covid) 2, 5, 201, 232
London Rowing Club 23, 150, 274
loyalty 264, 288
Lucerne Regatta 30, 85, 109, 272, 283
Lyon Rowing Club 142

Magdalen College, Oxford 140
Manchester 169
  Manchester City 169, 198, 257
  Manchester United 290, 294
Marathon(s) 3, 10, 49, 208
Marlow
  bypass 16
  Regatta 176, 211, 234, 274, 278
  Rowing Club 16
Mars
  factory 78, 292
  group vii, 162
Maasai people 177
mental health 229–231
Meole Brace School, Shrewsbury 39
Metropolitan regatta 115
Michigan State University 52
minibus(es) 30, 42, 46, 50, 74, 128, 217, 277
  1992 crash 28–9
MIT (US university) 164

309

Mitie (facilities management firm) 42, 133
mixed crews 187
Molesey Boat Club 24, 81, 107, 151, 152–3, 172
Monaco 179, 284
money 3, 16, 74, 103, 131–7, 163, 214, 250–1, 259, 261, 272
  'men, materials and money' 112, 260, 292, 295
Monkton Combe School 60, 82, 104–6
Monmouth School 16
Mortlake 150
Motivation 4, 7, 74, 135, 159 –160, 171, 195–9, 216, 231, 235, 260, 262, 266–7
  self-motivation 41
Mumford and Sons 216
Muscles 10, 11, 13, 92, 95, 98, 215, 218
music 123, 214–6, 220

national lottery 204
National Universities Championship (US event) 140
Nereus Rowing Club, Netherlands 56, 64, 92, 115, 125, 142, 174–5, 178, 206, 234
Netherlands rowing and rowers
  Dutch rowing style 97
  National rowing team 116, 206, 271–2, 285
  see also individual entries for clubs
New Zealand 90, 192
  crews and rowers 37, 168, 181, 182, 192, 283
Newcastle University 30, 50, 125, 126, 140, 141, 175, 180–1, 182–3, 189, 256–7, 260, 264, 277–8
Nihon University, Japan 20, 126
Northeastern University 138, 183
Norwegian rowing / rowers 147, 168, 174, 176
Nottingham 42, 48, 110

Nottingham University 20, 40
Notts County Rowing Association (NCRA) 85–6
novice rowing / rowers 1, 15–18, 69, 117–8, 122, 132, 137, 139, 187–8, 192, 195, 204, 235, 261, 289, 295

oar(s) xiii, 37, 42, 77, 95–8, 102, 156, 157, 159, 212, 273, 279
Olympics
  2004 Athens 109–110, 124, 136
  2008 Beijing 124, 130, 136
  2012 London 116, 130
  2016 Rio 136, 139, 190, 223, 224
  2021 Tokyo 140, 201, 203, 205
  2024 Paris 223–231
  2028 Los Angeles 90, 281, 286–7, 289
  medals and tables 1, 43, 66, 103, 104, 109, 116, 124–5, 130, 135–7, 139, 164, 168, 190, 281, 285–7, 294–5
Oxbridge 31, 56, 58, 80, 119, 161, 164
Oxford (the city) Council 213
Oxford Brookes University
  Campus 214, 217
  Headington Hall 213
  history 25, 31
  leadership 80, 193
  support to UBUBC 132, 137, 252, 260–1, 288
  Vice-chancellor 137, 190
Oxford Brookes University Boat Club
  annual dinner 267–270
  beating Brookes 259–260
  culture 31, 43, 48, 108, 133, 215, 246, 248, 258, 288, 289–91
  ethos 41, 43, 48, 74, 79. 80, 127, 134, 193, 199, 225, 246, 260, 277, 283, 289
  the Dark Side 256–9
  see also individual topics e.g. boathouse, coaches, humility, leadership,

psychology, recruitment, team spirit, training, etc.
Oxford colleges
  Brasenose College 32
  Oriel College 16–17
Oxford Falcon Rowing and Canoeing Club 16, 25, 69
Oxford Polytechnic 15–20, 29, 31, 40, 186, 297
Oxford University / University of Oxford 15, 81, 136, 248, 297
  boat club 16, 55, 56, 58, 64, 103, 106, 116, 126, 176, 202, 272
Oxpolycarbonate 16

pain 10–14, 37, 41, 109, 217, 220, 229, 254
Pangbourne College 101, 163
parents 104, 165, 203, 249
Paris regatta 45–6, 50
Paris St Germain 169
passport (lack of) 46
Pathe News 266
Pengwern Boat Club 39–40
Pergamon Press 214
Phyllis Court, Henley 267
planning permission 20, 71–72, 74, 77
polytechnics 25
postgraduate studies 82, 174, 176, 234
Poznan World Rowing Cup 272, 281
Premiership, the 257
press, the 202
pressure
  on athletes 9, 12, 37, 98, 143, 207, 219, 221, 242, 262
  on Richard Spratley 84, 103, 109
  on space (boathouse etc.) 70, 75
Prime Minister, the 201–2
Princeton Training Center 172
Princeton University 61, 91, 93, 211–2, 236, 277, 280
project management 26
Proteus-Eretes Rowing Club, Netherlands 115, 143

310

General index

psychology 11–14, 160
  Brookes approach 242–3, 246, 251, 283
  racing preparation 242, 245, 254
  "team" aspects 11–12, 14
punts and punting 26, 69, 71
Putney 150, 153

Queen's Tower Boat Club 87, 151
Quintin Head 202

race reports (Henley finals) 35, 64, 91, 119, 146, 172, 211, 254
racing
  preparation 30, 51, 174, 244
  tactics 63, 159–160, 245
  see also psychology
Radley College 164, 169
Raleghs Cross Inn 27
rating (strokes per minute) 44, 62, 65, 82, 96–9, 147, 175, 181, 216
  in training 193, 215, 221
Ratzenberg Regatta 179
Reading 1, 2, 22, 237
  Reading Blue Coat School 16, 191
  Reading College 22
  Reading Rowing Club 1
  Reading University 29, 41, 62
Real Madrid 198
recruitment 259–260
  British Rowing 225, 230
  Brookes approach 81, 127, 163–171, 176, 190, 251, 289, 291
  US universities 120, 164–8
Regatta Enclosure (Henley) 36, 66
Regatta magazine 58
regattas 9, 18, 30, 32, 40, 103, 149, 167, 174, 186, 194, 199, 270, 290, 294, 295
  see also Evesham, Henley, Henley Women's, Marlow, Stratford-upon-Avon
relaxation 51, 98, 141, 177

responsibility, personal 79, 247, 249, 291
Ridley College, Canada 31
risk 79, 137, 261
  flood risk 76
River Ouse 204
Rocky the dog 214
Row360 magazine and website x, 146, 207, 226
rowing tank / tank rooms 43, 265–6
Ruder Club Hansa Dortmund xvi

San Diego Crew Classic 9
Saudi Arabia 191
scholarships 120, 165, 219
Scotland 110–1, 140, 205
sculling 4, 7, 11, 111, 164, 219, 228, 257, 270, 295–6
Scumbag College 259
seat racing 29, 41, 48, 187, 195–6, 200, 246
selection (crew) 171, 249
  at Brookes 29, 41, 115, 195–200, 248, 251, 290–1
  national 47–8, 64, 84–5, 90, 104, 126, 169, 227–8, 272, 285, 295
Shanghai 9
Shiplake College 26, 163
Shrewsbury 39–40
Shrewsbury school 39, 163
side-by-side
  racing 56, 58, 74, 149–150, 156
  training 44, 69, 221, 259
Sir William Borlase's school 22, 164
social distancing 203
social life – see 'fun'
social media 170
South Africa 116
Southampton University 20
Spain national rowing squad 30
sponsorship 133–5
sport (not rowing)
  American football 52
  Basketball 12
  cricket 12

football viii, 12, 115, 155, 158, 164, 168–9, 257, 259
  rugby 12
Sports Science 106–7, 118
station (rowing "lane" at Henley) 36, 65, 106, 120, 147, 157, 211, 240–1, 254, 274–5, 277–8
St. Andrew's University 264
St. Edward's School 163
St. Mary's University, Twickenham 3
St. Paul's Girls School 163, 165
St. Paul's School 163, 166, 168–9
St. Petersburg University 129
standardisation 77–8, 187, 199, 292
Steps (pop group) 216
Stratford-upon-Avon regatta 16
stream (river flow) xvi, 45, 65, 70, 106, 147, 150, 158, 180, 184, 211, 241, 244, 267, 275
student fees 131–2, 164
submarine design 95
success breeds success 163, 166, 294
Sunderland vii
Sunderland Football Club viii, 257
Sunshine on a Rainy Day (song) 26, 28
Surbiton 164
Surbiton High School 163
surfing 105, 116–7
sweep rowing 166, 184, 194, 218, 228, 257, 270, 285, 295
swimming 1, 11, 157, 259
Syracuse University, USA 91–93, 180, 236–7

tailwind vii, 111, 267
taster days 170
Taurus Boat Club ix, 87
  committee ix, 49
  competing 138, 142, 176, 274
  newsletter 15, 52
team spirit 12, 27, 42, 134, 195, 200, 247, 251, 260, 290
technique, rowing 6–7, 41, 94–8, 100, 118, 141, 159, 219

311

telemetry 4, 29, 100–1, 200, 221, 244, 260, 292
television
 Gladiators 49
 GMTV 49
Temple Island 36, 53, 62, 254
Thames (river) 1, 3, 20, 26, 29, 39, 43, 45, 55, 68–75, 150, 163, 170, 202, 204, 263, 268, 273, 290
Thames Rowing Club 8, 151, 152, 238, 272
Thames Tradesmen (rowing club) 29, 164
tide 56, 150, 157
Tideway Scullers (School) 151, 152, 164, 188
Tourists 26, 69
Training 40, 61
 aerobic 93
 anti-doping 144
 camp 4, 27–9, 48, 170, 193, 250, 263
 during Covid 203
 facilities 20, 43, 68, 69, 215, 259
 programmes 6, 9, 24, 26, 39, 66, 74, 81, 106–7, 123, 160, 187, 190, 199, 220, 247, 260, 289–293
 purpose inc. selection 41, 150, 151
 sessions 42–44, 80, 111, 114–8
 weight training 26, 41, 42, 70, 107–8, 123, 215, 218, 220
triathlon 225
Trinity College Dublin 33, 52–3, 61
Trinity College, Hartford (USA) 114, 122
Triton Rowing Club, Netherlands 206, 233, 234
trousers, female HRR guests allowed to wear 206
trust
 in the boat 11–12, 161, 249, 269
 "trust the process" 245, 293
Twickenham 168, 208

UK anti-doping organisation 143
UK lottery 135, 186, 204, 229
umpire(s) 32, 35–6, 53, 61, 157, 175, 210, 212, 238, 241, 255, 280
underdog culture / spirit 26, 31, 41, 74, 80, 108, 125, 248, 258, 290
United States of America 37, 45
 Americans 88, 216
 national rowing team 86, 124, 172
 university rowing xiii, 129, 130, 133, 165–171
 see also individual US universities
University of Bristol 20, 45, 59
University of California *see* Berkeley, University of California
University of Galway 114
University of London 45, 56, 91, 153, 178, 192, 209, 233, 249, 295
University of Pennsylvania 120
University of Texas 119
University of the West of England 178
University of Virginia 129
University of Washington 10, 35–38, 61, 64, 86, 91, 93, 129, 146–148, 165–9, 180–1, 219, 233, 236, 241, 244, 250, 251, 256, 274, 278, 280
University of Western Ontario, Canada 129
Upper Thames Rowing Club 36, 92, 121
US universities (*see individual universities*)

Vale of Leven Academy 110
Varese (World Rowing Cup event) 240, 285
Venice 185
Vesta Rowing Club 29

Wallingford 43, 71, 123, 265
 Head race 263

Wallingford Rowing Club 26, 68–70, 72, 74
warning (in races) 201, 212, 255
weather 27, 44, 106, 146, 150, 153, 175, 220, 270, 276, 278
 floods 69, 71, 76
 rain 254, 263, 276, 278–80, 283
 thunder 146
weight 10, 32, 35, 40, 46–8, 88, 89, 96, 98, 112, 156, 166, 260, 266
Westminster School 49, 163, 176
Wimbleball 4, 27–9, 48, 131, 132, 139, 170, 193, 251, 263
Windsor Boys' School xvi, 164
women's rowing
 at Brookes 3–8, 15 –18, 25, 69, 108, 118, 120, 132, 137, 185–194, 205, 215, 221, 246, 257, 264, 268, 270–1, 283, 286–7, 295
 at Henley Royal Regatta xv, 185–6
 coxing 46, 156
 history 81, 185–6
 participation 193–4
 see also Henley Women's Regatta, Olympics, Island and Remenham events at Henley, and general Brookes entries
Worcester Rowing Club 86
world championships xiii, 41, 85, 88, 90, 104, 109, 110, 230, 258, 283, 286, 296
World Rowing Federation 46
World War Two 203
Wycliffe College 163
Wyfold Galleries 133–4

Yale University 43, 59, 103, 114, 133, 167, 168, 175, 177, 191, 192, 256, 262, 285
youth hostel 132, 251
YouTube 38, 62, 139, 141, 142, 155, 171, 175, 245